THE CLASSICS OF WESTERN SPIRITUALITY
A Library of the Great Spiritual Masters

PIETISTS
Selected Writings

EDITED WITH AN INTRODUCTION BY
PETER C. ERB

PREFACE BY
F. ERNEST STOEFFLER

PAULIST PRESS
NEW YORK • RAMSEY • TORONTO

Cover Art
Born, raised and educated in New York, free-lance designer/illustrator ROBERT
MANNING has received numerous commissions for religious theme books. The
"woodcut" seemed a natural style to suggest the bold, dramatic spirit of the Pietists.
The portrait is that of the movement's founder, Spener, and the burning heart symbol-
izes the active evangelical emphasis of Pietist Christianity.

Acknowledgements
The Publisher gratefully acknowledges the use of "Nine Public Lectures Concerning Saving
Faith" *reprinted by permission of the University of Iowa Press.*

Material from Pia Desideria *by Philipp Jakob Spener, translated by T. G. Tappert,* © *1964 by
Fortress Press is reprinted by permission of the publisher.*

6/92

Library of Congress
Catalog Card Number: 83-60125

ISBN: 0-8091-2509-9 (paper)
      0-8091-0334-6 (cloth)

Published by Paulist Press
545 Island Road, Ramsey, N.J. 07446

Printed and bound in the United States of America

Contents

Editor of this Volume

PETER ERB was born in 1943 in Tavistock, Ontario, Canada. He is presently Assistant Professor of English and Religion and Culture at Wilfrid Laurier University, Waterloo, Ontario, Canada. Dr. Erb's specialization is in late medieval spirituality. After serving as pastor of the Amish Mennonite Church in Tavistock, he re-entered the academic world, completing his M.S.L. at the Pontifical Institute of Medieval Studies, and his Ph.D. at the University of Toronto. He has published numerous articles, reviews and papers on Protestant spirituality. His books include *Schwenkfeld in His Reformation Setting* and *The Spiritual Diary of Christopher Wiegner*, and he is now working on a book entitled *Toward a Definition of the Contemplative Life*. He is the recent recipient of a Canada Council Grant to complete a book on Gottfried Arnold. Professor Erb has combined teaching and writing with an active career in research on Protestant monastic communities in North America, and Patristic scholarship among the Radical Reformers. Dr. Erb is Associate Director of the Schwenkfeld Library, Pennsburg, Pennsylvania and Managing Editor of *Studies in Religion/Sciences religieuses*, the Canadian journal for religious studies. He has supervised doctoral and masters students at various universities in Canada and the United States. He resides in Waterloo, Ontario, with his wife, Betty, and their two children, Catharine and Suzanne. Dr. Erb is a member of the Ostdeutscher Kulturrat, Kulterwerk Schlesiens, American Society of Reformation Research, American Society of Church History and the American Theological Library Association.

Author of the Preface

F. ERNEST STOEFFLER was born in Germany in 1911. He is a graduate of Yale Divinity School, New Haven, Connecticut and Temple University, Philadelphia, Pennsylvania and is currently Professor Emeritus of Religion at the College of Liberal Arts and Sciences, Temple University. Professor Stoeffler is the author of *The Rise of Evangelical Pietism* (Leiden, 1965), *German Pietism During the Eighteenth Century* (Leiden, 1973), and editor of *Continental Pietism and Early American Christianity* (Grand Rapids, Michigan, 1976).

PREFACE

Pietism is today considered to have been one of the most influential Protestant reform movements since the Reformation itself. For reasons difficult to understand historians of Christianity, as well as historians in general, have either paid only marginal attention to it or ignored it altogether. During the past two decades, however, there has come about a decided change of attitude in the western world. In both Europe and America interest in its development, its impact, as well as in the literature associated with it, has increased markedly.

In part this new interest has been the result of an initial recognition on the part of historians of religion and of culture that we are dealing here with a much neglected field of study which deserves to be subjected to historical investigation. In the process of such scrutiny it gradually became clear that the historical study of Pietism is by no means an exercise in the stirring up of dry bones. The evidence which presented itself took on increasing contemporary significance. It began to lay bare the roots of much that is widely recognized as belonging to the very nature of Protestantism as it is practiced in the world in which we live.

We now realize that, among other things, Pietism has been a powerful influence in the re-shaping of theological education so as to orient it toward the practical concerns of the churches. This has obviously remained an ongoing effort both on the theological and ethical levels. It strengthened the idea of the pastor's task as a "calling," which is to be entered into primarily for reasons of religious commitment rather than for the sake of other professional rewards. It profoundly influenced all components of both public and private worship within substantial segments of Protestantism. Thus preaching, which during the age of Protestant orthodoxy had been basically theological discourse, and not infrequently an exercise in theological polemics, was now oriented primarily toward the moral and religious commitment of the people in the pew. A vastly expanded hymnody had the same objective in mind. In some circles the singing of hymns,

PREFACE

linked with appealing tunes, became the most attractive feature of worship in the churches and in the homes. Public prayer was frequently detached from liturgical forms, thus becoming the expression of the most deeply felt needs of the hour.

Under the impact of Pietism, family worship became the norm rather than the exception among its adherents. To the father, and sometimes the mother, were delegated the priestly and intercessory functions of the entire household. The result was a new emphasis upon the need for, and the use of, devotional aids, with an appropriate explosion in the printing and distribution of such aids. Daily Bible reading, as well as frequent group discussion of the biblical message, was expected of anyone who professed to take his/her Christianity seriously. The difference between clergy and laity was thus minimized, and the sense of religious fellowship across traditional lines of ecclesiastical differentiation was enhanced. A "brother," or "sister," was anyone given to the same religious perspective, irrespective of his/her church affiliation. The universal insistence of Pietists that the religious renewal basic to the Pietist understanding of the meaning of religiousness must express itself in conduct eventuated in a decided pressure to "do good." Hence the rapid proliferation of a large variety of charitable institutions, including schools which were regarded as opportunities for the children of the poor to become productive members of society. Among the most profound changes which Pietism wrought within Protestantism was its bequest to the latter of a new vision of a world in need of the Gospel of Christ— hence the tremendous impulse it gave to the expansion of the Protestant missionary enterprise.

Though these and other concerns of early Pietism had to be modified in the course of time to meet the changing needs of successive generations of Christians, their influence upon the world Protestant community today can hardly be overlooked. Among Protestant groups in the East and in the West its subtly pervasive influence goes on. This would seem to be especially true of contemporary America where conservative Protestantism has become increasingly conspicuous, and where the religious self-understanding of today's conservative Protestants exhibits various similarities with that of the early Pietists.

Since the middle 1960's a number of efforts have been made to open up the field of classical Pietism to the English speaking public, as well as to create some appreciation of its influence upon our own religious

PREFACE

institutions. One of the major difficulties has been, however, that to most seminary students, pastors, and interested Christians in general the sources were inaccessible because they were largely unavailable in the English language. Thus Peter Erb's anthology, drawn from many of these sources and presented in readable English, is rendering a most important service. While to some the selections which have been chosen may in the main be of historical interest only, to others they may well continue to serve as a fountain of religious inspiration. To the unbiased reader they still breathe the spirit of profound religious devotion which may well penetrate the shell of conventional religiosity and confront him with a divine imperative never experienced before.

Fortunately the translator and editor of this volume has not restricted himself to an unduly narrow range of materials. The authors quoted represent a wide ecclesiastical and doctrinal spectrum which should serve to broaden reader interest among adherents of various Christian traditions. The religious perspective expressed in this anthology not infrequently met with implacable opposition, and sometimes with severe punishment, by fellow Protestants. One might wish that this example of past mistakes may strengthen our resolve to respect the religious convictions of our fellow human beings, and, if we must differ, we do so without rancor or recrimination.

FOREWORD

Pietism was the most important development in Protestant spirituality. Its roots can be traced to Lutheran and Calvinist-Puritan concerns with the practice of piety in the late sixteenth and seventeenth centuries, but the beginning of the movement itself can be located and dated with precision. In 1675 Philipp Jakob Spener, senior pastor of the Frankfurt am Main ministerium, wrote a preface to the postills of Johann Arndt. He entitled the piece *Pia desideria* (Pious desires) and in it he advocated a renewed emphasis on biblical preaching and on the experience of repentance and the new birth, the establishment of conventicles for the mutual edification and admonition of "reborn" believers, and a reform of pastoral training that would place less emphasis on scholastic polemical theology and more on the development of a sensitised ministry concerned with the practical devotional and moral life of parishioners.

Spener's *Pia desideria* was immediately popular and by the close of the century its principles had affected all German-speaking Protestant communities in Europe and America. Under Spener's protégé, August Hermann Francke, the Pietist interest in ecumenism, missions, social service, and lay and pastoral education was furthered at the new university of Halle (a.S.). In Württemberg, Pietism developed a special concern with biblical study (particularly under Johann Bengel), a concern that was reawakened in the nineteenth century and has continued to the present day. In Saxony under the influential Count Zinzendorf a closely knit Pietist program was initiated among the Moravian Brethren to whom Zinzendorf had granted protection and through them Pietist ideas reached John Wesley and early Methodism in its English and American forms. Most Pietist conventicles remained within the denominations in which they arose, but many, under the influence of earlier Radical Reformation traditions or of Boehmist and Quietist ideas, broke from the established denominations to form new sectarian groups.

In both its churchly and radical forms the influence of Pietism was great. Without it, it is difficult to understand the growth of "evangelical" Christianity in Europe and America, and its adherents played central roles in the development of Protestant, hymnological, devotional, theological, and biblical studies.

INTRODUCTION

To write the history of Pietism is to write the
history of modern Protestantism.
—Michel Godfroid,
"Le Pietisme allemand a-t-il existe?"

"We have every reason not to adopt a belittling attitude to Pietism," writes Ernst Käsemann, the contemporary New Testament scholar. "Our church life still continues to draw its nourishment from its roots in Pietism, the recruits from the ranks of theological workers even today are drawn from bourgeois pietistic circles, and [Pietism's] weakening is undoubtedly leading to a very threatening crisis over the whole area of the Church's activity."[1] Käsemann's statement may seem overly emphatic, particularly to English-speaking readers for whom the noun "Pietism" and its adjective "pietistic" have lost all specific meaning and now serve only to disparage a religious approach seen by its opponents as too emotionally intense. Likewise, English-speaking New Testament scholars may find Käsemann's comments on Pietism and his detailed discussion of pietist exegesis[2] misdirected and anglophone users of the histories of modern Protestantism by Karl Barth[3] and Paul Tillich[4] too regularly set aside these author's analyses of the pietist awakening as peculiarly German.

---

1. Ernst Käsemann, "New Testament Questions of Today," in his *New Testament Questions of Today,* trans. W. J. Montague (Philadelphia, Pa.: Fortress Press, 1969), p. 4.
2. See Ernst Käsemann, "Thoughts on the Present Controversy about Scriptural Interpretation," in ibid., pp. 260–285.
3. Karl Barth, *Protestant Theology in the Nineteenth Century,* trans. Brian Cozens and John Bowden (London, 1972), pp. 33–173. Note as well Eberhard Busch, *Karl Barth und die Pietisten* (München, 1978).
4. Paul Tillich, *Perspectives on 19th and 20th Century Protestant Theology* (New York, 1967), pp. 9–24. Cf. Emmanuel Hirsch, *Geschichte der neueren evangelischen Theologie* (Gütersloh, 1951) vol. 2, pp. 91–207. The misrepresentation of Pietism by many authors is to a large degree due to the influence of Albrecht Ritschl's negative three-volume study, *Geschichte des Pietismus* (Bonn, 1880–1886).

1

INTRODUCTION

But Pietism was not solely a German movement nor can it be reduced simply to its first sudden life in the Protestant world of the late seventeenth and early eighteenth centuries. Käsemann's words could, as well, be applied directly to the Protestanism of North America, for Pietism was a source for much of John Wesley's spirituality and through him (and members of the nineteenth-century pietist renewal in Germany), it touched North American nineteenth-century revivalism and the Evangelical movement of the twentieth century. Contemporary North American Evangelicals in particular, as they grapple with their recent and relatively sudden realization of political and social influence and as they continue to move haltingly toward theological self-identity, are increasingly required to study their pietist ancestors so as to understand the sources of their spirituality and the clearest existing analogues for their piety.

Nor may opponents of the Evangelicals ignore Pietism. In their acceptance and support of the modern world and its myths of a subjectively oriented individualism, freedom, and progress, they must not fail to note the importance of Pietism in shaping the thought of major modern figures. Immanuel Kant's reflection on the "interior" transcendental structures of human thought and on the categorical imperative is a development of his early pietist training, as are Friedrich Schleiermacher's meditations on religious "feeling." Modern biblical criticism, as already suggested, owes much to continuing pietist studies in this area.[5]

The Beginnings of Pietism

There has been much discussion regarding the sources of the pietist awakening and although these cannot be limited to the Lutheran tradition, it is within that tradition that the pietist movement first appeared in the distinctive form in which it was to develop. Following Luther's death in 1546 a number of controversies arose within Lutheranism over which theological principles were central to faith and which were not (*adiaphora*), whether good works were necessary for salvation, if or how far one cooperates in one's conversion, the role of

---

5. On Pietism and Evangelical concerns, note particularly the fine semi-popular work by Dale Brown, *Understanding Pietism* (Grand Rapids, Mich., 1978). For an overview of the continuing influence of Pietism see Martin Schmidt, *Pietismus* (Stuttgart, 1972), pp. 143–167.

INTRODUCTION

law, the precise role of the sacraments in the mediation of grace, sin and the essence of man, and whether justification is only forensic (that is, solely God's declaration, as Luther had taught) or whether it is infused.[6] These questions were eventually resolved in the *Formula of Concord* (1580). In their attempts to defend their respective theologies both Lutherans and Calvinists developed a precise theological methodology and a vocabulary that characterized an academic theology known as Protestant Orthodoxy or Scholasticism.[7] Scholasticism's method owed much to the work of Philip Melancthon, and was influenced by the Spanish-Jesuit scholastics of the sixteenth century.[8] It insisted legalistically on the acceptance of precisely worded doctrinal confessions. To its enemies, the later Pietists, it was seen as dry, polemical, and intolerant, lacking concern with practical piety; but the Pietists did learn much from Orthodoxy, and in spite of their rhetorical rejection of the Scholastics, they did in fact owe much to the methodology they so vehemently attacked.[9] From its beginnings Lutheran Orthodoxy was opposed by men who were primarily interested in personal renewal, individual growth in holiness, and religious experience. This opposition found a spokesman in the Lutheran pastor and

---

6. For an outline of these controversies see F. Bente, *Historical Introduction to the Book of Concord*, in *Concordia Triglotta* (St. Louis, Mo., 1921) and *Die Bekenntnisschriften der evangelisch-lutherischen Kirche* (Berlin, 1930), vol. 1, pp. xi–xliv.

7. On the history of scholastic orthodoxy within Protestantism, see Isaac A. Dorner, *History of Protestant Theology*, trans. George Robson and Sophia Taylor, 2 vols. (Edinburgh, 1871); Otto Ritschl, *Dogmengeschichte des Protestantismus*, 3 Bde. (Göttingen, 1908–1926); Hans Emil Weber, *Reformation, Orthodoxie und Rationalismus*, 2 Bde. (Gütersloh, 1937–1951); and the relevant sections in Hans Leube, *Kalvinismus und Luthertum im Zeitalter der Orthodoxie* (Leipzig, 1928). On the introduction of the scholastic method into Protestant theology see also Hans Emil Weber, *Der Einfluss der protestantischen Schulphilosophie auf die orthodox-lutherische Dogmatik* (Leipzig, 1980) and Robert P. Scharlmann, *Thomas Aquinas and John Gerhard* (New Haven and London: Yale University Press, 1964), pp. 13–43. Note as well Paul Althaus, *Die Prinzipien der deutschen reformierten Dogmatik im Zeitalter der aristotelischen Scholastik* (Leipzig, 1914). A more recent though much narrower and less useful work (despite its bulk) is that of Robert D. Preuss, *The Theology of Post-Reformation Lutheranism, A Study of Theological Prolegomena*, 2 vols. (St. Louis, Mo., 1970). Note as well the compendiums of scholastic doctrine by Heinrich Heppe, *Reformed Dogmatics*, trans. G. T. Thomsen (London, 1950) and Heinrich Schmidt, *The Doctrinal Theology of the Evangelical Lutheran Church*, trans. Charles A. Hay and Henry E. Jacobs (Philadelphia, Pa., 1876).

8. See Scharlemann, *Thomas Aquinas*, vol. 5, pp. 13–28.

9. Pietism was as deeply indebted to Orthodoxy as it was opposed to it. See Hans Leube, *Die Reformbestrebungen der deutschen lutherischen Kirche im Zeitalter der Orthodoxie* (Leipzig, 1924) and his *Orthodoxie und Pietismus* (Witten, 1975), as well as Heinrich Bornkamm, *Mystik, Spiritualismus und die Anfänge des Pietismus im Luthertum* (Giessen, 1926).

3

devotional author Johann Arndt (1555–1621), who in his *True Christianity* and numerous devotional works[10] established the direction of a movement that would shape Lutheran thought throughout the seventeenth century.

But Arndt's concern with practical piety was not alone responsible for the Pietism that would break upon the European Protestant Church half a decade after his death. Equally important for developing pietist ideals was Calvinism.[11] Calvin's publication of *Institutes* was, as he said, intended for direction in "Godliness"[12] and the movement he founded was in its seventeenth-century Dutch and English Puritan forms in particular concerned with sanctification. William Ames summed up this concern perhaps better than any in his definition of theology as "the doctrine of Living to God."[13] How far the practical concerns of Radical Reformation groups such as the Mennonites and the Schwenckfelders[14] stimulated the development of Pietism is not certain, but early pietist proponents were acquainted with writers from these groups and looked postively on mystical spiritualists such as Jacob Boehme (1575–1624) and his followers[15] as well as later Quietists.[16]

Early Lutheran Pietism

The basic premises of all practically directed reform groups in seventeenth-century Protestantism found expression in a single trea-

---

10. For bibliography and discussion on Arndt see my introduction to Johann Arndt, *True Christianity* (New York, 1979), pp. 1–17.

11. On this influence see Wilhelm Goeters, *Die Vorbereitung des Pietismus in der Reformierten Kirche der Niederlande* (Leipzig und Utrecht, 1911); Heinrich Heppe, *Geschichte des Pietismus und der Mystik in der Reformierten Kirche* (Leiden, 1879); and F. Ernst Stoeffler, *The Rise of Evangelical Pietism* (Leiden, 1970). Note also August Lang, *Puritanismus und Pietismus* (Neukirchen Kreis Moers, 1941) and James R. Tanis, *Dutch Calvinistic Pietism in the Middle Colonies: A Study of the Life and Theology of Theodorous Jacobus Freylinghuysen* ('s Gravenhage, 1967).

12. John Calvin, *Institutes of the Christian Religion*, trans. Ford Lewis Battles, ed. John T. McNeill (Philadelphia, Pa., 1960), vol. 1, p. 9.

13. William Ames, *The Marrow of Theology*, trans. John Dykstra Eusden (Boston, 1968), p. 77.

14. See George H. Williams, *The Radical Reformation* (Philadelphia, Pa., 1962), pp. 810–814. Note as well Robert Friedmann, *Mennonite Piety through the Centuries* (Goshen Ind., 1949), and Egon W. Gerdes, "Pietistisches bei Kaspar von Schwenckfeld," *Miscellanea Historiae Ecclesiasticae II*, (Louvain, 1967), pp. 105–137.

15. For details see introduction to my translation of Jacob Boehme, *The Way to Christ* (New York, 1978), pp. 1–26.

16. See below, n. 53.

4

INTRODUCTION

✓ tise issued in 1675. In that year Philipp Jakob Spener (1635–1705), *senior* of the *ministerium* in Frankfurt am Main, published an introduction to the postills of Johann Arndt. The treatise, reissued separately a year later under the title *Pia Desideria: or Heartfelt Desires for a God-pleasing Improvement of the true Protestant Church*,[17] was to spur a concern for the practice of piety within Protestantism, and, before the author's death in 1705, it had passed through four editions and was translated into Latin to make it more widely available.[18] As Lutheran pastor to a community that had known the turmoil and disillusionment of the Thirty Years War, Spener was sadly aware of the low ebb of Christian life in his city and throughout Germany, and, pressing the need for repentance and rebirth on the part of individual believers, he attempted to remedy the situation in 1670 by the introduction of small prayer and study groups or conventicles of awakened Christians, who met for mutual encouragement in individual faith and practice.

Spener's *Pia Desideria* outlined his hopes and intentions. After noting the decline in moral life at the time, it detailed at length the defects of political and clerical authorities as well as those of the populace, clarified the possibility of reform, and set down proposals to enact it. The section of the work discussing Spener's proposals for improving the Christianity of his contemporaries called for a renewed study of the Scriptures, the initiation of group meetings or conventicles to stimulate Christian growth, the practice of the priesthood of all believers, and the practice of piety. All Christians—not only ministers—are to function as priests and to fulfill the office of sacrifice by offering their bodies, free of sin, to God. Likewise, their spiritual natures are to be tamed and submitted in passive obedience before him. The tongue and mind are to be offered in prayer and meditation on the Scriptural text. If this is done, the Holy Spirit will illumine the mind of each committed believer. Study is to be assiduously undertaken and to be directed to the conversion of the erring and the comfort of the weak. Rather than maintain polemical attack, Christians should endeavor to come to agreement through dedicated

---

17. Philipp Jakob Spener, *Pia desideria*, hrsg. Kurt Aland, 3, Aufl. (Berlin, 1964). See also Allen C. Deeter, *An Historical and Theological Introduction to Philipp Jakob Spener's Pia desideria: A Study in Early German Pietism* (Ph.D. Diss., Princeton, 1963). For biographical details see Paul Grünberg, *Philipp Jakob Spener*, 3 Bde. (Göttingen, 1893–1906), and above all Johannes Wallmann, *Philipp Jakob Spener und die Anfänge des Pietismus* (Tübingen, 1970).

18. See Kurt Aland, *Spener-Studien* (Berlin, 1943), pp. 1–21.

prayer, examples of moral well-being, and heartfelt love. Antagonistic scholastic disputation must be ended. The role of the pastor must be reemphasized and pastoral education revamped with greater attention given to the daily life of a pastor in its devotional and moral aspects.

The whole of Spener's *Pia Desideria* was written within an eschatological context, a "hope for better days." The sinfulness of the church, he felt, is a sign of the end. Through the actions of the whore of Babylon, the Roman Catholic Church, the true people of God within the Protestant tradition will be made aware of their evil ways (Spener's ecumenical concern extended only to other Protestant traditions). Regeneration is necessary for the church as well as for the individual. Before the end of time the Jews will be converted, Rome will fall, and a new millennial era will begin for the people of God.[19]

Unlike his Orthodox opponents, Spener focused more on the subjective appropriation of the believer's redemption than on God's objective saving act in history in the incarnation. The pattern by which the grace of the Holy Spirit in the redemption is applied to the individual believer had been worked out during the seventeenth century and was known as the *ordo salutis* (order of salvation).[20] The believer is elected (*electio*), called (*vocatio*), illumined (*illuminatio*), converted (*conversio*), regenerated (*regeneratio*), justified (*justificatio*), united mystically with Christ (*unio mystica*), renovated (*renovatio*), and preserved to the end (*conservatio*) to be glorified with the Son (*glorificatio*). Not only did Spener place emphasis on the *ordo* in general, but he accented illumination (directing attention away from the illumination of theological knowledge to direct, inner, psychological illumination in the believer) and conversion and renovation or sanctification.

Such principles seemed to many of Spener's contemporaries to be based on a questionable theology, which relegated doctrine to a secondary position and elevated experiential piety, personal assurance, and a high moral and devotional life, in practice if not in theory, to the rank of saving graces. For men whose thought moved within the *simul justus et peccator* (the believer is at once justified and a sinner) paradox of Luther, such a theology was seen as a return to a concept of justification based on merit, the use of conventicles (*ecclesiolae in ecclesia*) was viewed as a base for the development of separatism, and

---

19. See especially Wallmann, pp. 307ff.
20. On the *ordo* see Schmidt, *Doctrinal Theology*, pp. 407–499.

INTRODUCTION

the conventicles themselves were seen as a "fourth species of religion" outlawed by the Treaty of Westphalen (1648), which allowed only Catholics, Lutherans, and Calvinists free exercise of faith. To emphasize both these dangers, its enemies maligned the movement with the designation "Pietism."

What offended Pietism's opponents perhaps more than anything was its emphasis on the emotional aspect of religious life. As one modern scholar has put it, Pietists insisted on

> the need for, and the possibility of, an authentic and vitally significant experience of God on the part of individual Christians; the religious life as a life of love for God and man, which is marked by social sensitivity and ethical concern; utter confidence, with respect to the issues of both life and death, in the experientially verifiable authenticity of God's revelation in Christ, as found in the biblical witness; the church as a community of God's people, which must ever be renewed through the transformation of individuals, and which necessarily transcends all organizationally required boundaries; the need for the implementation of the Reformation understanding of the priesthood of all believers through responsible lay participation in the varied concerns of the Christian enterprise; a ministry which is sensitized, trained, and oriented to respond to the needs and problems of a given age; and finally, the continual adaptation of ecclesiastical structures, practices, and verbal definitions to the mission of the church.[21]

Pietist concerns spread rapidly and by the close of the century had affected Protestant denominations in Germany, Holland, Switzerland, and Scandinavia and were carried to the areas settled by these peoples in North America.[22] Many of the adherents of the

---

21. F. Ernest Stoeffler, *German Pietism during the Eighteenth Century* (Leiden, 1973), p. ix. The search for a definition of Pietism has been particularly troubled because the movement had not only theological but also wide sociological and political effects. See Carl Hinrich, *Preussentum und Pietismus* (Göttingen, 1971); Wolf Oschlies, *Die Arbeits- und Berufs-pädegogik August Hermann Franckes (1663–1727)* (Witten, 1969). On Pietism and the role of women see the excellent work of Fritz Tanner, *Die Ehe im Pietismus* (Zurich, 1952).

22. For general histories of Pietism, see the useful articles by Carl Mirbt in *The Schaff-Herzog Encyclopaedia of Religious Knowledge* (vol. 9, pp. 53–67) and Martin

INTRODUCTION

movement, often called Church Pietists, remained within the organized churches of their birth, and saw in the pietist spirit the form
and power by which their various congregations and traditions might
be revitalized. Many others, however, conveniently designated Radical Pietists, moved in the direction toward which Spener's enemies
saw the whole revival oriented. Some of these, in fact, separated
themselves from the churches with which they had initially been associated, forming new sectarian bodies as they did. In some cases this
movement to separation was furthered by Spiritualist and Anabaptist
communities in the areas, in others by the theosophic tradition of
Jacob Boehme.

The Pietist Flowering

A brief history of Pietism is useful in illustrating the relationships between Church and Radical Pietists. Early in his career,
Spener had met the former Jesuit, reformed church pastor, and later
separatist Jean de Labadie (1610–1674),[23] and had refused to take up a
clear position against Boehme.[24] It is little wonder, as a result, that he
raised antagonisms during his life at Frankfurt am Main (1666–1686),
Dresden (1686–1691), and Berlin (1691–1705). Supporters came quickly to his side in all German cities and controversy began immediately.
In Hamburg under Johann Friedrich Mayer (1650–1712), in Witten-

---

Schmidt, *Pietismus.* The best available histories are Stoeffler, *Rise,* and *German Pietism;*
Horst Weigelt, *Pietismus-Studien, I. Teil; Der Spener hallische Pietismus* (Stuttgart, 1965);
W. Hardorn, *Geschichte des Pietismus in der schweizerischen Reformierten Kirche* (Konstanz
und Emmishofen, 1901). On the spirit of the movement see Martin Fischer and Max
Fischer on the theme "Die bleibende Bedeutung des Pietismus" in Oskar Sohngen,
hrsg., *Die Bleibende Bedeutung des Pietismus ... Zur 250-Jahrfeier* (Witten und Berlin,
1960), pp. 76ff., 93ff. The structure of Pietist conventicles is well outlined in Friedrich
Baum, *Das schwäbische Gemeinschaftleben,* 2. Aufl. (Stuttgart, 1929). For most recent Pietist studies see Martin Greschat *Zur neueren Pietismusforschung* (Darmstadt, 1977),
which includes excellent articles on Spener, Francke, Zinzendorf, and Bengel as well
as on the movement in general. Above all see the journal *Pietismus und Neuzeit* published annually since 1974. Bibliographies on each of the major authors treated in this
volume are also available in Martin Schmidt und Wilhelm Jannasch, hrsg., *Das Zeitalter
des Pietismus* (Bremen, 1965).
　　23. See Kurt Dietrich Schmidt, "Labadie und Spener," *Zeitschrift für Kirchengeschichte* 46 (1928): 566–683, but note Aland, *Spener-Studien,* pp. 41–62.
　　24. See Philipp Jakob Spener, *Theologische Bedencken* (Halle, 1700–1702), vol. 3, pp.
595, 924, 944; cf. vol. 1, pp. 368, 369, 373, 377, and vol. 2, p. 409, and his *Erfordertes Theologisches Bedencken* (Ploen, 1690), pp. C3ff., and *Sieg der Wahrheit und der Unschult* (Cölln
an der Spree, 1693), pp. vi, 7, 13 passim.

INTRODUCTION

berg under Valentine Ernst Loescher (1673–1749), and in Gotha under Ernst Saloman Cyprian (1673–1745), opposition was especially strong.

Chief among Spener's defenders was August Hermann Francke (1663–1727).[25] An avid and pious student, Francke studied first at Kiel, and after entering the university at Leipzig in 1684, took a leading role in a *collegium biblicum* there that was formed on the model and under the inspiration of Spener's conventicles. In 1687 he experienced a conversion, and in several pastoral offices thereafter supported Spenerian reforms. On the latter's recommendation he was appointed to the newly established university at Halle in 1692. Francke was not a theologian in the formal sense of the word, but his theological direction left an indelible mark on the movement. Like Spener, he emphasized the experience of the new birth (*Wiedergeburt*), and his own experience in coming to this new birth led him to give special attention to the radical shift indicated by it. At conversion, he believed, one begins to move from the kingdom of Satan to the kingdom of God. The new birth is initiated by a battle with a deep sorrow over past sins and an experience of repentance (*Busskampf*). God initiates man's redemption, Francke taught, but man is required to accept the proffered grace, which comes at special points in a believer's life (*Gnadenstunden* or hours of grace). The new birth is experienced, Francke writes using medieval mystical language, as a *Durchbruch*, a breakthrough. Thereafter, one must move forward in the footsteps of one's Savior, rejecting the old way of life, its thought structure, and the natural desires that go with it. Such a life will have its trials and sufferings but these can be borne in the newly gained trust and joy in God.

Under Francke's direction, Halle rapidly became a center for pietist study. There a new interest was taken in pastoral training and in education at all levels, an orphanage was built, and an extensive foreign mission service begun.[26] Francke's work, with its mystical orientation and ecumenical concern (far more open than Spener's

---

25. See Erich Beyreuther, *August Hermann Francke 1663–1727* (Hamburg, 1958), and Erhard Peschke *Bekehrung und Reform. Ansatz und Wurzeln der Theologie August Hermann Franckes* (Bielefeld, 1977).

26. See Ernst Benz, "Pietist and Puritan Sources of Early Protestant World Missions," *Church History* 20 (1951): 28–55.

INTRODUCTION

ecumenism),[27] was quickly broadcast through an active printing program under Carl Hildebrand von Canstein (1667–1719).[28] That program was responsible above all for inexpensive readable editions of the Bible for the laity, songbooks (including that with the foreword by Johann Anastasius Freylinghausen [1670–1739]), prayer books, and devotional guides. The most famous of the prayer books printed at Halle was the collection by Johann Friedrich Starck (1680–1756), published first in 1728 and popular throughout German-speaking denominations for over a century and a half.[29] The popularity of Starck's prayer book reflects the popularity of Halle's printing program at large and Pietism generally. Among the Radical Reformation traditions, for example, Mennonites were early influenced by Pietist concerns, and some members of that community still continue to use the Lutheran prayerbook *Geistliches Lustgärtlein Frommer Seelen* (*Spiritual Garden of Desires for Pious Souls*, 1787) and its introductory guide for edification.[30] To Halle too came Henry Melchoir Mühlenberg (1711–1787) and from there in 1742 he traveled to Pennsylvania to serve the German Lutherans in the new world.[31]

Supported by the political leadership of Prussia[32] and defended in its orthodoxy by men like Joachim Lange (1670–1744),[33] the Halle Pietists had, nevertheless, much in common with those Pietists labeled Radical. Francke was particularly interested in Quietism and published Miguel Molinos's (1640–1697) *Spiritual Guide*.[34] At Halle, too, Christian Thomasius (1655–1728) taught (and his liberal attitude

---

27. See Martin Schmidt, "Der ökumenische Sinn der deutschen Pietismus und seine Auswirkungen in der Bibelverbreitung," in Sohngen, *Die Bleibende*, pp. 60–75.
28. Cf. Carl Hildebrand von Canstein, "Ohnmaszgeblicher Vorschlag" in ibid., pp. 109ff. See also Peter Schicketanz, *Carl Hildebrand von Cansteins Beziehungen zu Philipp Jacob Spener* (Witten, 1967).
29. Available for this study was Starck's *Tägliches Handbuch in guten und bösen Tagen* (vollständige Ausgabe; Konstanz, o.J.).
30. For details on this work see *The Mennonite Encyclopaedia* (Scottsdale, Pa., 1956), vol. 2, pp. 447–448, and Robert Friedmann, *Mennonite Piety through the Centuries* (Goshen, Ind., 1949).
31. On Muhlenberg see above all *The Journals of Henry Melchior Muhlenberg*, trans. Theodore G. Tappert and John W. Doberstein, 3 vols. (Philadelphia, 1942).
32. Kurt Deppermann, *Der hallesche Pietismus und der preussische Stadt unter Friedrich III* (Göttingen, 1961). Note also Carl Hinrich's *Preussentum und Pietismus*, pp. 1–125.
33. See R. Dannenbaum, *Joachim Lange als Wortführer des hallischen Pietismus gegen die Orthodoxie* (Ph.D. Diss, Göttingen, 1952).
34. See Weigelt, *Pietismus-Studien*, pp. 46ff. Note as well Stoeffler, *Pietism*, p. 9, n. 4.

INTRODUCTION

toward Church history influenced pietist historiography);[35] as did Joachim Justus Breithaupt (1658–1732), who in the treatise *De heresi* redefined the term *heresy* as had the earlier work of George Calixtus (1586–1656)[36] so as to make it applicable only to those who rejected basic Christian truths (*Hauptwahrheiten*), that is, those truths that directed a man to a full experiential relationship with God. Assent to Lutheran symbolic books was thereby set aside. Under such a principle Boehme could be defended, the Reformed Church praised, and Roman Catholics accepted as fellow believers; in addition, radicals such as Johann Kaspar Schade (1666–1698) were seen as spiritual brethren,[37] and Halle could play an important role in aiding Gottfried Arnold (1666–1714)[38] and, through Arnold, all radicals who came under his influence.

Radical Pietism

Of all the first-generation Pietists, Gottfried Arnold is the most important for students of pietist spirituality, because of his interest in mysticism, his dissemination of mystical texts, and his wide influence on both Church and Radical Pietists. A young scholar at Wittenberg, he had initially chosen for himself an academic career. After graduation with a master's degree he took up a position as a private tutor at Dresden and moved progressively to the more radical fringes of the pietist movement. By 1698, he had come to be seen as a representative of Radical separatistic Pietism and a supporter of Boehmists and Quietists. After a short-lived career as an academic (he accepted a position as professor of history at Giessen only to reject it dramatically one year later), he published his most influential work, the *Unparteiische Kirchen-und Ketzer Historie* (*Non-partisan history of church and heresy,* 1699–1700),[39] much of his poetry, a series of editions of patristic, me-

---

35. See Erich Seeberg, *Gottfried Arnold: Die Wissenschalft und die Mystik seiner Zeit* (Meerane i.S., 1923), pp. 498–515.

36. On Calixtus theology of church history and ecclesiology, see J. L. Neve, *The Lutherans in the Movements for Church Union* (Philadelphia, Pa., 1921), pp. 81–109.

37. Note Spener's edition *Christliches Ehren-Bedächtnusz . . . Johann Caspar Schadens* (Daselbst gedruckt, o.J.).

38. On Arnold see above all Seeberg, *Arnold.* Note as well my *The Role of Late Medieval Spirituality in the Life and Work of Gottfried Arnold (1666–1714),* (Ph.D. Diss., Toronto, 1976), which includes a full biography of Arnold.

39. *Unparteiische Kirchen-und Ketzer-Historie, Von Anfang des Neuen Testaments Bisz auf das Jahr Christi, 1688,* 2 Bde. (Franckfurt a.M., 1699–1700).

11

dieval, sixteenth- and seventeenth-century mystical compositions, and a history of mystical theology.[40] In September of 1701 he suddenly married (he had earlier preached celibacy) and took up a position as a pastor in the established church. Until his death in 1714, he continued to uphold his earlier theological position, although he softened its most radical aspects.

On a first reading, Arnold's work seemed to uphold a theology opposed to the Lutheran doctrine of forensic justification and supporting in its Boehmist and Quietist mystical language a doctrine of infused justification. Like Spener and Francke, Arnold molded his thought within the framework of the *ordo salutis*, but whereas Spener had emphasized illumination, conversion, and renovation, and Francke repentance, as a background to conversion and renovation, Arnold turned his attention to the *unio mystica* and renovation. In his first major book, *Die Erste Liebe (First love*, 1696)[41] a study of the life of the early Christians, for example, Arnold opens his discussion on illumination calling readers' attention to the role of the inner spiritual voice that will continue in the believer to his death. This inner voice he opposes to the outer dead letter, but in proper Lutheran fashion he also indicates the necessary use of the outer word of Scripture.

A discussion of the new birth (*Wiedergeburt, conversio*) follows, as expected, the treatment of illumination. The new birth is the *sine qua non* of Christian life, a supernatural act worked solely by the divine to the increase of a holy life and the renewal of the image of God in man (*regeneratio*). Borrowing heavily from Arndt, Arnold developed the latter's teaching within a threefold anthropology. A Christian is body, soul, and spirit. The spirit is God's gift, his image and likeness received in faith (*justificatio*). It is through this spirit that the image of God is renewed at conversion, and it is toward the fulfillment of that image that the soul is directed for final perfect renewal in heaven.

Through the spirit as well, man is made like the angels and united with God in Christ (*unio mystica*). Man thus becomes a participant in the very nature of God, receiving the gifts of the Spirit, chief among which is faith. Faith is for Arnold an act that progresses experientially in love from the time of the new birth through to its com-

---

40. *Historie und Beschreibung der Mystischen Theologie/oder geheimen Gottes Gelehrtheit/wie auch derer alten und neuen Mysticorum* (Franckfurt a.M., 1703). Among the authors edited by Arnold in the years earlier were Marcarius Angelus Silesius, Ruusbroec; in 1712 he published a complete translation of Thomas a Kempis.

41. Gottfried Arnold, *Die Erste Liebe* (o0), 1696).

pletion, full renovation, and perfect union. Such love gains its end only in heaven, but it can achieve ecstatic insights while on earth, although its ultimate goal here is peace and joy in the Holy Spirit.

The same structure is found in Arnold's *Geheimnis der göttlichen Sophia* (*Mystery of divine Sophia*, 1700).[42] In it he makes extensive use of Boehmist themes, for example, but they are discontinuous; they are used as rhetorical techniques to call lost persons to a new creation and the redeemed to a mature Christian life. Certainly Arnold does speak of an essential, substantial union of the believer with Sophia (Wisdom), but this union is a union by faith in Christ. The righteousness it brings and its progress in the Christian do not belong properly to the believer; Sophia is God's gift living with men, not man's own work.

This theological pattern is likewise described by Arnold in an emblem inserted in his edition of the *Vitae Patrum* (1700).[43] The emblematic insert too is to be read according to the Lutheran *ordo*. Christian life begins with the breaking of the heart; faith rises out of divinely inspired prayer (point 3); purification grows from renewal (point 6); and the new life is the natural result of divine birth (point 11). All acts and growth following the new birth are the work of God. They are received and strengthened and blossom forth in the spirit. The fruits of the spirit that are listed extend beyond those noted in Galatians 5:22 and are deliberately listed in a hierarchical order. That order is firmly within the rhetoric of mysticism, but Arnold does not deny the Lutheran doctrine of *simul iustus et peccator*. Yet his attention is directed not solely to the union of each believer with Christ in faith but, concerned mainly with sanctification rather than justification, it is directed toward that special union, peace, vision, and perfection to which a contemplative is called. The democratization in Protestantism of the aristocratic medieval mystical ascent is still in effect, however:[44] Union is not the goal of a few; it is the necessary direction of all true, as opposed to pharisaic, Christians.

Arnold's division of Christianity into true and false Christians is

---

42. *Das Geheimnisz der Göttlichen Sophia oder Weischeit* (Leipzig, 1700).

43. *Vitae Patrum Oder: Das Leben der Altväter* (Halle, 1700); exemplar; Schwenkfelder Library, Pennsburg, Pa.

44. For details see Heiko A. Obermann, *The Harvest of Medieval Theology* (Cambridge, Mass. 1963), pp. 341–343, and his "*Simul gemitus et raptus.* Luther und die Mystik," in Ivan Asner, hrsg., *Kirche, Mystik, Heiligung und das Natürliche bei Luther* (Göttingen, 1967), pp. 20–59.

most clearly outlined in his famous work *History of Church and Heresy.*
In the "General Remarks" that introduce the *History* and on which
the whole work is constructed,[45] Arnold outlines the change that took
place in the approach to, treatment of, and resulting redefinition of
heresy in the first four Christian centuries. Early Christian leaders attacked evil teaching where they found it, Arnold taught, but as time
went on they extended the definition to teachings they did not understand. These they attacked with great ferocity, driving the persecuted
into greater error. In their arrogance, these powerful, hypocritical
clerics came to believe that only they upheld the truth, with the result
that anyone who spoke against them, or against their manifest crimes,
was automatically defined as a heretic. Although defined as heretics,
those who stood against the institution, those who upheld the simplicity of Christ's gospel, were the true witnesses to the truth, the true
Church. Actual heresy was that teaching pressed by the so-called Orthodox.

For Arnold, the witnesses to the truth (*Zeugen der Wahrheit*)
throughout history are the true followers of Christ, the true successors to his apostles, and are to be recognized by the persecution they
suffer. They are taught by God and protected by him in their battle
against pharisaic, institutional Christianity. At the beginning of
Christian history, the truth of God was immediately available to the
reborn. Among these Arnold placed the mystics. As time went on the
clerics forced their definitions into narrow confines, building not
only the Scriptural Canon but the symbols and conciliar statements
by which they insisted all truth must be judged, although the work of
the Holy Spirit in renewing the image of God in man ought to have
been followed. The true witnesses experienced the working of the divine, by the guidance of the Spirit in them were able to interpret the
Scriptures properly and make correct theological judgements, and, established as the true Church, witnessed against the institutional heresy about them.

Arnold's emphasis on the experience of the mystical union with
Christ and on a radical distinction between witnesses to the truth and
members of the established, theologically "orthodox" churches, between God's children and Babel, was widely attractive to separatistic
Pietists. Thus, radicals like Heinrich Horche (1652–1729), Johann

---

45. See Gottfried Arnold, *Unparteiische Kirche-und Ketzer-Historie* (Franckfurt a.M.,
1699), "Allgemeine Anmerckungen."

INTRODUCTION

Porst (1668–1728), Johann Heinrich Reitz (1655–1720), as well as the Swiss separatists associated with Samuel Koenig (1670–1750), found stimulation in Arnold's work.[46] Perhaps his thought and career also played a role in the formation of the more revolutionary bodies aligned with the Radical Pietists, in particular the Inspirationalists,[47] a group related to the Camisards, Huguenots who fled France after the revocation of the Edict of Nantes in 1685 and whose worship centered on prophesyings (in these meetings the prophet would go into a trance and speak ecstatically). Certainly Arnold's Boehmist-oriented works were of major importance in the career of Johann Conrad Dippel (1673–1734),[48] the individualist and mystical spiritualist whose peregrinations throughout Germany, Denmark, and Sweden strengthened the Radical Pietist bodies in those countries. Arnold's support of Radical Reformation groups influenced Ernst Christian Hochmann von Hohenau (1670–1721),[49] a central figure in the establishment of the Church of the Brethren founded by a separated pietist conventicle at Schwartzenau in 1708 and which in America was parent to the first significant Protestant monastic community, the Ephrata Cloisters near Lancaster, Pennsylvania.[50] The Ephrata Cloisters was founded in 1732 by the superintendent, Johann Conrad Beissel (1690–1768), and flourished until the late eighteenth century. His thought was influenced by Boehmism and Sabbatarianism but was, in its general outlines, formed by Radical Pietism. During the seventy

---

46. The fullest modern study of separatist Pietism is David Ensign Chauncey, *Radical German Pietism (c. 1675–c. 1760)* (Ph.D. Diss., Boston University School of Theology, 1955); but note as well Max Goebel, *Geschichte des christlichen Lebens in der rheinischen-westphälischen evangelischen Kirche*, 3 Bde. (Coblenz, 1852–1860), vol. 2, pp. 681ff., III, and Seeberg, *Auswahl*, pp. 4–5.

47. See Goebel, vol. 2, pp. 778–809. Note especially Donald F. Durnbaugh, "Johann Adam Gruber: Pennsylvania Prophet and Poet," *Pennsylvania Magazine of History and Biography* 83 (1959): 382–408.

48. See Goebel, vol. 2, pp. 166–193.

49. See Goebel, vol. 2, pp. 809–855, and Heinz Renkewitz, *Hochmann von Hochenau (1670–1721)* (Breslau, 1935).

50. See Donald F. Durnbaugh, *European Origins of the Brethren* (Elgin, Ill.: 1958); Donald F. Durnbaugh, *The Brethren in Colonial America* (Elgin, Ill., 1967); Julius Friedrich Sachse, *The German Sectarians of Pennsylvania 1708–1800: A Critical and Legendary History of the Ephrata Cloister and the Dunkers*, 2 vols. (Philadelphia, 1899–1900); F. Ernest Stoeffler, *Mysticism in German Devotional Literature of Colonial Pennsylvania* (Allentown, Pa., 1950); Donald E. Miller, "The Influence of Gottfried Arnold upon the Church of the Brethren," *Brethren Life and Thought* 5, no. 3 (1960): 39–50; Donald F. Durnbaugh, "Work and Hope: The Spirituality of the Radical Pietist Communitarian," *Church History* 38 (1970): 72ff.

years the community flourished it produced a large body of poetry, art, music, and theological treatises and under its second prior, the learned Peter Miller (1710–1792), came to the attention of Europeans as well as Americans. Arnold also was seen as a supporter of the Boehmist movement known as Philadelphianism, founded in England by Jane Leade (1623–1704) and represented in Germany by Johann Petersen (1649–1727) and his "spiritual wife," Johanna Eleanora Von Merlau; Petersen was an active defender of Arnold.[51]

All of the Radicals mentioned to this point were especially attracted by Boehmist thought, but Quietism too shaped the movement. Both Francke and Arnold edited Molinos's *Spiritual Guide;* Arnold also edited the works of Gertrude More and Cardinal Petrucci and borrowed much from the Quietist Pierre Poiret (1646–1719).[52] A quarter of a century before the founding of Ephrata, Johann Kelpius (1673–1708) had traveled to America and established a monastic community in what is now North Philadelphia, Pennsylvania. Kelpius's most significant work, his treatise on prayer, reflects this Quietist influence on Pietism.[53] The most important of all the Quietistic Pietists, however, was Gerhard Tersteegen (1697–1769) of Muhlheim an der Ruhr.[54] He was of Reformed Church tradition and clearly a separatist. Tersteegen carried on an extensive correspondence, remaining in close contact with the Pietists in America as well as those in Europe. Although deeply influenced by Poiret and Madame Guyon (1648–1717) and editor of Bernies-Louvigny (1602–1659),[55] Tersteegen was a Pietist first and a Quietist only thereafter. Certainly Tersteegen's wide use of mystical vocabulary can lead one to suppose that his goal is the experience of an ecstatic, world-denying union with the

---

51. On Leade and the Philadelphians see Nils Thune, *The Boehmenists and the Philadelphians* (Uppsala, 1948).

52. On Poiret see Max Weiser, *Peter Poiret* (München, 1934) and his earlier *Der sentimentalische Mensch* (Gotha und Stuttgart, 1924). On Quietism in general see Ronald A. Knox, *Enthusiasim* (Oxford, 1961), pp. 231–254.

53. The fullest discussion of Kelpius is Julius F. Sachse, *The German Pietists of Provincial Pennsylvania* (Philadelphia, 1895).

54. See Goebel, *Geschichte des christlichen Lebens,* pp. 289–477; Emanuel Hirsch, *Geschichte der neuern evangelischen Theologie* (Gütersloh, 1949–1954), vol. 2, pp. 274–277; and my article "Gerhard Tersteegen, Christopher Saur and Pennsylvania Sectarians," *Brethren Life and Thought* 20 (1975): 153–157, which includes a more detailed bibliography.

55. See *Das verborgene Leben mit Christo in Gott, aus den Schriften des erleuchteten Johann v. Bernies Louvigne.* Ins. Deutsche übertragen und kurz zusammengezogen von Gerhard Ter-Stegen ... (Stuttgart, o.J.).

divine, but, like Arnold, all such rhetoric must be read within the context of traditional Protestant thought if one is not to err in interpreting the author's intention.

Pietism in Württemberg

Strikingly different from Halle Pietism and the Radical Pietism of Arnold and Tersteegen is that which developed in the Duchy of Württemberg in the late seventeenth century and continues strong to the present day.[56] Chief among the representatives of Württemberg Pietism are the biblical scholar Johann Albrecht Bengel (1687–1752) and the theosophical pietist philosopher Friedrich Christoph Oetinger (1702–1782). Biblical scholarship and theosophical speculation are seen as distinctly separate by modern thought, but in seventeenth- and eighteenth-century Württemberg they were bound together. Before the advent of Pietism in the duchy, Johann Valentin Andreä (1586–1654) had developed a pansophistic theology that was tied closely to biblical study; by the turn of the century Johannes Andreas Hochstetter (1637–1720) and his son Andreas Adam (1668–1717), among others, were developing biblical studies within a Pietist context. Bengel[57] shared their interests and the general concerns of the Spener-Halle pietistic school, although he softened the emphasis on the *Busskampf.* With the Lutherans at Halle, Bengel shared an interest in Reformed theology as it was applied to the study of Scripture, particularly the covenant theology of Johann Cocceius (1603–1669) and the work of his follower Campegius Vitringa (1659–1722).[58] Bengel was early troubled by the fact of variant biblical readings, particularly as he found them in the *Oxford Greek Testament.* Working toward an answer, Bengel never doubted that the Bible was essentially one in spite of the variants and that its chief purpose was to provide man insight into the full glory of God. His exegesis was directed toward the one purpose of the Bible and to this end he published his *Gnomon on*

56. See Hartmut Lehmann, *Pietismus und weltliche Ordnung in Württemberg von 17. bis zum 20. Jahrhundert* (Stuttgart, 1969).
57. See Gottfried Mälzer, *Johann Albrecht Bengel: Leben und Werk* (Stuttgart, 1970).
58. Cf. Hermann Bauch, *Die Lehre vom Wirken des Heiligen Geistes im Frühpietismus: Studien zur Pneumatologie und Eschatologie von Campegius Vitringa, Philipp Jakob Spener und Johann Albrecht Bengel* (Hamburg, 1974). On Cocceius see Dorner, *History of Protestant Theology,* vol. 2, pp. 31–35.

the New Testament in 1742 after almost a quarter-century of study,[59] a volume particularly praised by and influential on John Wesley.

Bengel's study of the Scripture and attraction to Spener's Pietism led him as well to speculate extensively on the last days, concluding that the world would end in 1836.[60] Bengel's eschatological speculations had great influence in later pietist circles and even after the fated year came and went without direct divine intervention, the influence of his biblical commentary continued. Part of the reason for this was undoubtedly the warmth, tolerance, and sensitivity of his personality, which shone through in writings as it had in his person, directing the reader to the same goal toward which he directed himself: *Te totum applica ad textum, textum totum applica ad te* (Apply yourself totally to the text; apply the text totally to yourself).

Like Bengel, Oetinger too summed up the orientation of his life and what he felt should be the orientation of the lives of others in a personal admonition: "Like Socrates seek the most useful and the simplest from learning. . . . Time is eternity wrapped up; eternity is time unwrapped."[61] His words reflect his philosophical position, his search to understand time and eternity, nature and supernature, man and the universe.

After seeking to understand himself as a youth, he underwent a conversion in 1721, entered theological study at Tübingen, but dissatisfied with the answers provided by the Orthodox theologians, Bengel (to whom he remained close throughout his life), and others, he spent time traveling, meeting such persons as the Inspirationalist Johann Friedrich Rock at Berleberg (Rock was part of a group who completed an eight-volume translation of the Bible, which included a lengthy mystical commentary on the text),[62] and visiting Halle and the Moravians under Count Zinzendorf in Saxony. Oetinger was soon attracted to Cabbalistic literature and above all the works of

---

59. *Gnomon Novi Testamenti in qvo ex natvra verborum vi simplicitas, profunditas, concinnitas, salvbritas, sensvvm caelestium indicatur* (Tübingen, 1742). In relation to Bengel's concern with the Bible, note that of Pietism in general; see Kurt Aland, hrsg., *Pietismus ind Bibel* (Witten, 1970).

60. See his *Erklärte Offenbarung Johannes und viel mehr Jesu Christi . . .* (Franckfurt a.M., 1740) and *Sechzig erbauliche reden uber die Offenbarung Johannes* (Stuttgart, 1748).

61. See Friedrich Christoph Oetinger, *Inquisitio in Sensum Communem et Rationem* (Tübingen, 1753), p. 270.

62. See Goebel, *Geschichte des christlichen Lebens*, vol. 3, pp. 71–125. See above all Walter Grossmann, *Johann Christian Edilmann, from Orthodoxy to Enlightenment* (The Hague, 1976).

INTRODUCTION

Boehme. Boehme's attempt to reconcile Creator and creation, and his distinction between natural reason (*Vernunft*) and the understanding (*Verstand*) that comes from new life in Christ, were developed by Oetinger so as to move behind the philosophical systems of Newton, Leibnitz, and Wolff. Oetinger published the fullest explication of his thought, the *Theologia ex idea vitae deducta* (*Theology drawn from the idea of life*), in 1765,[63] teaching that the human person is directed toward his perfection in the creation of a new spiritual body. The dynamic movement in man is not reason or being, but "life." The path of life toward the new spiritual body is the path marked by the traditional *ordo*, and the attainment of its goal is made possible by the death and resurrection of Christ. In the *sensus communis* one is opened to knowledge of the universe and the Scripture by the Holy Spirit. At the root of man, beyond the division of subject and object, there is a unified center where one can contact wisdom and truth.

Oetinger's attraction to Boehme, his ontological and epistemological speculations (only recently receiving the attention they deserve[64]), and his interest in the visions of the seer Emanuel Swedenborg (1688–1772) seem distant from the concerns of the Pietists, but they are not. In his sermons and his numerous theological and pastoral works, Oetinger shared the pietist vision of a practical experiential Christianity.

Count Zinzendorf and the Renewed Moravianism

Among the Radical Pietists and between the Radical and Church Pietists, as might be expected, theological battles raged. The greatest disagreements, however, were those that developed against the Pietism of the Saxon Nicolaus Ludwig, Count Zinzendorf (1700–1760).[65] Bengel wrote a lengthy work against him and in Europe and

---

63. See Friedrich Christoph Oetinger, *Theologia ex Idea Deducta*, hrsg. von Konrad Ohly, 2 Bde. (Berlin, 1979). Particularly valuable is Sigrid Grossmann, *Friedrich Christoph Oetingers Gottesvorstellung* (Göttingen, 1979).

64. Note in particular the preface by Hans-Georg Godamer to the reprint edition of Oetinger's *Inquisitio* (Stuttgart, 1964).

65. For a general biography see John R. Weinlick, *Count Zinzendorf* (New York, 1956). A good overview of critical difficulties in the interpretation of Zinzendorf's theology is available in Stoeffler, *German Pietism*, pp. 140ff. On the Moravians at the time see J. Taylor and Kenneth G. Hamilton, *History of the Moravian Church* (Bethlehem, Pa., 1967) and above all Gillian Lindt Gollen, *Moravians in Two Worlds* (New York, 1967) and Jacob John Sessler, *Communal Pietism among Early American Moravians* (New York, 1933).

INTRODUCTION

America he and his movement continually stirred up animosity in spite of their deeply irenic and ecumenical concerns.[66]

Zinzendorf had been much influenced by Spener and Francke; his theology was a further development of their thought. Born in 1700, Zinzendorf lost his father at only six weeks of age. When he was four his mother married a Prussian marshal and moved to Berlin, leaving her son in the care of his pietist grandmother at Gross-Hennersdorf in Upper Lusatia. A highly precocious and religious child, Zinzendorf matured quickly. After a period of study at Halle, he was sent at sixteen to Wittenberg by a guardian who was opposed to the young student's religious bent and Zinzendorf found himself in an institution the exact opposite of his liking. Here, however, he was able to learn the various social skills so necessary for a man of the court. With further studies in Germany, Holland, and France he completed his education. Not allowed by his family to enter the Lutheran ministry, Zinzendorf accepted his role as a public figure but chose to make it one that would serve to the fullest his ideals for Christian life.

Early in 1722 Zinzendorf heard of the plight of the Bohemian Brethren, or the Moravians. Except for one other group, the Waldensians in northern Italy and southern France, the Moravians were the oldest of the Protestant communities. In direct spiritual descent from the fifteenth-century Hussite movement, they had maintained their existence despite intensive persecution. By the eighteenth century, the few who remained were rallied by the efforts of Christian David (1691–1751), a former Catholic who came out of Bohemia in 1722 and worked avidly as a missionary of the Moravian cause for the rest of his life. For a man of Zinzendorf's character, the Moravians' cry for help did not go unheard. He offered them asylum on his estate at Berthelsdorf, where they immediately set to work to build homes for themselves. They began on June 17, 1722, and they named their village Herrnhut (the Lord's Watch) since it was under God's care that they had arrived and since they continued to maintain watch for his purposes. The ties between the major figures in the renewed Moravian Church were close. All the leaders were attached in some way to the Pietist awakening. Christian David had been converted in Görlitz in 1717 under the influence of Melchior Schäffer, the pastor at Holy Trinity, and his friend Johann Andreas Rothe (1688–1758).

---

66. Johann Albrecht Bengel, *Abriss der sogenannten Brudergemeine* (Stuttgart, 1751). See also Gottfried Mälzer, *Bengel und Zinzendorf* (Witten, 1968).

INTRODUCTION

In the early years at Herrnhut, under the strain of continuing immigration and newly developing social structures, religious differences rose to the forefront. The Lutheran Rothe could not always understand or appreciate certain Moravian traditions and the presence of various other groups of religious enthusiasts made the situation volatile. Nevertheless, unanimity was growing through 1726–1727. By February of 1727, the group had divided into bands, small groups of similarly situated members—bachelors, young girls, widows, and so forth—and on August 13, 1727, the whole community experienced a deep spiritual awakening. From that moment on the movement blossomed and evangelists spread out in diaspora from Saxony into other areas of Europe and the world, in particular to the New World colonies of Georgia and Pennsylvania.

The theology these evangelists carried with them was shaped in large part by that of Zinzendorf. Opposed to theological system, Zinzendorf placed attention on the heart and its feeling or experience of Christ in faith. Christ's redemptive act was central for Zinzendorf. Emphasizing Luther's distinction between a hidden and a revealed God, he spoke of Christ as a *Spezial-Gott,* a special God in whom the fullness of the divinity was revealed. The God revealed through creation and redemption is God the Son. Faith in this God brings further experience of love for his redemptive presence in the believer, an experience of love that Zinzendorf is fond of describing in terms of bride-bridegroom imagery or images such as "little Jesus" or "sweet Jesus," which at times strike a modern reader (as they did many of Zinzendorf's contemporaries) as being in bad taste. The most extreme images of this kind as well as the most vivid description of Christ's wounds and blood are found in the works written by Zinzendorf between 1743 and 1750.

Like all the Pietists, Zinzendorf placed great emphasis on conversion and new birth, but he opposed Francke's emphasis on extreme sorrow over sin and repentance (*Busskampf*). For Zinzendorf the conversion experience was joyous and brought with it assurance of salvation. In his treatment of renovation, too, he differed from Francke and Luther, holding to a theology of the imitation of Christ, of growing more like Christ, rather than to one of following Christ in discipleship alone.

The most striking elements in Zinzendorf's thought, however, were his views on marriage and his ecclesiology. For him the relationship between the marital couple was the best analogy for understand-

21

ing the relationship between Christ and the believer, and he made, as a result, wide use of bridegroom imagery and of the images from the Song of Songs when describing either. Because of the seriousness with which the analogy was held among the Moravians and because of Zinzendorf's familial model of the trinity (Father, Mother, and Son) the institution of marriage was much more respected among that tradition than elsewhere in the Protestant world. Whereas the radicals either rejected marriage completely, insisting on strict celibacy, or allowed "spiritual marriages," Zinzendorf and the Moravians exalted sexuality in marriage. The love between man and wife was to be as creative and open as the love of the Father, Mother (Holy Spirit), and Son in the heart of the believer.

Of all the Pietists, Zinzendorf's ecumenism was the widest. He believed, broadening Spener's concept of pietist conventicles as *ecclesiolae in ecclesia*, that the various denominations were "schools" divinely instituted to direct believers in faith. None of these denominations were final, he believed; even the Moravian tradition in its renewed form was not the "true church" toward which all were moving. In the early 1740s Zinzendorf seemed to think that the true church might come into being in the American wilderness. But his hope for a "Congregation of God in the Spirit" was to be disappointed; many of the traditions saw Zinzendorf's plan as a plot on the part of a spiritually aggressive leader to draw all into his own denomination, and accordingly rejected his proposal.[67]

Although Zinzendorf failed in his attempt to bring the German-speaking Protestants of America together, he was to have an influence on English-speaking American spirituality in a way he never expected, namely through John Wesley and the Methodists. Wesley first met the Moravians on his way to Georgia. The day after his arrival he spoke with August Gottlieb Spangenberg (1704–1792), next to Zinzendorf the most important Moravian of the time.

> Saturday, 7.—Mr. Oglethorpe returned from Savannah with Mr. Spangenberg, one of the pastors of the Germans. I soon found what spirit he was of and asked his advice with regard

---

67. Note the debate in *The Journals of Henry Melchior Muhlenberg*, trans. Theodore G. Tappert and John W. Doberstein (Philadelphia, 1942), vol. 1, pp. 76–81, 109ff., 156ff.

to my own conduct. He said, "My brother, I must first ask you one or two questions. Have you the witness within yourself? Does the Spirit of God bear witness with your spirit that you are a child of God?" I was surprised, and knew not what to answer. He observed it and asked, "Do you know Jesus Christ?" I paused and said, "I know He is the Saviour of the world." "True," replied he, "but do you know He has saved you?" I answered, "I hope He has died to save me." He only added, "Do you know yourself?" I said, "I do." But I fear they were vain words.[68]

After numerous difficulties in America, Wesley returned to England, where he was in close contact with Peter Böhler, leader of the Moravians in Great Britain. In 1738, he reports conversations with Böhler as follows:

In the evening I went very unwillingly to a society in Aldersgate Street, where one was reading Luther's preface to the Epistle to the Romans. About a quarter before nine, while he was describing the change which God works in the heart through faith in Christ, I felt my heart strangely warmed. I felt I did trust in Christ, Christ alone, for salvation; and an assurance was given me that He had taken away my sins, even mine, and saved me from the law of sin and death. . . .
        After my return home, I was much buffeted with temptations, but I cried out, and they fled away. They returned again and again. I as often lifted up my eyes, and He "sent me help from his holy place." And herein I found the difference between this and my former state chiefly consisted. I was striving, yea, fighting with all my might under the law, as well as under grace. But then I was sometimes, if not often, conquered; now, I was always conqueror.
        Thursday, 25.—The moment I awakened, "Jesus, Master," was in my heart and in my mouth; and I found all my

---

68. *The Journal of John Wesley* (London, 1872), vol. 1, p. 35.

strength lay in keeping my eye fixed upon Him and my soul
waiting on Him continually.[69]

Immediately after this experience Wesley went on a three-month
trip to Germany, where he met with many Pietists. In the years to
follow he was to work out the implications of pietist theology in his
own linguistic tradition.

Later Developments

By the time Wesley made his trip to Germany, the theological
climate had changed radically from the one Spener had faced some
fifty years earlier. The Enlightenment had begun. There was a new
interest in the natural order as scientific study of the universe developed, and under the influence of thinkers such as Leibnitz (1646–
1716) and Christian Wolff (1679–1754) an optimistic belief in the progress of history and the possibilities and end of man was developing.
Those Pietists who lived and worked before the death of Francke in
1727 did not need to speak to the new situation; many of those who
were active immediately after that date (Zinzendorf and Oetinger in
particular) met the changed circumstance with varying degrees of understanding and success. By the mid-eighteenth century, however, it
was almost impossible for Pietism to ignore the Enlightenment. The
first-generation Pietists opposed seventeenth-century Orthodoxy,
even while developing out of it; the Pietists of the second half of the
eighteenth century, often called Neo-Pietists, opposed the Enlightenment, but they too were much affected by the position they resisted.
Joined with the remnants of their early opponents, the Orthodox,
they upheld revelation against reason, grace against nature, and
God's redemptive activity against man's freedom. Nevertheless, there
was much in their pietistic background that fitted well with the new
age—first with Enlightenment ideals, then with *Sturm und Drang*, and
finally with Romanticism—and that they accented accordingly.

They too stood in awe before the beauty of nature and the majesty of the universe, accented inner illumination and personal growth,
and looked toward a better age. Even though their view of man was
not that of a belief in human freedom and their vision of better days

---

69. Ibid., pp. 103–104.

INTRODUCTION

not that of the myth of progress, Neo-Pietists, aware of the similarities between their own positions and those of their opponents, were able to open fruitful dialogues with a now more secularized world. Thus Johann Caspar Lavater (1741–1801) could speak glowingly of Herder, and the greatest of the Neo-Pietists, Johann Heinrich Jung-Stilling (1740–1817), could maintain friendship with Johann Wolfgang von Goethe (1749–1832).[70]

How far one can trace the direct influence of Pietism following the era of the Neo-Pietists is difficult to ascertain.[71] Its most important impact was initially with the German-, Dutch-, and Scandanavian-speaking areas of Europe, but the significance of its influence for and through the religious groups within these linguistic communities in North America must not be overlooked, particularly as they were affected by the stepchild of Pietism, Wesleyan Methodism. What is clear is that as Pietism developed it underwent significant changes, not always for the best. Among Pietism's North American descendants the emphasis on subjective individual experience, initially directed against an arid scholastic concern with "pure" doctrine, soon forced a peculiar semantic shift within the language of piety. By this shift, "knowledge" of God was reduced to an "emotional experience" undergone at conversion and in devotion, and the emphasis on faith soon turned that gift into a near-Pelagian work. Pietism's radical division of head and heart would, in time, support anti-intellectualism. The movement's love ethic, originally committed to a social gospel, shifted to attention on caring and duty and may well have played a role in the development of totalitarian attitudes on both sides of the Atlantic. Confidence in salvation moved by way of Wesleyan assurance to certainty and the conventicles, once formed for mutual encouragement, became the basis for an intolerant division of true against false Christianity and Christians. Pietism's concern with the priesthood of all believers tended in popularist democratic circles to merge with anti-intellectualism and support only the most simplistic theological positions.

But Pietism must not be finally judged by its offspring, whether

---

70. For details see Stoeffler, *German Pietism*, pp. 253ff., and Heinrich's *Preussentum und Pietismus*, pp. 352 ff. Note also Harry Lowen, *Goethe's Response to Protestantism* (Bern, 1972).

71. See Stoeffler, *Rise*, pp. 3ff. for suggestions regarding the influence of Pietism in the English-speaking church.

INTRODUCTION

liberal or conservative. Too often in the past has its proper interpretation been hampered by prejudice and hatred. In its initial form it was committed to a new view of Christian existence, always judged in light of eschatological expectations, to renewed ethical requirements both for individuals and for society at large, to a reformed concern with experience and the religious nature of the whole person, to a radical questioning of earlier simplistic approaches to state-church relationships and religious tolerance, to ecumerical endeavors, and to an intensification of personal and communal spirituality.

Note on the Texts

The texts below have been selected to reflect, as fully as possible, the scope of Pietist spirituality in the eighteenth century. Primarily designed to treat the Spener-Halle school and persons under its immediate influence, the collection places heavy emphasis on the Lutheran origins of the pietist awakening, is limited to German-speaking members of the movement, and omits texts by Neo-Pietists. Nevertheless, even with the limitations of narrowing the volume to represent "first-generation" Pietism, it was possible to include some persons who reflect later concerns (Zinzendorf, Oetinger). Unfortunately, a section on Reformed Pietists had to be removed and it has not been possible for reasons of space to include a section on Pietism in America. It is my hope to expand material gathered for such a section into a future volume on Pietism in America.

Where possible, I have chosen shorter texts. In the case of longer texts, I have necessarily edited (Pietists were not only prolific writers, but also extremely repetitive and for this reason I have not followed the normal practice of the Classics series and included full translations of a single book-length work) and deletions are indicated. The collection is intended to reflect pietist spirituality but almost all the genres used by pietist authors are included: the theological treatise, the sermon (used by Pietists as an aid to meditation), the sermon note, the autobiography, the biography, the prescriptive guide, the hymn and poem (translated literally in most cases), the prayer book, the biblical commentary, the personal letter, the catechism, emblem, confessional, and liturgical text.

I wish particularly to thank Charlotte Cox, who aided greatly and graciously in typing and proofreading, and Cyndi Holbrook, who helped with the assembly of the final typescript. I wish also to express

INTRODUCTION

my gratitude to Fortress Press, Philadelphia, Pennsylvania, for permission to reprint the selection from Spener's *Pia desideria*, Pathway Publishing, Aylmen, Ont., for permission to reprint sections from *A Devoted Christian Prayerbook*, and the University of Iowa Press, Iowa City, Iowa, for permission to reprint selections from Zinzendorf's *Nine Public Lectures*. Full bibliographical details for sources of all texts included are indicated at the end of the volume.

Philipp Jakob Spener
1635–1705

Philipp Jakob Spener

FROM THE
PIA DESIDERIA*
1675

1

Thought should be given to a more extensive use of the Word of God among us. We know that by nature we have no good in us. If there is to be any good in us, it must be brought about by God. To this end the Word of God is the powerful means, since faith must be enkindled through the gospel, and the law provides the rules for good works and many wonderful impulses to attain them. The more at home the Word of God is among us, the more we shall bring about faith and its fruits.

It may appear that the Word of God has sufficiently free course among us inasmuch as at various places (as in this city [Frankfurt am Main]) there is daily or frequent preaching from the pulpit. When we reflect further on the matter, however, we shall find that with respect to this first proposal, more is needed. I do not at all disapprove of the preaching of sermons in which a Christian congregation is instructed by the reading and exposition of a certain text, for I myself do this. But I find that this is not enough. In the first place, we know that "all Scripture is inspired by God and profitable for teaching, for reproof, for correction, and for training in righteousness" (2 Tim. 3:16). Accordingly all Scripture, without exception, should be known by the congregation if we are all to receive the necessary benefit. If we put together all the passages of the Bible which in the course of many years are read to a congregation in one place, they will comprise only

*Reprinted with permission from Philipp Jakob Spener, *Pia desideria*, translated, edited, and with an Introduction by Theodore G. Tappert (Philadelphia: Fortress Press, 1964), pp. 87–122.

31

a very small part of the Scriptures which have been given to us. The remainder is not heard by the congregation at all, or is heard only insofar as one or another verse is quoted or alluded to in sermons, without, however, offering any understanding of the entire context, which is nevertheless of the greatest importance. In the second place, the people have little opportunity to grasp the meaning of the Scriptures except on the basis of those passages which may have been expounded to them, and even less do they have opportunity to become as practiced in them as edification requires. Meanwhile, although solitary reading of the Bible at home is in itself a splendid and praiseworthy thing, it does not accomplish enough for most people.

It should therefore be considered whether the church would not be well advised to introduce the people to Scripture in still other ways than through the customary sermons on the appointed lessons.

This might be done, first of all, by diligent reading of the Holy Scriptures, especially of the New Testament. It would not be difficult for every housefather to keep a Bible, or at least a New Testament, handy and read from it every day or, if he cannot read, to have somebody else read. . . .

Then a second thing would be desirable in order to encourage people to read privately, namely, that where the practice can be introduced the books of the Bible be read one after another, at specified times in the public service, without further comment (unless one wished to add brief summaries). This would be intended for the edification of all, but especially of those who cannot read at all, or cannot read easily or well, or of those who do not own a copy of the Bible.

For a third thing it would perhaps not be inexpedient (and I set this down for further and more mature reflection) to reintroduce the ancient and apostolic kind of church meetings. In addition to our customary services with preaching, other assemblies would also be held in the manner in which Paul describes them in 1 Corinthians 14:26–40. One person would not rise to preach (although this practice would be continued at other times), but others who have been blessed with gifts and knowledge would also speak and present their pious opinions on the proposed subject to the judgment of the rest, doing all this in such a way as to avoid disorder and strife. This might conveniently be done by having several ministers (in places where a number of them live in a town) meet together or by having several members of a congregation who have a fair knowledge of God or desire to increase their knowledge meet under the leadership of a minister, take up the

Holy Scriptures, read aloud from them, and fraternally discuss each verse in order to discover its simple meaning and whatever may be useful for the edification of all. Anybody who is not satisfied with his understanding of a matter should be permitted to express his doubts and seek further explanation. On the other hand, those (including the ministers) who have made more progress should be allowed the freedom to state how they understand each passage. Then all that has been contributed, insofar as it accords with the sense of the Holy Spirit in the Scriptures, should be carefully considered by the rest, especially by the ordained ministers, and applied to the edification of the whole meeting. Everything should be arranged with an eye to the glory of God, to the spiritual growth of the participants, and therefore also to their limitations. Any threat of meddlesomeness, quarrelsomeness, self-seeking, or something else of this sort should be guarded against and tactfully cut off especially by the preachers who retain leadership in these meetings.

Not a little benefit is to be hoped for from such an arrangement. Preachers would learn to know the members of their own congregations and their weakness or growth in doctrine and piety, and a bond of confidence would be established between preachers and people which would serve the best interests of both. At the same time the people would have a splendid opportunity to exercise their diligence with respect to the Word of God and modestly to ask their questions (which they do not always have the courage to discuss with their minister in private) and get answers to them. In a short time they would experience personal growth and would also become capable of giving better religious instruction to their children and servants at home. In the absence of such exercises, sermons which are delivered in continually flowing speech are not always fully and adequately comprehended because there is no time for reflection in between or because, when one does stop to reflect, much of what follows is missed (which does not happen in a discussion). On the other hand, private reading of the Bible or reading in the household, where nobody is present who may from time to time help point out the meaning and purpose of each verse, cannot provide the reader with a sufficient explanation of all that he would like to know. What is lacking in both of these instances (in public preaching and private reading) would be supplied by the proposed exercises. It would not be a great burden either to the preachers or to the people, and much would be done to fulfill the admonition of Paul in Colossians 3:16, "Let the word of Christ dwell in you richly, as you teach and admonish one another in all wisdom, and as you sing psalms and hymns and spiritual songs." In fact, such songs may be used in the proposed meetings for the praise of God and the inspiration of the participants.

This much is certain: The diligent use of the Word of God, which consists not only of listening to sermons but also of reading, meditating, and discussing (Ps. 1:2), must be the chief means for reforming something, whether this occurs in the proposed fashion or in some other appropriate way. The Word of God remains the seed from which all that is good in us must grow. If we succeed in getting the people to seek eagerly and diligently in the book of life for their joy, their spiritual life will be wonderfully strengthened and they will become altogether different people. . . .

One of the principal wrongs by which papal politics became entrenched, the people were kept in ignorance, and hence complete control of their consciences was maintained was that the papacy prohibited, and insofar as possible continues to prohibit, the reading of the Holy Scriptures. On the other hand, it was one of the major purposes of the Reformation to restore to the people the Word of God which had lain hidden under the bench (and this Word was the most powerful means by which God blessed his work). So this will be the principal means, now that the church must be put in better condition, whereby the aversion to Scripture which many have may be overcome, neglect of its study be counteracted, and ardent zeal for it awakened.

2

Our frequently mentioned Dr. Luther would suggest another means, which is altogether compatible with the first. This second proposal is the establishment and diligent exercise of the spiritual priesthood. Nobody can read Luther's writings with some care without observing how earnestly the sainted man advocated this spiritual priesthood, according to which not only ministers but all Christians are made priests by their Savior, are anointed by the Holy Spirit, and are dedicated to perform spiritual-priestly acts. . . . [A]ll spiritual functions are open to all Christians without exception. Although the regular and public performance of them is entrusted to ministers appointed for this purpose, the functions may be performed by others in case of emergency. Especially should those things which are unrelated to public acts be done continually by all at home and in everyday life.

Indeed, it was by a special trick of the cursed devil that things were brought to such a pass in the papacy that all these spiritual functions were assigned solely to the clergy (to whom alone the name "spiritual," which is in actual fact common to all Christians, was therefore arrogantly allotted) and the rest of the Christians were excluded from them, as if it were not proper for laymen diligently to study in the Word of the Lord, much less to instruct, admonish, chastise, and comfort their neighbors, or to do privately what pertains to the ministry publicly, inasmuch as all these things were supposed to belong only to the office of the minister. The consequence has been that the so-called laity has been made slothful in those things that ought to concern it; a terrible ignorance has resulted, and from this, in turn, a disorderly life. On the other hand, members of the so-called spiritual estate could do as they pleased since nobody dared look at their cards or raise the least objection. This presumptuous monopoly of the clergy, alongside the aforementioned prohibition of Bible reading, is one of the principal means by which papal Rome established its power over poor Christians and still preserves it wherever it has opportunity. The papacy could suffer no greater injury than having Luther point out that all Christians have been called to exercise spiritual functions (although not called to the public exercise of them, which requires appointment by a congregation with equal right) and that they are not only permitted but, if they wish to be Christians, are obligated to undertake them.

Every Christian is bound not only to offer himself and what he has, his prayer, thanksgiving, good works, alms, and so forth, but also industriously to study in the Word of the Lord, with the grace that is given him to teach others, especially those under his own roof, to chastise, exhort, convert, and edify them, to observe their life, pray for all, and insofar as possible be concerned about their salvation. If this is first pointed out to the people, they will take better care of themselves and apply themselves to whatever pertains to their own edification and that of their fellow men. On the other hand, all complacence and sloth derives from the fact that this teaching is not known and practiced. Nobody thinks this has anything to do with him. Everybody imagines that just as he was himself called to his office, business, or trade and the minister was neither called to such an occupation nor works in it, so the minister alone is called to perform spiritual acts, occupy himself with the Word of God, pray, study, teach, admonish, comfort, chastise, and so forth, while others should not trouble themselves with such things and, in fact, would be meddling in the minister's business if they had anything to do with them. This is not even to mention that people ought to pay attention to the minister, admonish him fraternally when he neglects something, and in general support him in all his efforts.

No damage will be done to the ministry by a proper use of this priesthood. In fact, one of the principal reasons the ministry cannot accomplish all that it ought is that it is too weak without the help of the universal priesthood. One man is incapable of doing all that is necessary for the edification of the many persons who are generally entrusted to his pastoral care. However, if the priests do their duty, the minister, as director and oldest brother, has splendid assistance in the performance of his duties and his public and private acts, and thus his burden will not be too heavy. . . .

3

Connected with these two proposals is a third: The people must have impressed upon them and must accustom themselves to believing that it is by no means enough to have knowledge of the Christian faith, for Christianity consists rather of practice. Our dear Savior repeatedly enjoined love as the real mark of his disciples (John 13:34–35, 15:12; 1 John 3:10, 18, 4:7–8, 11–13, 21). In his old age dear John . . . was accustomed to say hardly anything more to his disciples than "Children, love one another!" His disciples and auditors finally became so annoyed at this endless repetition that they asked him why he was always saying the same thing to them. He replied, "Because it is the Lord's command, and it suffices if this be done." Indeed, love is the whole life of the man who has faith and who through his faith is saved, and his fulfillment of the laws of God consists of love.

If we can therefore awaken a fervent love among our Christians, first toward one another and then toward all men (for these two, brotherly affection and general love, must supplement each other according to 2 Peter 1:7), and put this love into practice, practically all that we desire will be accomplished. For all the commandments are summed up in love (Rom. 13:9). Accordingly the people are not only to be told this incessantly, and they are not only to have the excellence of neighborly love and, on the other hand, the great danger and harm in the opposing self-love pictured impressively before their eyes (which is done well in the spiritually minded John Arndt's *True Christianity*, IV, ii, pp. 22–28), but they must also practice such love. They must become accustomed not to lose sight of any opportunity in which they can render their neighbor a service of love, and yet while performing it they must diligently search their hearts to discover whether they are acting in true love or out of other motives. If they are offended, they should especially be on their guard, not only that they refrain from all vengefulness but also that they give up some of their rights and insistence on them for fear that their hearts may betray them and feelings of hostility may become involved. In fact, they should diligently seek opportunities to do good to their enemies in order that such self-control may hurt the old Adam, who is otherwise inclined to vengeance, and at the same time in order that love may be more deeply implanted in their hearts.

For this purpose, as well as for the sake of Christian growth in general, it may be useful if those who have earnestly resolved to walk in the way of the Lord would enter into a confidential relationship with their confessor or some other judicious and enlightened Christian and would regularly report to him how they live, what opportunities they have had to practice Christian love, and how they have employed or neglected them. This should be done with the intention of discovering what is amiss and securing such an individual's counsel and instruction as to what ought now to be done. There should be firm resolution to follow such advice at all times unless something is expected that is quite clearly contrary to God's will. If there appears to be doubt whether one is obligated to do this or that out of love for one's neighbor, it is always better to incline toward doing it rather than leaving it undone.

4

Related to this is a fourth proposal: We must beware how we conduct ourselves in religious controversies with unbelievers and heretics. We must first take pains to strengthen and confirm ourselves, our friends, and other fellow believers in the known truth and to protect them with great care from every kind of seduction. Then we must remind ourselves of our duty toward the erring.

We owe it to the erring, first of all, to pray earnestly that the good God may enlighten them with the same light with which he blessed us, may lead them to the truth, may prepare their hearts for it, or, having counteracted their dangerous errors, may reinforce what true knowledge of salvation in Christ they still have left in order that they may be saved as a brand plucked from the fire [Zech. 3:2]. This is the meaning of the first three petitions of the Lord's Prayer, that God may hallow his name in them, bring his kingdom to them, and accomplish his gracious will in and for them.

In the second place, we must give them a good example and take the greatest pains not to offend them in any way, for this would give them a bad impression of our true teaching and hence would make their conversion more difficult.

In the third place, if God has given us the gifts which are needful for it and we find the opportunity to hope to win the erring, we should be glad to do what we can to point out, with a modest but firm presentation of the truth we profess, how this is based on the simplicity of Christ's teaching. At the same time we should indicate decently but forcefully how their errors conflict with the Word of God and what dangers they carry in their wake. All of this should be done in such a way that those with whom we deal can see for themselves that everything is done out of heartfelt love toward them, without carnal and unseemly feelings, and that if we ever indulge in excessive vehemence this occurs out of pure zeal for the glory of God. Especially should we beware of invectives and personal insinuations, which at once tear down all the good we have in mind to build. If we see that we have made something of a beginning in this fashion, we should be so much the more energetic in advancing what has been begun, perhaps with the assistance of others. On the other hand, if we see that they have been so captivated by their preconceived notions that, although we perceive in them a disposition to serve God gladly without being able for the present to comprehend what we have said, they are to be admonished at the very least not to slander or speak evil of the truth which they have heard from us, to reflect further on the matter in the fear of the Lord and with fervent prayer, and in the meantime to try seriously to advance in the truth and to serve their God according to the practical principles and rules of conduct which most people who call themselves Christians have to some extent in common.

To this should be added, in the fourth place, a practice of heartfelt love toward all unbelievers and heretics. While we should indicate to them that we take no pleasure in their unbelief or false belief or the practice and propagation of these, but rather are vigorously opposed to them, yet in other things which pertain to human life we should demonstrate that we consider these people to be our neighbors (as the Samaritan was represented by Christ in Luke 10:29–37 as the Jew's neighbor), regard them as our brothers according to the right of common creation and the divine love that is extended to all (though not according to regeneration), and therefore are so disposed in our hearts toward them as the command to love all others as we love ourselves demands. To insult or wrong an unbeliever or heretic on account of his religion would be not only a carnal zeal but also a zeal that is calculated to hinder his conversion. A proper hatred of false religion should neither suspend nor weaken the love that is due the other person.

In the fifth place, if there is any prospect of a union of most of the confessions among Christians, the primary way of achieving it, and the one that God would bless most, would perhaps be this, that we do not stake everything on argumentation, for the present disposition of men's minds, which are filled by as much fleshly as spiritual zeal, makes disputation fruitless. It is true that defense of the truth, and hence also argumentation, which is part of it, must continue in the church together with other things instituted to build it up. Before us are the holy examples of Christ, the apostles, and their successors, who engaged in disputation—that is, vigorously refuted opposing errors and defended the truth. The Christian church would be plunged into the greatest danger if anybody wished to remove and repudiate this necessary use of the spiritual sword of the Word of God, insofar as its use against false teachings is concerned. Nevertheless, I adhere to the splendidly demonstrated assertion of our sainted Arndt in his *True Christianity*, "Purity of doctrine and of the Word of God is maintained not only by disputation and writing many books but also by true repentance and holiness of life" (*True Christianity*, vol. 1, p. 39). . . .

I therefore hold (1) that not all disputation is useful and good. . . . Just as all disputing is not praiseworthy and useful, so (2) proper disputation is not the only means of maintaining the truth but requires other means alongside it. Even if one resolves to limit debate to occasions in which everything is well arranged and confine it to that which is the sole and entire purpose of disputation . . . God may not add his blessing, nor will he always allow the truth to prevail. This is the case with those whose thoughts hardly extend beyond making many people Lutheran and do not deem it important that with this profession such people become genuine Christians to the very core. They therefore regard true confession of faith merely as a means of strengthening their own ecclesiastical party and not as an entrance upon a life of zealous future service of God. If the glory of God is to be properly advanced, disputation must be directed toward the goal of converting opponents and applying the truth which has been defended to a holy obedience and a due gratitude toward God. Such a *convictio intellectus* or conviction of truth is far from being faith. Faith requires more. The intention must be there to add whatever is necessary to convert the erring and remove whatever is a hindrance to him. Above all, there must be a desire, in promoting God's glory, to apply to ourselves and to all others what we hold to be true, and in this light to serve God. . . .

From all this it becomes apparent that disputing is not enough either to maintain the truth among ourselves or to impart it to the erring. The holy love of God is necessary. If only we Evangelicals would make it our serious business to offer God the fruits of his truth in fervent love, conduct ourselves in a manner worthy of our calling, and show this in recognizable and unalloyed love of our neighbors, including those who are heretics, by practicing the duties mentioned above! If only the erring, even if they cannot as yet grasp the truth which we bear witness to, would make an effort (and we ourselves should point them in this direction) to begin to serve God, in love of God and fellow man, at least to the extent of the knowledge which they may still have from Christian instruction! There is no doubt that God would then allow us to grow more and more in our knowledge of the truth, and also give us the pleasure of seeing others, whose error we now lament, alongside us in the same faith. For the Word of God has the power, if it is not viciously impeded either by those who declare it or by those who hear it, to convert men's hearts. Thus holiness of life itself contributes much to conversion, as Peter teaches (1 Pet. 3:1–2).

5

Since ministers must bear the greatest burden in all these things which pertain to a reform of the church, and since their shortcomings do correspondingly great harm, it is of the utmost importance that the office of the ministry be occupied by men who, above all, are themselves true Christians and, then, have the divine wisdom to guide others carefully on the way of the Lord. It is therefore important, indeed necessary, for the reform of the church that only such persons be called who may be suited, and that nothing at all except the glory of God be kept in view during the whole procedure of calling. This would mean that all carnal schemes involving favor, friendship, gifts, and similarly unseemly things would be set aside. Not the least among the reasons for the defect in the church are the mistakes which occur in the calling of ministers, but we shall not elaborate on this here.

However, if such suitable persons are to be called to the ministry they must be available, and hence they must be trained in our schools and universities. May God graciously grant that everything necessary thereunto may be diligently observed by the professors of theology and that they may assist in seeing to it that the unchristian academic life, which prevails among students of all faculties and which has been sorrowfully lamented . . . by many pious persons, may by vigorous measures be suppressed and reformed. Then the schools would, as they ought, really be recognized from the outward life of the students to be nurseries of the church for all estates and as workshops of the Holy Spirit rather than as places of worldliness and indeed of the devils of ambition, tippling, carousing, and brawling.

The professors could themselves accomplish a great deal here by their example (indeed, without them a real reform is hardly to be hoped for) if they would conduct themselves as men who have died unto the world, in everything would seek not their own glory, gain, or pleasure but rather the glory of their God and the salvation of those entrusted to them, and would accommodate all their studies, writing of books, lessons, lectures, disputations, and other activities to this end. Then the students would have a living example according to which they might regulate their life, for we are so fashioned that examples are as effective for us as teachings, and sometimes more effective. . . .

The professors should therefore exercise good discipline among those who eat at their table and not permit mischief for the sake of gain. Edifying conversation should be carried on by them at table. Unseemly talk, especially talk in which texts of the Bible, parts of hymns, and similar words are misused by twisting their meaning to evil purpose (whereby more harm is done than one may imagine, for godly persons are often disturbed in their devotions the rest of their lives whenever they come upon such words), should be averted and earnestly rebuked, not complacently tolerated.

Besides, students should unceasingly have it impressed upon them that holy life is not of less consequence than diligence and study, indeed that study without piety is worthless. . . . Students should constantly be reminded that the rule in human life is, *Qui proficit in literis et deficit in moribus, plus deficit quam proficit,* that is, whoever grows in learning and declines in morals is on the decrease rather than the increase. This is even more valid in spiritual life, for since theology is a practical discipline [*Theologia habitus practicus est,* a common assertion of orthodoxist theologians in the seventeenth century] . . . everything must be directed to the practice of faith and life. . . .

Surely, students of theology ought to lay this foundation, that during their early years of study they realize that they must die unto the world and live as individuals who are to become examples to the flock, and that this is not merely an ornament but a very necessary work, without which they may indeed be students of what may be called a philosophy of sacred things but not students of theology who are instructed and will be preserved only in the light of the Holy Spirit. Many, instead, hold that while it would be a good thing for a student of theology to lead a decent life, it is not necessary or important, provided he studies diligently and becomes a learned man, whether he allows himself to be governed by a worldly spirit during these years and participates with others in all the pleasures of the world, for there is time enough to change his manner of life when he becomes a minister—as if this were always in our power and as if a deeply ingrained love of the world did not generally cling to people throughout their lives, give them a bad reputation, and accordingly do harm to the ministry. On the other hand, if at the beginning of their study of theology all this were told to students and impressed upon them, I should hope that it would bear much fruit throughout the entire time of their study and, indeed, the rest of their lives.

It would be especially helpful if the professors would pay attention to the life as well as the studies of the students entrusted to them and would from time to time speak to those who need to be spoken to. . . . [T]he professors should openly and expressly show those who lead a godly life, even if they are behind the others in their studies, how dear they are to their teachers and how very much they are to be preferred to the others. In fact, these students ought to be the first, or the only, ones to be promoted. The others ought to be excluded from all hope of promotion until they change their manner of life completely. This is the way it ought in all fairness to be. It is certain that a young man who fervently loves God, although adorned with limited gifts, will be more useful to the church of God with his meager talent and academic achievement than a vain and worldly fool with double doctor's degrees who is very clever but has not been taught by God. The work of the former is blessed, and he is aided by the Holy Spirit. The latter has only a carnal knowledge, with which he can easily do more harm than good.

It would not be a bad thing if all students were required to bring from their universities testimonials concerning their piety as well as their diligence and skill. Such testimonials would have to be given only after careful reflection, and never to students who do not deserve them. These measures might bring it about that students doing theology would see how necessary that is to which most of them now seldom give a thought.

It would also be helpful if the professors would employ their skills to observe which studies might be useful and necessary to each student according to his intellectual gifts, his homeland, his professional goals, and the like. Some should pursue polemics with more zeal in preparation for their profession, because it is necessary that the church always have adequately equipped men to contend with enemies of the truth; rather than allowing every Goliath fearlessly to taunt the ranks of Israel, it must have some Davids who can step forward and face the Goliaths [cf. 1 Sam. 17]. . . . Other students need not make polemics their chief study, but they must also be sufficiently equipped to be able to stop the mouths of adversaries when the occasion requires and protect their congregations from error. We especially wish that those who come from lands in which there are Jews would be more diligent in learning about our controversies with these people in order that they might minister to them. On the whole, however, it would be desirable (and several excellent theologians have often expressed this wish) that disputations be held in the schools in the German language so that students may learn to use the terminology which is suited to this purpose, for it will be difficult for them in the ministry when they wish to mention something about a controversy from the pulpit and must speak to the congregation in German, although they have never had any practice in this. Alongside of students who study polemics more thoroughly are others who will be adequately trained if they have a good understanding of our doctrines and know only so much of opposing doctrines as may be necessary to be secure from error and be able to show their auditors what is true and not true. When it comes to more difficult matters such men may make use of the help and advice of others.

Unless he has somebody to lead him faithfully by the hand, a beginning student will hardly know what he needs and what he does not need in these matters. . . .

It might also be useful to make more effort to put into the hands of students, and recommend to them the use of, such simple little books as the *Theologia Germanica* and the writings of Tauler, which, next to the Scriptures, probably made our dear Luther what he was. Such was the advice of Luther himself, who in a letter to Spalatin wrote thus of the man of God (as he called Tauler elsewhere): "If you desire to read the old, pure theology in German, you can obtain the sermons of the Dominican friar, John Tauler. Neither in the Latin nor in the German language have I found a purer, more wholesome theology or one that agrees more with the Gospel" [Luther to George Spalatin, Dec. 14, 1516, in WA, Br, 1, 79]. Again Luther wrote: "Once again I beg you, believe me in this case, follow me, and buy Tauler's book. I have admonished you before to get it wherever you can. You will have no trouble finding a copy. It is a book in which you will find such a skillful presentation of pure and wholesome doctrine that in comparison all other books, whether written in Greek, Latin, or Hebrew, are like iron or clay" [Luther to George Spalatin, May 6, 1517, in WA, Br, 1, 96]. Elsewhere Luther said: "I have found more of pure, divine teaching in it than I have found or am likely to find in all the books of the scholastics in all the universities" ["Explanations of the Disputation Concerning the Value of Indulgences" (1518), in WA, 1, 557]. Concerning *Theologia Germanica* (which Luther also ascribed to Tauler, although it was written later, and which I look upon as a particular honor to this city inasmuch as it is supposed to have been written here in Frankfurt), Luther expressed this opinion: "To boast with my old fool, no book except the Bible and St. Augustine has come to my attention from which I have learned more about God, Christ, man, and all things" ["Preface to the Complete Edition of a German Theology" (1518), in WA, 1, 378]. Hence this little book was republished and furnished with a foreword by our dear Arndt in the interest of Christian edification. Moreover, it is in order to praise him rather than criticize him that we mention that the dear man often made use of Tauler and extolled him in his *True Christianity.* Thomas a Kempis's *Imitation of Christ* is to be placed beside these other two books; a few years ago it was republished for the common good together with a guide. . . .

There is no doubt that such little books, to which something of the darkness of their age still clings, can and may easily be esteemed too highly, but an intelligent reader will not go astray in them. In any case, if diligently used they will accomplish much more good in students and give them a better taste of true piety than other writings which are often filled with useless subtleties and provide a good deal of easily digested fodder for the ego of the old Adam. . . .

Just because theology is a practical discipline and does not consist only of knowledge, study alone is not enough, nor is the mere accumulation and imparting of information. Accordingly, thought should be given to ways of instituting all kinds of exercises through wbich students may become accustomed to and experienced in those things which belong to practice and to their edification. It would be desirable if such materials were earnestly treated in certain lectures, especially if the rules of conduct which we have from our dear Savior and his apostles were impressed upon students. It would also be desirable if students were given concrete suggestions on how to institute pious meditations, how to know themselves better through self-examination, how to resist the lusts of the flesh, how to hold their desires in check and die unto the world . . . how to observe growth in goodness or where there is still lack, and how they themselves may do what they must teach others to do. Studying alone will not accomplish this. . . .

How these exercises are to be introduced must be left to the judgment of pious and sensible professors. If I am permitted to make a suggestion, I think it would be of advantage if a godly theologian would at first take up exercises not with many students but with only those among his auditors in whom he has already observed a fervent desire to be upright Christians. With these he should undertake to treat the New Testament in such a way that, disregarding whatever has academic association, attention may be given only to what is useful for their edification. This should be done in such fashion that each student may be permitted to say what he thinks about each verse and how he finds that it applies to his own and to others' benefit. The professor, as the leader, should reinforce good observations. If he sees,

45

however, that students are departing from the end in view, he should proceed in clear and friendly fashion to set them right on the basis of the text and show them what opportunity they have to put this or that rule of conduct into practice. Such confidence and friendship should be established among the students that they not only admonish one another to put what they have heard into practice but also inquire, each for himself, where they may have failed to observe the rules of conduct and try at once to put them into practice. They should also come to a mutual agreement to keep an eye on one another and, with brotherly admonitions suitable thereto, see how one or another may accommodate himself. In fact, they ought to give an account to one another and to their professor of how, in this or that situation, they have acquitted themselves in the light of the given rules.

In such a confidential relationship in which every matter that concerns the participants (for they must quickly learn not to make rash judgments about others or pass sentence on anyone outside the group) is examined according to the Word of God, it should soon become evident how far one has progressed and where in particular there may still be need for help. The professor would exercise no other authority over the consciences given into his care than, as one who is more experienced, to point out, on the basis of the sole authority of the Word of God, what his opinion in any given case may be; and as the students become more and more experienced the professor should be able to confer with them as colleagues. If this practice were continued for a while with fervent and earnest prayers to God, and each person, especially when he wished to prepare himself for the Lord's Supper, were to describe the condition of his conscience to the whole group and were always to act according to its counsel, I have no doubt that within a short time a glorious advance in piety would result. If the proposal really got into motion, more and more would be attracted, to their advantage, and finally the participants could become young men who are upright Christians (before they enter the ministry, where they should make others Christians) and who take pains to do rather than to teach. This is what real teachers in the school of our Savior ought to be. . . .

6

In addition to these exercises, which are intended to develop the Christian life of the students, it would also be useful if the teachers made provision for practice in those things with which the students will have to deal when they are in the ministry. For example, there should be practice at times in instructing the ignorant, in comforting the sick, and especially in preaching, where it should be pointed out to students that everything in their sermons should have edification as the goal. I therefore add this as a sixth proposal whereby the Christian church may be helped to a better condition: that sermons be so prepared by all that their purpose (faith and its fruits) may be achieved in the hearers to the greatest possible degree.

There are probably few places in our church in which there is such want that not enough sermons are preached. But many godly persons find that not a little is wanting in many sermons. There are preachers who fill most of their sermons with things that give the impression that the preachers are learned men, although the hearers understand nothing of this. Often many foreign languages are quoted, although probably not one person in the church understands a word of them. Many preachers are more concerned to have the introduction shape up well and the transitions be effective, to have an outline that is artful and yet sufficiently concealed, and to have all the parts handled precisely according to the rules of oratory and suitably embellished, than they are concerned that the materials be chosen and by God's grace be developed in such a way that the hearers may profit from the sermon in life and death. This ought not to be so. The pulpit is not the place for an ostentatious display of one's skill. It is rather the place to preach the Word of the Lord plainly but powerfully. Preaching should be the divine means to save the people, and so it is proper that everything be directed to this end. Ordinary people, who make up the largest part of a congregation, are always to be kept in view more than the few learned people, insofar as such are present at all.

As the [Luther] Catechism contains the primary rudiments of Christianity, and all people have originally learned their faith from it, so it should continue to be used even more diligently (according to its meaning rather than its words) in the instruction of children, and also of adults if one can have these in attendance. A preacher should not grow weary of this. In fact, if he has opportunity, he would do well to tell the people again and again in his sermons what they once learned, and he should not be ashamed of so doing.

I shall here gladly pass over additional observations that might well be made about sermons, but I regard this as the principal thing:

Our whole Christian religion consists of the inner man or the new man, whose soul is faith and whose expressions are the fruits of life, and all sermons should be aimed at this. On the one hand, the precious benefactions of God, which are directed toward this inner man, should be presented in such a way that faith, and hence the inner man, may ever be strengthened more and more. On the other hand, works should be so set in motion that we may by no means be content merely to have the people refraim from outward vices and practice outward virtues and thus be concerned only with the outward man, which the ethics of the heathen can also accomplish, but that we lay the right foundation in the heart, show that what does not proceed from this foundation is mere hypocrisy, and hence accustom the people first to work on what is inward (awaken love of God and neighbor through suitable means) and only then to act accordingly.

One should therefore emphasize that the divine means of Word and sacrament are concerned with the inner man. Hence it is not enough that we hear the Word with our outward ear, but we must let it penetrate to our heart, so that we may hear the Holy Spirit speak there, that is, with vibrant emotion and comfort feel the sealing of the Spirit and the power of the Word. Nor is it enough to be baptized, but the inner man, where we have put on Christ in Baptism, must also keep Christ on and bear witness to him in our outward life. Nor is it enough to have received the Lord's Supper externally, but the inner man must truly be fed with that blessed food. Nor is it enough to pray outwardly with our mouth, but true prayer, and the best prayer, occurs in the inner man, and it either breaks forth in words or remains in the soul, yet God will find and hit upon it. Nor, again, is it enough to worship God in an external temple, but the inner man worships God best in his own temple, whether or not he is in an external temple at the time. So one could go on.

Since the real power of all Christianity consists of this, it would be proper if sermons, on the whole, were pointed in such a direction. If this were to happen, much more edification would surely result than is presently the case. We have a glorious example of this in the sermon collection of the precious, gifted, and sainted John Arndt to which these lines are a preface. . . .

I have no doubt that the Christian reader will have abundant pleasure in the present edition and that in his use of it he will be able, with God's grace, to edify himself magnificently. I do not propose to add anything more to this report about our new edition. As I have indicated above, I prefer to leave to the reader's own experience and judgment what sort of profit he may find in this book in its present form.

At the same time I earnestly admonish the reader not to jump to hasty conclusions if he should at times find, in this and other works of the beloved author, some expressions or teachings which at first sight may seem strange to him. He should thoroughly ponder their true meaning and employ fervent prayer. I have no doubt that he will himself discover that everything is in accord with the Scriptures and the method of teaching prescribed for us there and that it is far removed from all heresy. On the contrary, it is directed toward an honest cultivation of true orthodoxy (not the vain reputation of an orthodoxy that consists merely of doctrinal statements but a living knowledge of effective Christianity) and what such orthodoxy is aimed at, namely, the inner man. . . .

In conclusion, I call fervently on the gracious God and giver of all good things that, as he has once allowed many good seeds of his Word to be scattered abroad through his faithful servant who has long since entered into his peace, and as he has hitherto powerfully blessed many of these grains that fell into godly hearts and bore not a little fruit (for which thanks be to God forever!), so he may continue to give his blessing to the book which is still extant and is now prepared for wider use in this edition, that many who with devout and simple hearts seek their edification on Sundays in these sermons as well as in the Holy Scriptures may also abundantly find it here and return to God their fruits of thanksgiving. May many preachers themselves be revived thereby to preach the heart of Christianity after this model with simplicity and power. In general, may it also be a means for some further reform of the wretched condition of our church which we deplored so heartily above. Everything, however, be to the glory of God himself and (which has the same outcome) the advance of his kingdom for the sake of Jesus Christ. Amen.

Philipp Jakob Spener

FROM

THE SPIRITUAL PRIESTHOOD*

Briefly described according to the word
of God in seventy questions and answers

1677

1. What is the spiritual priesthood?

It is the right which our Savior Jesus Christ purchased for all
men, and for which he anoints his believers by his Holy Spirit, in the
power of which they may and shall bring sacrifices acceptable to
God, pray for themselves and others, and edify themselves and their
neighbors.

2. Is anything concerning it recorded in the Scriptures?

Yes, certainly: Revelation 1:6, 5:10; 1 Peter 2:9.

3. Why is it called a spiritual priesthood?

Because they are to bring not *bodily*, but *spiritual* sacrifices, and
in their office have to do with *spiritual* acts (1 Pet. 2:5).

4. From whom has such a spiritual priesthood come?

From Jesus Christ, the true High Priest according to the order of
Melchizedek (Ps. 110:4), who has no successor in his Priesthood, but
remains High Priest alone and forever. He has thus made his Christians priests before his Father; their sacrifices however are holy and

*Translated from Philipp Jakob Spener, *Hauptschriften*, bearbeitet und eingeleitet
von Paul Grünberg (Gotha, 1889), pp. 93–114.

made acceptable to God only by his holiness (Heb. 8:1–6, 7:23–28; cf. Question 2, 1 Pet. 2:5).

5. How do Christians become priests?

As in the Old Testament priests were not elected, but were born to the office, so also the new birth in Baptism gives us the divine adoption as sons and the spiritual priesthood connected with it (James 1:18).

6. Does not anointing belong to the priesthood?

Yes, and just as the ancient priests were consecrated with holy oil (Exod. 28:41), and as Christ also was anointed with the oil of gladness (Ps. 45:7), the Holy Spirit, and therefore is called Christ, that is, the *Anointed;* so he has also by grace (John 1:16) made his believers partakers of this anointing, but in a lower degree (Ps. 45:8; Heb. 1:9).

7. Are then all believing Christians partakers of the anointing?

Yes, all have *received* the anointing, and as long as they continue in the way of God, it will *abide* with them (1 John 2:20, 27).

8. But for what was Christ anointed?

To be a *King*, a *High Priest* and a *Prophet*, these being the classes of persons in the Old Testament who were anointed.

9. For what are his believers anointed?

Likewise to be *kings, priests,* and *prophets,* or, since the prophetic office is embraced in the priestly, to be kings and priests. (Cf. Question 2.)

10. Who then are such spiritual priests?

All Christians without distinction (1 Pet. 2:9), old and young, male and female, bond and free (Gal. 3:28).

11. Does not the name "priest" belong only to ministers?

No. Ministers, according to their office, are not properly priests, nor are they so called anywhere in the New Testament, but they are *servants of Christ, stewards of the mysteries of God, bishops, elders, servants of the Gospel,* of the Word, and so forth. Rather, the name "priest" is a general name for all Christians and applies to ministers not otherwise than to other Christians (1 Cor. 4:1, 3:5; 1 Tim. 3:1, 2, 5:17; Eph. 3:7; Acts 26:16; Luke 1:2).

12. But are not ministers alone the spiritual?
No. This character also belongs to all Christians (Rom. 8:5, 9).

13. What are the offices of a spiritual priest?
They are manifold. But we can divide them into three chief offices: (1) The office of *sacrifice;* (2) of *praying* and *blessing;* and (3) of the *divine Word.* The first two are always called *priestly offices;* the last is also called a *prophetic office.*

14. But what must spiritual priests sacrifice?
First of all *themselves* with all that they are, so that they may no longer desire to serve themelves, but him who has bought and redeemed them (Rom. 6:13, 14:7, 8; 2 Cor. 5:15; 1 Cor. 6:20; Ps. 4:5, 110:3; 1 Pet. 3:18). Therefore, just as in the Old Testament the sacrifices were *separated* from other animals (Exod. 12:3–6), so they must also *separate* themselves from the world and its uncleanness (Rom. 12:2; 2 Cor. 6:14–18; James 1:27). For this reason they are called the chosen generation (Lev. 20:26; 1 Pet. 2:9).

15. How in particular must we offer our bodies and their members to God?
By not using our bodies for sins, but *alone* for the glory and service of God (Rom. 12:1, 6:13; cf. Question 14), accordingly by keeping them in subjection (1 Cor. 9:27) and by suppressing evil desires which wish to work evil through our members, what the Scriptures call cutting off our members (Matt. 5:29, 30; 18:8, 9; 19:12).

16. How shall we offer our souls to God?
By letting them as well as our bodies be holy *temples* and abodes of God (1 Cor. 3:16, 17); by allowing our *reason* to be brought into captivity to the obedience of Christ (2 Cor. 10:5); by surrendering our *wills* to the divine will in true submission and obedience (1 Sam. 15:22; Matt. 6:10, 26:39; Heb. 10:5–7); and by making an acceptable *sacrifice* of our *spirits and souls* in true *repentance* (Ps. 51:16, 17).

17. How else shall we offer ourselves in sacrifice to God?
By being willing to receive the *cross* from his hand; by submitting

ourselves to him, that he may send us what is pleasing to him (2 Sam. 15:26), and by being willing to lay down our *lives* for his glory, if it be his *will* (Phil. 2:17, 18; 2 Tim. 4:6).

18. Shall we not also offer up our old man to God?

As in the Old Testament a devoted thing was killed, sanctified to God, and so offered to him (Lev. 27:28, 29), in like manner we should also slay our old man, and *in this sense* sacrifice him (Rom. 6:6; Gal. 5:24; Col. 3:5).

19. What else shall we offer to God?

Our *hearts and tongues* for prayer, praise, and thanks to him (Ps. 141:2, 50:14, 23, 69:30, 31; Heb. 13:15; Ps. 27:6, 107:22, 116:17, 18; Hos. 14:2); also our *earthly possessions,* wherever we see an opportunity to promote his glory thereby and to show mercy to those in distress, especially to the members of Christ (Heb. 13:16; Matt. 25:40; Acts 24:17; Phil. 4:18; Luke 21:1–4).

20. Is there anything else that we should offer to God?

Yes; namely, the *doctrine of the Gospel* and thereby *our fellow man,* who by it is converted and sanctified to God (Mal. 1:11; Rom. 15:16; Isa. 60:7; Phil. 2:17, 18. Cf. Question 17).

21. Ought we not also to bring such sacrifices to God the Lord in order to make atonement for our sins?

No, for Christ alone has made satisfaction for us by his sacrifice, and he who wishes to add to it his own sacrifice for atonement blasphemes the sacrifice of Christ (Heb. 10:14).

22. Are the aforementioned sacrifices, which we bring to God, altogether pure?

In themselves they would not be perfectly pure, but by virtue of the holy sacrifice of Jesus our sacrifices are also sanctified and acceptable to God for his Son's sake (1 Pet. 2:5).

23. How often and when should we make such offerings to God?

Always, through our whole life. For although we surrender and offer ourselves to God with body and soul once for all when we first yield our hearts to his service, nevertheless this purpose should be repeated, and sacrifices of this kind should be brought by us to God the Lord daily and even hourly.

24. What else besides sacrifice belongs to the priestly office of Christ? As the high priest of the Old Testament blessed the people (Num. 6:23–27) and prayed for them (Num. 16:47; 2 Chron. 30:27), so Christ also, as the true High Priest of the New Testament, laid his blessing upon us (Mark 10:16; Luke 24:50; Acts 3:25, 26; Eph. 1:3) and prayed for us (John 17:9, 20; Luke 22:31, 32, 23:34) and still prays for us (Rom. 8:34; 1 John 2:1; Heb. 9:24, 7:25. Cf. Question 4). In like manner it is the duty of Christians not only to offer *prayers to God for themselves*, but also *to make intercession for their fellow men* (1 Tim. 2:1–3; James 5:14–16; Eph. 6:18, 19; Acts 12:5) and *to bless them* (Matt. 5:44; Rom. 12:14; 1 Pet. 3:9). For Christ's sake such prayer and blessing are not in vain, but effectual (Matt. 18:19, 20; James 5:16; 1 Tim. 2:3).

25. What is the third office of a priest?
As the priests were occupied with the law of God (Mal. 2:7), so also is it the office of spiritual priests to let *the Word of God* dwell richly among them (Col. 3:16). This is also called their *prophetic office.*

26. Are then all Christians preachers and are they to exercise the preaching office?
No. To exercise the office publicly in the congregation before all and over all requires a *special call.* Hence if anyone were to arrogate this to himself as a power over others, or were to encroach upon the office of the ministry, he would commit sin (Rom. 10:15; Heb. 5:4). For this reason some are *teachers* and others *hearers* (1 Cor. 12:28–30), whose respective duties toward each other are treated in the *Table of Duties* [in the Catechism].

27. But how shall they occupy themselves with the Word of God?
They shall use it for *themselves* and *among or with* others.

28. How shall they use the Word of God for themselves?
Not only shall they *hear* it, when it is preached and proclaimed in the congregation, but they shall also diligently *read* it and have it read to them.

29. Is it proper for all Christians diligently to read the Scriptures?
Yes. Since they are the letter of the heavenly Father to *all* his children, no child of God can be excluded from them, but all have both the *right* and *command* to read them (John 5:38).

30. But would it not be better that they simply believe what they hear from their preachers?

No. They also are to search the Scriptures, so that they may test the teaching of their preacher, in order that their faith may not be founded upon the reputation and faith of a man, but upon divine truth (Acts 17:11).

31. Are not the Scriptures too difficult for the uneducated to understand?

No, for already in the Old Testament the divine Word was given to instruct the simple (Ps. 19:7, 119:130), and fathers were required to teach it to their children (Deut. 6:6, 7). Now the New Testament is still more clear (Rom. 13:12; 1 John 2:8). Christ thus did not direct his doctrine to the wise and intelligent of this world, but to the simple (Matt. 11:25, 26). Indeed, he who would understand Jesus must put aside all worldly wisdom and become a child (Matt. 18:3; Luke 18:17). Paul likewise, and all the other apostles, went forth not with high words, but with the power of God, which is hidden from the wise but is revealed to babes according to the inscrutable wisdom of God, who through foolish preaching put to shame the wise of this world (1 Cor. 1:18–24, 2:1–5; 2 Cor. 1:12, 10:4, 5). So also the apostles wrote their epistles for the most part to uneducated and plain people, who could not have understood them by heathen science and philosophy, but who by the grace of God understood them for their salvation without these (1 Cor. 1:2, 2:6–10).

32. But are not many things in the Scriptures obscure and too high for the uneducated?

The Scriptures in themselves are not obscure, for they are light and not darkness (Ps. 119:105; 2 Pet. 1:19). However, there are many things in them too high not only for the uneducated, but also for the learned, which, on account of our darkened eyes, appear obscure to us (1 Cor. 13:9, 10).

33. Would it not be better for this reason if the uneducated did not read them?

No. The learned are not deterred from searching more and more in them, although they must confess that in many places they often miss the meaning. Just as little can uneducated pious souls be prohibited from the Word, in which they can seek and find the strengthening of their faith.

34. Can they in their simplicity also learn to understand them?

Indeed. First of all the principal points of doctrine and rules of life are given in the Scriptures so clearly and according to the letter that each uneducated person can learn and comprehend them as well as the learned. Thus, when pious hearts have comprehended these and obediently used the first measure received, as they continue to read the Scriptures with meditation and prayer, God the Holy Spirit will open their understanding more and more, so that they may also learn and understand the higher and more difficult matters as far as is necessary for strengthening of their faith, instruction in life, and comfort (Matt. 13:12; John 14:21; 2 Tim. 3:15–17).

35. But they are not able to use the ancient languages and the helps of scholarship like the learned; how then is it possible for them to understand the Scriptures?

It would be desirable if all Christians would try more earnestly to learn the *Hebrew and Greek languages,* in which the Scriptures were written (just as is done with other foreign languages that are learned for secular business) and thus to understand, as far as possible, the Holy Spirit in its own language. But since, by the grace of God, the Scriptures have now been translated into other languages, so that anyone can find enough for the necessary knowledge of Christianity, the ignorance of foreign languages is no hindrance for pious Christians to the true knowledge of what God finds useful for the edification of their souls. Much less can the lack of other *scholarly aids* hinder them, since even in the case of the learned these are not properly means for the *saving knowledge* of the truth, but only are able to serve, when rightly used, *to explain further* the truth known through the Spirit, to present it to others, and to establish and defend it against the gainsaying of others.

36. Whence do simple pious Christians receive the understanding of the Scriptures?

From the enlightenment of the Holy Spirit, by whose inspiration the Scriptures were first recorded, so that they cannot be understood without his light (2 Pet. 1:21; 1 Cor. 2:12). Now God has promised the Holy Spirit to all who call upon him in simplicity and, therefore, not only to the learned (Luke 11:13; James 1:5; 1 John 5:14, 15). By his anointing and illumination they, therefore, understand all in the Scriptures that they need for their salvation and growth in the inner man (according to the measure of grace appointed to each one) (1 John 2:20; Eph. 1:17, 18).

37. How shall they conduct themselves when they read the Scriptures, that they may be assured of the truth?

(1) They should not take the Scriptures into their hands without *sincere prayer* for the grace of the Holy Spirit, nor without the purpose to admit a place in themselves for his working and power, and they should not stop with *knowledge*, but should obediently apply what they have learned to God's glory. (2) They should not let their *reason* be master, but should *give close attention* to the words of the Holy Spirit, how they are framed, compare them with what precedes and follows, consider their meaning, believe that every word is recorded by the Holy Spirit designedly as it is, and also *compare* the portion read *with other passages* of Scripture. (3) They should read all *with application to themselves*, how far it concerns them and may be serviceable for their edification. (4) They should lay hold of that *first* which is altogether clear and build their faith upon that, and also immediately seek to order their life according to the duty perceived. (5) They should pass over what at first they cannot understand at once and what they find *too difficult and high*, and commit it to God until after repeated reading and prayer, when they have been faithful to God in the truth previously perceived, gradually they attain more light even in the passages not understood before. (6) They should always in *humility* receive, keep, and practice whatever God has granted them to know, and be content with his grace. (7) They should eagerly speak about the Scriptures to godly *ministers* and other *Christians*, and obtain their advice where they cannot get on themselves, and when by God's grace they are shown the true meaning of a passage, they should receive it in humility and the fear of God.

38. Is it necessary to a saving and living knowledge of the Scriptures to desire to be made better by them?

Yes, indeed. Otherwise we will read them not as the Word of the great God (which they are), our regard for whom must effect in us not only deep reverence, but also *obedience* to do what we hear from his Word and mouth immediately and much more promptly than if a great worldly potentate had commanded us to do something. He who does not read the Scriptures in this way does not read them as God's Word. He deprives himself of their power, and, therefore, will not come to the true spiritual knowledge of them (John 7:17; Ps. 111:10, Wisd. 1:5, 6; 2 Pet. 1:8, 9, 3:16; 2 Cor. 4:3, 4; 2 Thess. 2:10, 11; 1 John 2:3, 4, 4:7, 8).

39. How many readers hinder the benefit and do harm to themselves?
(1) If, contrary to such rules, they read the Scriptures without sincere prayer and the purpose to obey God, but only to get knowledge, to make a show, and to exercise their curiosity upon them. (2) If they follow the judgment of their *reason* and let it count for more than the words of the Holy Spirit. (3) If they do not observe what is useful for *their edification,* but only what they can use for their *glory and against others.* (4) If they *despise* what the Scriptures simply stated and what is *easy to comprehend.* (5) If, on the contrary, they take up only *difficult passages,* about which there is much dispute, in order to discover in them something unusual and to make a show before others. (6) If they use what they have learned with *pride* and for *their own* glory. (7) If they *think they alone are wise,* obstinately refuse better instruction, love to quarrel, and receive nothing from others with modesty. (8) But, above all, if they *lead a carnal life,* so that the Holy Spirit cannot dwell in them. In such the reading of the Scriptures produces no effect. They attain only a natural knowledge of the letter of the Scriptures, without the inward power of the Spirit in them, and therefore by God's judgment can only become more hardened thereby and more incapable of the truth (2 Tim. 3:7–9; Titus 1:15, 16; Jude 10. Cf. the passages in question 38).

40. Would it not be better to leave the more careful searching of the Scriptures to ministers, and for the rest to abide by simplicity?
All Christians are bound to *this* simplicity: not to desire to search out what God has not revealed, and also not to make their reason master in matters of faith. But if by simplicity is meant that they who are not ministers shall *not seek* nor exert themselves to *grow in knowledge,* this is against God's will and is disgraceful ignorance, laziness, and ingratitude toward the rich divine revelation. Here we ought to seek not to be simple but wise and understanding, and by practice to exercise the senses to discern good and evil (Heb. 5:14; Rom. 10:10; 1 Cor. 14:20; Eph. 1:15–19, 4:14; Col. 1:9–12, 28).

41. What would such a person do, who directed people to such simplicity?

He would thereby directly oppose *God's command* and will, diminish his honor, put himself in the way of the extension of his kingdom, and hinder all the good which could and should arise by such growth in knowledge, to the greatest peril of other souls and to his own condemnation.

42. But is there not danger that disorder will arise when all study the Scriptures so much?

If such study aims only at showy and carnal knowledge, whereby one seeks great conceit and love of disputation with others, it leads to no good. But if it is carried on according to the rules given above, there will follow from it divine and saving wisdom, which rather prevents than produces disorder (James 3:17, 18).

43. But shall Christians always be so busy with the Word of God as to neglect secular affairs?

It is, indeed, their greatest joy to be occupied with their God and his Word, as the one thing needful (Ps. 119:102f.). But as they still live in the world and need to work for the support of their bodies, and are also placed by God in certain *positions* for the general good, when they have bodily work and business, they do so diligently according to the ability that God gives, avoid all idleness, and so prove even in such service their obedience to God and their love to their fellow men (Luke 10:39–42; 1 Cor. 7:20f.; 1 Thess. 4:11f.; 2 Thess. 3:11f.).

44. Must Christians only use the Word of God alone each for himself?

No. They should also use it together with others for mutual edification (1 Pet. 4:10, 2:9; 1 Thess. 5:11; cf. Questions 25–27).

45. What is the proclamation to which Peter admonishes [us] (1 Pet. 2:9)?

That they also speak of it to others and praise the great grace, goodness, and faithfulness of the heavenly Father, who has redeemed us all from the dominion of darkness, from sin, death, the devil, and hell, and has called us through the Holy Spirit to the wonderful light of righteousness and blessedness; for which reason also we should no longer walk in darkness, but in light. This is the sum of all their proclamation.

46. Is a Christian also responsible to care for the salvation and edification of others?

Yes, certainly. This is shown in God's Word everywhere. *All the parts of the Catechism* also direct us to it.

47. How are we directed to it in the Ten Commandments?

In the *second table* we have the general command to love our neighbor *as ourselves*, in the fifth commandment his life, that is, his entire welfare, is enjoined upon us. If now I am to love myself so that I care first of all for my soul and its spiritual and eternal welfare, then I also owe like love to my fellow man. Again, if I am bound by love to avert all danger of body and life from my neighbor, I am bound by this love all the more to help according to my ability that he may not perish in peril of soul (James 5:19, 20).

48. What does the Apostles' Creed teach us in this matter?

In it we confess the *communion of saints*. This consists not only of the communion in heavenly *blessings*, which we enjoy together and with one another, but also of the fellowship of fraternal *love*, which is directed to spiritual ends (1 Cor. 12:25, 26).

49. What do we find in the Lord's Prayer in regard to this duty?

As we know and call upon a *common Father*, we should have a loving and brotherly mind toward all, and this brotherly love includes care for the welfare of our neighbor. Moreover, as we pray in this prayer not only for ourselves, but also for our brethren, it is our duty to seek, according to our ability, that the name of God may be hallowed also in our fellow man, that his kingdom may be established and confirmed and his will may be done in him and by him. For what I earnestly *pray for*, I will also seek *to promote* all I can.

50. How does Baptism point to it?

Since by it we are *united to Christ*, and so all become *members of one spiritual body*, this communion also imposes the obligation that one member shall, according to his ability, further the best *welfare* of the other (1 Cor. 12:18; Eph. 4:15f.).

51. Does the Holy Communion also look to this?

Yes. Because it is a *feast of love* (we all partake of *one* bread), it signifies that we are *one* body, and hereby the duty referred to is confirmed (1 Cor. 10:17).

52. But how shall believing Christians use the divine Word among their fellow men?

The Scriptures have been given for teaching, for reproof, for correction, for discipline in righteousness (2 Tim. 3:16) and also for comfort (Rom. 15:4). Accordingly, believing Christians are to use the Scriptures to all these intents and to *teach, convert* from error, *admonish, reprove,* and *comfort,* as the Scriptures themselves everywhere indicate.

53. Is this proper for all Christians?

Yes, according to the gifts bestowed by God upon each one; but [with the restriction] that this is *not* to be done *publicly* before the whole congregation, but privately as occasion offers and *without hindrance to the public office of the regular ministry.*

54. How shall Christians teach?

When dealing with uninstructed persons, they should seek to instruct them in the elements of the faith and *to lead them to the Scriptures.* When godly hearts come together and read in the Scriptures with one another, each one should modestly and in love tell for the edification of the others what God has enabled him to understand in the Scriptures, and what he thinks will be serviceable for the edification of the others (1 Cor. 14:31; Col. 3:16. Cf. Question 25).

55. How can they convert the erring?

By showing them their error simply from the Word of God and reminding them to give way to the truth (James 5:19, 20. Cf. Question 47).

56. How is admonishing to be done?

They should frequently, on every occasion, admonish and exhort each other earnestly to put into practice, by God's help, what they perceive ought to be done. By such admonition hearts are greatly strengthened in doing good (1 Thess. 5:14; Heb. 3:13, 10:24f.; Rom. 15:14).

57. How shall Christians exercise reproof?

When they see their brethren sin, they should reprove them in kindness, meekness, and love, show them their wrong, and thereby try to win them over to amendment (Lev. 19:17; Prov. 24:24, 25; Matt. 18:15; Gal. 6:1, 2; Eph. 5:11; 1 Cor. 14:24, 25).

58. How ought they to comfort?

When they are with the sorrowful, they should speak to them words of divine comfort, and cheer them all they can (1 Thess. 4:18). This includes that in time of need, when no ordained minister can be had, they may also impart the comfort of the forgiveness of sins or absolution (Luke 17:3, 4; 2 Cor. 2:10).

59. Do all these offices, enumerated above, concern all Christians?

Yes, and that too not only in the sense that fathers and mothers should faithfully do these things among their children and domestics, but that every Christian has the *power* and *right* to do these things among his brethren on other occasions, as the passages referred to prove. (Cf. Question 31; Deut. 6:6, 7; Eph. 6:4; 2 Tim. 3:15).

60. But do women also share in these priestly offices?

Yes, indeed. Here is neither Jew nor Greek, bond nor free, male nor female, but all are *one* in Christ Jesus (Gal. 3:28). In Christ, therefore, the difference between man and woman, in regard to what is spiritual, is abolished. Since God dignifies believing women also with his spiritual gifts (Joel 2:28, 29; Acts 21:9; 1 Cor. 11:5), the exercise of them *in proper order* cannot be forbidden. The apostles themselves make mention of those godly women, who worked together with them and edified their fellow men; and far from censuring them for this, they accorded them love and praise for it (Acts 18:26; Rom. 16:1, 2, 12; Phil. 4:2, 3; Titus 2:3–5).

61. But are women not forbidden to teach?

Yes, namely, in the *public congregation*. But that it is permitted to them outside of the public congregation is clear from the passages and apostolic examples cited (1 Cor. 14:34; 1 Tim. 2:11, 12).

62. In what way are Christians to exercise these offices?

As God and love present the occasion to them. They must *not forcibly obtrude themselves* upon anyone, but deal only with those who are willing to accept such help in love.

63. May a number also meet together for such a purpose?

They may mutually edify each other when *occasion* arises. In the same way it cannot be wrong if several good friends sometimes meet *expressly to go over a sermon* together and recall what they heard, *to read in the Scriptures,* and *to confer* in the fear of the Lord how they may put into practice what they read. Only *the gatherings should not be large,* so as not to have the appearance of a *separation* and *a public assembly.* Nor should they, by reason of them, *neglect the public worship or contemn it, or disdain the ordained ministers.* They should also otherwise *keep within their bounds,* not omit *their necessary work and not neglect their calling* against the will of employers or parents, be willing to *render an account* of their doings, and *avoid every form of evil.*

64. Shall anyone set himself up as a teacher or allow others to appoint him as such?

No. This priesthood is common to all, and according to it each must be just as willing *to learn* from others as *to teach* in divine order.

65. Is it right for uneducated persons to take up the deep questions and difficult passages of Scriputre and try to explain them?

No. It would be presumption. (Even *preachers* endowed with greater gifts may easily commit this mistake.) The office of spiritual priests is this: to seek in the Word of God only how all may be established in the faith and edified in godly life (cf. Question 37, 5).

66. Does their office also extend to the sacraments?

As to *Baptism* (God, according to his promise, wills children to be saved, and it is our duty to grant them the means, namely, Baptism), in a case of necessity, when no minister can be had, *any pious Christian* may perform the Baptism, and such a Baptism, if otherwise administered according to the divine ordinance, is a true, valid Baptism. But as to the *Lord's Supper,* no case of necessity can ordinarily arise, because, when an ordained minister cannot be had, a person desiring comfort may be referred to the *spiritual communion* (of faith). Therefore this sacrament is not of the same necessity (as Baptism).

67. But is it not to be feared that disgraceful confusion and disorder will arise in the Church from all this?

If *proper care* is not exercised *to keep all within bounds,* this, like every other good thing, may by the fault of men result in harm. But this is not to be feared if *both* the *ministry* and the *spiritual priests* perform their duty according to the rules of Christ.

68. What shall the ministry do to prevent all disorder?
They should sometimes *instruct* their hearers in regard to this spiritual priesthood, and not hinder but direct them *in the exercise of it.* They should *observe* how their hearers do their duty, and occasionally *call them to account.* If they are acting prudently, they should *encourage* them; but if from lack of understanding they make mistakes, they should *correct* them in love and gentleness; and they should especially use precautions to keep them from falling into conceit, contention, and erroneous doctrine as well as from going farther than Christian edification demands. In short, *they should keep the supervision and Christian direction of the work in their hands.*

69. How have the spiritual priests to conduct themselves so as to prevent disorder?
They should make their own edification and that of their neighbors their object in *pure love,* and do nothing for *vain glory* and from other carnal motives. They should undertake nothing that is *too high* for them. They should *associate faithfully with godly ministers,* avail themselves of their advice, get their help where it is possible, and open for them opportunities to exercise their office. They should willingly give them *an account* of their doings and follow their Christian counsel, and especially refrain from all *disparagement* of them, *picking flaws in them and injuring their office with anyone,* because discord arising from such a cause will tear down more than they can build up.

70. But have not spiritual priests the right to judge their ministers?
Yes, insofar as that they should *examine their teaching faithfully,* whether it is in accordance with the Word of God; and if they find it grounded in the Scriptures, they should *follow* it. But if they perceive it to be erroneous, and the ministers, in spite of previous consultation, persist in it, they should thereafter guard themselves against such false teaching (Acts 17:11; 1 Thess. 5:21, 22; 1 John 4:1; Matt. 7:15).

Philipp Jakob Spener

FROM
ON HINDRANCES
TO THEOLOGICAL STUDIES*
1680

[Each person who wishes to enter the pastorate must first undertake studies. For the good of the church it is necessary that these persons be instructed and formed during their period of study in such a
way that thereafter they might serve the church in the most useful
way. Although we have examples of some people who enter the service of the church for worldly reasons, but set aside their earlier evil
life and become new men and true instruments of the grace of God
through the power of the Word, nevertheless there are, unfortunately, many more examples at hand of persons who throughout their
lives, although they are serving the church, maintain their worldly
orientation since they have not been purified of their youthful and
worldly loves. Far too many parents encourage their children to enter
the ministry for reasons other than the reasons they ought to. Although there is not a great deal of wealth to be gained in the church,
still it is not to be denied that some parents believe that their children
can, as pastors, earn their bread with less work and toil. In our
church the pastors are associated with the middle class, and parents of
lower classes often see the position of pastor as securing a pleasanter
mode of life. A far greater hindrance to theological study, however, is
the thoughtless and unwholesome manner in which parents raise
their children. Few learn self-denial. Pride is not rooted out.]

Insofar as piety is concerned, its practice is often reduced to the
requirements that children learn by memory and repeat prayer for-

---

*Translated from Philipp Jakob Spener, *Hauptschriften*, bearbeitet und eingeleitet
von Paul Grünberg (Gotha, 1889), pp. 184–231.

mulae, but their words have an empty ring and are repeated without thought or understanding for they do not know what the significance of those words is and are not required to follow them through in life. Indeed, as far as they see, the whole of their parents' religion consists in externals and in going to public worship. How few are those parents who direct their children from early childhood on to an earnest fear and love of God and who lead them to true knowledge of God and to the practice of inner worship!

[Parents who have not properly raised their children send them at a very young age to school. Here they spend more time learning Latin than the language which they must later use in the pastorate. Far better that they be taught Greek and Hebrew so that they might read the Holy Scriptures. In the schools religious instruction is poorly taught, teachers seldom know what a Christian is, and students who go on to further education take to the university all the evils they have learned earlier. When they enter the universities they are therefore hindered in their proper direction.]

The first hindrance which they bring with them is ignorance or a false conception of the true nature of theology. They consider this only a human discipline which like the other liberal arts has its foundation in human reason and is intended to sharpen and intensify reason.... But theology, according to the words of my teacher Dahnhauer, is "a continual, heavenly, powerful light in a spiritual, pure, and enlightened eye—a light which leads man, as one driven out of heaven, once again in a most loving way to the blessedness of the heavenly fatherland." It is my belief that the person who brings such a concept of theology to the university has a good basis for a blessed study. Such a student will have the firm conviction that in theology which properly bears the name of theology, he will not be able to do anything zealously without the proper teacher, namely the Holy Spirit, and that he cannot have this teacher if he is not already purified by him from worldly love and many defilements, and allows himself to be made ready for so holy a spirit to dwell within him. But if a person, as most today have, has a different concept of the nature of theology, many other hindrances will grow out of this major hindrance. (1) Such a person will never ascribe anything to divine grace during his period of study, but will ascribe everything to his own understanding and to his own industry. Certainly, as a youth, he learned the words that we must thank God for everything, but he did not interiorize any concept of these words. Since it belongs to the first of our duties that we ascribe all goodness to God and particularly that we are aware of our incapability in spiritual things, it follows that the studies of such people can never be pleasing to God. . . . (2) From this a second error follows; such people spend little time in prayer and other practices of godliness in spite of the fact that they have to admit that Luther himself insisted that one provide room during the study of theology for prayer, meditation, and experience (*Oratio, Meditatio, Tentatio*). I am not suggesting that most of them are so indifferent that they do not say their prayers in the mornings or at other specified times, but I only wish that they would not practice these prayers so dully and out of mere custom, but that they would do so in the spirit and in truth, indeed, that they would repeat their prayers throughout the whole day, during their work and study in quiet, and in this manner hallow all their endeavors. What has been learned by heart without continual and active prayer in this name affects the understanding and the thought, but does not strike the heart which God alone must open (Acts 16:14). Yet, the heart is a tablet on which true theology must be written and on which alone it is worthy to be written. (3) To this a new evil is added. If one values learning about God the same as one values other human disciplines, one who so thinks believes it is not necessary to lead a holy life, which is of course necessary for all true Christians. . . . (4) As a result the goal of study at large remains a temporal goal. . . . (5) In such circumstances, undoubtedly most of those people who seek and find education in the universities discover nothing other than a certain literal knowledge of spiritual things and an empty learning bereft of all divine power. . . .

From all this a second hindrance arises, namely, a purposeless treatment and choice of basic disciplines for study. [Among the disciplines most poorly used, the first is philosophy, the methodology of which influences theology far too much. More attention ought to be given to philology. We must look now at the specific sections of theology: catechetics, symbolics, polemics, exegesis, church history, practical theology, homiletics.]

I must now speak of mystical theology. The term itself was already used in the ancient church and the material it treats is very old. Even if we dare not ascribe an early date to Dionysius, we do know that before and after him there were those who put great emphasis on mystical teaching even if not in a systematic form.

Earnest and upright men complain that philosophical errors, particularly Platonic errors, have entered into mystical treatises and that these errors have contaminated a matter which in itself is praise-worthy. I am assured that in the dark ages of the papacy there was present in mysticism, however, more power and light than in the thorny polemic scholastic theology which spoke little to the heart. I therefore doubt if Luther owed as much to any scholastic as he did to Tauler and similar writers. In saying this I do not deny that these pious men as children of their time did have much papal filth in their minds and perhaps also certain concepts which their predecessors had taken from Platonic philosophy. Nor will I oppose the position of anyone if he shows to me that, in their speculations, the mystics many times fell into a certain enthusiasm, that is, the fantasy of direct divine revelation. But, just as one does not cast aside gold, silver, or precious stones if they are covered with filth, but cleanses them and according to the proverb does not throw out the baby with the bath water, in a like manner according to this principle one ought not to move against mystical theology.

I find the significant distinction between scholastic dogmatics and that of the mystics only in the fact that they deal with the same material but in different ways. Dogmatics is customarily directed to designate what is true and correct according to single articles, to bring this to the attention of hearers, to convince them by written or logical procedures and to impress all of this upon their thought. Mysticism, on the other hand, is not satisfied with mere knowledge. It takes the whole mind and all the powers of the soul into its realm and, in these, wishes to establish once again the divine image. It stresses practical purification, illumination, and union with God. It seems to me that it is the responsibility of every teacher of theology to indicate in his discussion of each article to his hearers how the truth contained in that article is to be understood as practical. This is particularly so in regard to doctrines concerning repentance, justification, sanctification, union with God, and other like matters. He is to treat these questions in such a way that each person will know what he is to do and will be encouraged to do it in the most zealous manner. If a teacher of dogmatics uses this method he will scarcely be distinguished from a mystic, except in the fact that a teacher of dogmatics teaches many different topics, whereas a mystic is predisposed to certain dogmas, and, further, that the teacher of dogmatics is preeminently and always concerned with the formation of understanding, whereas the mystic is concerned more with the formation of the will.

If this is what we mean by mystical theology, no one can damn it with justification; indeed, all the subdisciplines of theology will be able to learn something from it. A pious reader will discover thoughts, counsels, and observations in the works of Tauler, Kempis, Gerson, the author of the *German Theology*, and other writers of this kind of book. Their style of writing, in spite of its simplicity and even if it is not especially learned and sophisticated, does move and grasp the heart. Anything that is in these books which arises out of the papal filth and the errors ascribed to Platonism can be noted and avoided without difficulty by anyone who understands our true doctrine.

If, for example, it is pointed out that among the mystics something enthusiastic (radical) has slipped in, it will be not difficult for someone to avoid it. One must only note that our formula of concord rejects the enthusiastic doctrine. It states "ancient as well as modern enthusiasts have taught that God converts a person through his spirit and brings him to saving knowledge of Christ without any created means or instrument, that is, without external proclamation and hearing of the Word of God." Further "they imagine that God draws men to himself and enlightens them, justifies them, and makes them blessed without any means, without hearing the Word and without use of the Sacraments." Further, "enthusiasts are those who await a divine revelation of the Spirit and despise the preaching of the divine Word." The person, however, who gives his whole attention to remain with the written, spoken and read word of God and, insofar as possible, by ceaseless meditation brings it into the interior of his heart is in no way to be called an enthusiast (radical) if he reads the mystical writings and according to their counsel he observes, inclines himself to, and endeavors to fulfill those actions which the divine Spirit brings forth in his heart through the Word. An enthusiast is the person who wishes to uphold, out of his own inner revelation, this or that dogma which is not to be found in the Holy Scripture.

But that person is certainly not an enthusiast and will not be one who experiences the working presence of the Holy Spirit, the sealing, the illumination (by virtue of that which the Spirit brings to us from the truth created from the Word), the Spirit's consolation, the loving taste of eternal things. All these things are indicated in the Holy Scripture and are promised to believers and thus are not empty names or fantasies. He is not an enthusiast who rejoices in such experiences, and with all zeal, and by all holy means endeavors to share in them. This is, according to my belief, the goal to which all mysticism is directed, a goal which is placed before all in the Holy Scripture. If, however, here and there the mystics make use of strange words and manners of speech—many of them have no clear and precise way of thinking—one can separate these aside, as far as I am concerned, and attend to those which are clearer, revealed in the Holy Scripture, and better represented by the experience of the pious. Clearly, one is also able to attack scholastic theology for coining expressions which are not common, just as one can attack mystical theology if these expressions are not often found in our common usage. Yet, as I said, there is no need to raise great concern about this. Uncommon and questionable mystical expressions can be easily left out. From this, I hope that one can easily see what my understanding of mystical theology is and how far I value it, namely, if it expresses perfectly our true teachings, if all its revelations are taken from the revealed word, and if it sets for itself that goal alone that we do not merely learn what the pleasures of God are but that by daily repentance we be ever more illuminated and ever more inwardly united with God. Everything which is not directed to this end among individual mystics nor which does not fit this rule, cast aside! The person who wishes to travel his path will find, among others, a preeminent guide in Johann Arndt. Some have even tried to make Arndt into an enthusiast but among others Heinrich Varenius defended him in such a manner that the shining glory of this holy man who triumphs in heaven, after he directed many to righteousness, remains unsullied. Whoever reads Arndt should read him with the intention with which he wrote, bound to his faith in our true doctrine! If one finds in Arndt any questionable manners of speech, let him go either to explanations which the holy Arndt himself made in other writings or which were indicated by the aforementioned Varenius. . . .

Philipp Jakob Spener

FROM

THE NECESSARY AND USEFUL READING OF THE HOLY SCRIPTURES*
1694

From the heavenly Father through Jesus Christ, his only begotten Son, I wish for the Christian reader the Spirit of wisdom and enlightened eyes of understanding to see the depths of the saving truth, given us by the gift of his Word so that he may walk with that Word and reach the Father by means of proper Bible reading. . . .

(1) The first means to proper Bible reading is heartfelt prayer, as Luther says, "Two things belong together: active reading of the divine Word and prayer." Luther discusses this more specifically in the following: "In the first place, you are to know that the Holy Scripture is the type of book which makes all other books of wisdom foolishness because none of them teach of eternal life aside from it. As a result, you are not to reject its thought and understanding for without them you will never reach eternal life but you are to kneel down in your inner closet and pray in proper humility and earnestness before God so that by his dear son he will give you his Holy Spirit who will enlighten you, lead you, and give you understanding. So David prayed in Psalm 1:19: Teach me, Lord, instruct me, guide me, direct me. . . . He knew the text of Moses and other books, read them daily, and listened to them being read. In addition, he wished to have the proper masters of the Scriptures so that he would not fall with his reason and be his own teacher. There were factious Spirits about who thought that the Scriptures were below them and could be easily un-

---

*Translated from Philipp Jakob Spener, *Hauptschriften*, bearbeitet und eingeleitet von Paul Grünberg (Gotha, 1889), pp. 232–271.

derstood with their own reason, as if it were a fable by Aesop which needed no enlightenment by the Holy Spirit or prayer." We see from this that Luther, who read the Scriptures zealously and counseled others to do what he experienced in practice, considered prayer necessary because the Scripture treated things which our understanding did not grasp, and for this reason we have need of the Holy Spirit. One could indeed say that the Scripture itself is a light and that there is no need for the Holy Spirit and its light. Indeed the Scripture is a light for our enlightenment but it is a word of the Spirit and if we could separate the Holy Spirit from the Word (which we cannot do), the Scripture would no longer work. On the necessity of binding the Holy Spirit to the Word of God (so that that doctrine might not be despised), I wish to now add a few more passages of Luther's: "The Scripture," he says, "is a book which is not given over solely to reading, but also to the proper exegete and revealer, namely the Holy Spirit. Where the Spirit does not open the Scripture, the Scripture is not understood even though it is read." Now if the Holy Spirit is to be required in and with the Word, we must in the most humble fashion request this of the heavenly Father. As a result, it is necessary as often as we begin to read to first at all times turn ourselves in prayer, weeping and lifting up of the soul to the Father of light from whom cometh every good and perfect gift from above (James 1:19) and for ourselves to pray for that for which the whole church prays in the litany; "you wish to give your spirit and power to the Word" so that his Spirit might prepare our hearts for the knowledge of truth and open them as they did that of Lydia (Acts 16:14), so that he might open to us the Scripture and the understanding of it (Luke 24:32, 45), so that he might purify us in reading from all forwardness, fleshly wisdom, and improper intention, so that this holiness might thus be handled by us with holy hands. We are to pray during our reading and are often to lift up our souls anew to God that he might give to us the ability to properly understand himself and his will and likewise open to us one door after the other into his Word. We are to close off our reading with prayer so that the Holy Spirit might also hallow what we have read and seal it in us that not only do we hold the Word in our thoughts but that the Spirit's power might impress itself into our soul and that we might hold the Word in a good heart and bring forth fruit in patience (Luke 8:15). We need all this prayer as Paul told us . . . in Eph. 1:17 f. . . .

(2) Prayer, if it is to be heard, must come out of the heart pleas-

ing to God for God does not hear sinners but he hears those who fear him and do his will (John 9:31). As a result, the prayer which is given in reading must come from such a heart, which stands in true repentance, for wisdom does not come into an evil soul and does not live in a body which is given over to sin. For the Holy Spirit which teaches correctly flees from the idolatrous and turns from the lawless (Wisd. 1:4–5). Therefore, the mind of the person who wishes to read in a fruitful manner must stand in true repentance, have in particular a heartfelt desire to truly know the divine will, and out of such a desire direct its reading. Those people who go to the Scripture for the sake of curiosity, or to practice their own arts in reading it and wish to seek their own disciplines in it, Luther directed to Homer, Ovid, Vergil, and other similar writers. It is indeed a sin to misuse time by reading such authors and to read them without careful consideration but it is less of a sin than to misuse the holy Word. And even if the sin is not the seeking of vain honor on the part of a Christian, nevertheless the sin is at its most serious when one endeavors to fill one's desire in the holiness of the Lord and thus reads in the Scripture only so that one might know many things from it and with this information might boast and be proud. The Scripture is given to us only to learn of God, and to understand from it his will and our blessedness. The person who now comes with such a heart to the Scriptures that at all times he speaks with Samuel: Lord, speak, your servant hears (1 Sam. 3:9–10), he prays correctly; his desires the Lord fills, and to him the Lord gives the necessary grace to make holy use of his reading.

(3) All knowledge of God and his will according to the law and the gospel, however, does not exist in mere knowing but must come forth in praxis and action. Likewise, the aforementioned desire for the knowledge of God must also be so directed. There must continually be a holy intention to put into practice that which one comes to know as the divine will in one's reading according to the grace which one has. Thus the Lord himself said in John 7:17: "If anyone wishes to do the will of the heavenly Father who sent me, he must turn inwardly (through inner enlightenment, conviction, and sealing of the Holy Spirit) to see if this doctrine which I bring is from God or if I speak of myself." The person who comes to his reading with this intention and endeavors in it rapidly and willingly to do what he comes to understand as the pleasure of the divine Father will not only in his soul be more and more convinced that what he reads is divine truth but such truth will then truly enlighten his heart. . . . Obedience is a true

thanks for a good received and divine goodness will be further sowed as seed on the land which will soon bear fruit. The general rule (Matt. 25:29) remains: He who has (who has gained the knowledge of the divine Word and has invested it according to his ability as a true servant), to him it will be given (by the power of further light of grace and wisdom to grasp more), and he will have the fullness (namely, that he will not only understand as much as is necessary but much more with which he can serve others); but he who does not have (he who does not use truly what has been entrusted to him nor invests it for the Lord in thankfulness but holds it by himself uselessly), from him also that which he has (his earlier light) will be taken away....

(4) ... Careful attention must be given to that which one reads. At all times it must be said: "May he who reads let him take note of what he reads" (Matt. 24:15). Even he who reads the simplest thing without paying attention to it has no use of it. He, however, who reads difficult matters in worldly circumstances without attention will do his work for no result. The Holy Scripture places before us the most weighty of truths which have the greatest seriousness; it is thus easy to see that reading of the Holy Scripture demands the greatest care. To make this clear to us it is useful to note that the reader, as often as he takes the precious book in his hands, ought ever to consider that it contains in itself the words of the living God and that thus in it the highest majesty speaks with us. Such a consideration works a holy respect in our souls and drives us on to give more careful attention to everything. This careful attention to the Scripture is the seeking which our dear Savior demanded (John 5:39). ... I know that all readers are not graced with the same gifts nor so to speak with the same abilities; however, God will be satisfied with the efforts of the simple and will not leave their zeal unblessed where they have not ceased to study according to their own abilities, even though more can be demanded from a learned person, and properly so, since he also has received more ability. According to Gregory's metaphor, Scripture is water in which a lamb can touch bottom and walk on it but an elephant must swim. This we can understand in the following sense: A simple person can discover his need in it and come to it even though he can only wade; on the other hand, the person who has greater understanding will meet with so many difficulties in the text that he must swim through them with great struggle, that is, he must turn all his powers toward overcoming those difficulties.

Every person [reading the Scriptures must first pay attention how the verses fit together and then pay attention to each individual word. Various parts of the Scripture must be compared with one another. As Luther has said, one must remain with the literal word and not add too much typological or allegorical understanding. One must be particularly careful not to allow reason to rule where faith ought to.]

(5) It must be added further that because the Holy Scripture is a book which is not directed to a particular time but to all times and not to a particular person but to all men, one ought not to read in it other than insofar as possible to direct it continually to the reader himself and to attend in it how our God speaks not only generally or only to those to whom the words were immediately directed, but to each person who reads these words. God is an unchangeable God and his will always remains the same. . . . Therefore, his Word, which expresses his will, is always the same and thus is to be directed to each person. When we read divine commandments and laws, they are directed, insofar as they are not expressly meant for specific people, to all of us in the same way, for we are all God's servants. Indeed, even if there is a special commandment to a particular person . . . we can still find, if we pay particular attention to it, a general duty on which it is grounded and we are guided to the zealous observance of that commandment. With regard to the evangelical promises of grace which we read, since they rose out of the common and nonpartisan love, we can certainly at all times apply them to ourselves as if they were immediately and specially spoken to us if we on our side stand in the order required. . . .

[Further help for finding a deeper meaning can be found in Arndt's *True Christianity* Book I, Chapter 6. Here Arndt treats the proper spiritual interpretation and allegorical interpretation. Furthermore, the order in which the books of the Bible are read is important. Some read them through in the order in which they are printed. The New Testament should be read more often than the rest of the books. Thereafter, one should read the books of Moses, then again the New Testament, and thereafter the historical books of the Old Testament. In the fourth place one should devote attention to the so-called hagiographic writings, Job, the Psalter, and the writings of Solomon, and finally to the prophets and the Aprocrypha. Both testaments are one word of God and have been given by one Holy Spirit and therefore they both have the same authority. At a first reading one may go through quickly, on the second reading more time should be taken.]

Philipp Jakob Spener

MEDITATION ON THE SUFFERING OF CHRIST*
Luke 18:31–43

INTRODUCTION

All the articles of our faith ought to be meditated upon with zeal, but there are some which are more important and more weighty than others and which are to be considered more often and with greater zeal.

Among these, however, there is none which is more necessary and more important than the article concerning the suffering and death of our Savior Jesus Christ which we properly look to as the most important base on which the rest of the building of divine truth rests, as that truth is pursued in our Christianity and it is to be grasped by us. . . .

Since this article is so important and useful, we must commit ourselves to grasp it at its very basis and we are particularly to direct our attention to meditate on it. Although we are to meditate on this article continually throughout the whole year and to consider how Jesus remains the daily food for our faith, nevertheless, the Christian church, from the very earliest period, set aside a number of weeks before the Easter celebration during which attention was to be directed chiefly to meditation on the suffering of Christ, and this period of time was called the Passion Time. Dearly Beloved, we have now entered the Passion Time once again through God's grace and now, according to our practice, after we have meditated on Christian virtues and responsibilities in life, we take up meditation on the sufferings of Christ. . . .

---

*Translated from Philipp Jakob Spener, *Die Evangelische Lebens-Pflichten In einem Jahrgang der Predigten* . . . (Franckfurt am Main, 1715), pp. 391–341.

First, however, we turn to our heavenly Father and pray to him humbly that, as he gave us his beloved son to suffer for us, he might now also give to us his Holy Spirit to properly understand the heights of that precious act of goodness and to understand what we are, as a result, bound to do, and to make us capable of presenting in a saving way in our whole life that holy meditation so as to bring about everything for the hallowing of his name, the establishing of his kingdom, and the perfection of his will. Lift up your hearts in song and prayer.

EXPLANATION OF THE TEXT

It is not clearly taught in the gospel how we are to carry out such a meditation but we do find the basis for such a meditation there. Something of the manner of that suffering is presented to us and following it we will hear, and consider the suffering of Christ on the basis of the gospel as a necessary, satisfactory and holy suffering.

We thus look upon the suffering of Christ as a necessary suffering because it was proclaimed earlier from God to the Prophet and God is a God of truth . . . (Acts 2:23 . . . Isaiah 53:5. . . .) The suffering of Christ is also a sufficient suffering in that the heavenly Father wisely set down what was necessary for our reconcilation and through it was was needed for his justice. . . . We also see the suffering of Christ as a holy suffering particularly since in it he was obedient to the Lord his heavenly Father (Phil. 2:9).

CHIEF POINTS

Let us consider now the chief matter, the saving meditation of the suffering of Christ.

If we wish to meditate on the suffering of Christ in a proper, saving way, we must note that it does not consist in one's considering what the Lord suffered moment to moment or what happened in the Garden, on the Mount, in the palace of the high priest, before Pilate; what terrible things followed and what circumstances occurred at each point. For although knowledge of this history is the basis of further meditation, and therefore is not useless for the energy which must be directed toward it, nevertheless, it is a fruitless meditation if it does not go any further. . . .

True meditation does not consist in one's considering the Jews and their faithlessness, the high priests and their enmity, the apostles' inconstancy, Pilate's injustice, the evil of the people, and the soldiers who crucified, mocked, and treated the Lord evilly, were angry against him, cursed him, and made fun of him. . . .

Moreover, the proper art and fruit of meditation do not consist in one's considering that he must suffer and empathize with Christ in his great suffering or weep over him and his suffering. In such an act many people may seek to place a large piece of their meditation. But Christ, so to speak, always says to us (Luke 23:28), "Do not weep over me but weep over yourselves and over your children." We might add to this verse "and over your sins." For, insofar as the suffering of Jesus occurred because of our sins, it is clearly worth weeping over and we must weep because we have made our Savior suffer so greatly. But, insofar as Christ fulfilled the will of his heavenly Father, redeemed us truly, won for us eternal glory, there is much greater worth in faithful joy than in natural compassion.

As a result, all meditation on the suffering of Jesus which remains with these mere considerations alone is not saving meditation. . . .

Proper saving meditation, in which Christian duty consists, grounds itself on the aforementioned threefold meditation upon the suffering of Christ. Since the suffering of Christ is a necessary suffering and occurred because of our sins, and for the reconciliation of our sins, we must meditate carefully upon it with heartfelt meditation upon our sins, which made such suffering necessary. Because Christ's suffering is a sufficient suffering through which divine justice was truly satisfied, we must look to it with faithful meditation on the deep use and fruit which we gain from it. Because the suffering of Christ is a holy suffering, directed in heartfelt obedience to the heavenly Father, we must look upon it with the same heartfelt intention to follow the example of that obedience in every way. Wherever such meditation is properly carried out, the results will follow.

Thus it is demanded first that meditation on the suffering of Christ must be carried out with heartfelt meditation on our sins, and in such a manner that we understand the power of divine righteousness and God's great anger against human sins. . . . Second, we must call to memory that it was our sins, that is, mine and yours, which brought such great suffering to the Lord. Our sins were the whips, the thorns, the fists, the nails, which wounded the Lord and mistreated him in his suffering. . . . Third, we must consider that what Jesus suffered we ought to have suffered as our merit. For example, when the Lord was badly treated by his disciples, I am to consider that I deserve all creatures to be faithless to me. When I consider that on the Mount he suffered with eternal death and sweated blood, I am to know that I deserve such an eternal death in all eternity, indeed, that I deserve to taste here its bitterness as well.... Fourth, such a meditation will be more fruitful insofar as we treat our particular sins and the particular suffering of Christ and see how divine righteousness was practiced in Christ as a *jus talionis* [a law of eye for eye]. This means that he had, at all times, to suffer to the extent to which man sinned against God.... Because of the lust of the flesh and all its sins which one wishes to do with one's body, one particularly deserves the suffering of the body insofar as one sought the lusts of the flesh and one deserves this in time and eternity....

If meditation on the suffering of Christ is so carried out, one will have the true fruit and use of it; insofar as we meditate and through it have contrition and hatred of sin, thus far will true living faith be strengthened and continued in the soul....

Both Augustine and Luther indicated that one is to look upon the sufferings of Christ in a twofold manner as a gift, the power and fruit of which are given to us for blessedness, and as an example to follow. It is not enough that we grasp and look to it merely as a gift, but we must endeavor to look upon it as an example. As a result, it belongs to saving meditation on the sufferings that as often as one undertakes such a meditation one is to think on those things which we see in Christ so that we may be like-minded with him and might truly and properly follow him. We are then clearly to see in the whole life of Christ and particularly to see in his suffering a deep and pure mirror of the noblest and chief virtues. We see in him first his obedience toward God his heavenly Father.... Moreover, we see in him his deep trust in his heavenly Father.... We also see the example of the thoughtful prayer of our loving Savior ... and his patience, in suffering....

Just as we see in the Lord Jesus great virtues which he manifested in his suffering toward his heavenly Father, likewise we see in that suffering those which he had toward men and which we are directed to follow and thus to consider. He manifested first by his whole suffering the warm love for us, since we can properly say that he was the Passover Lamb burned in the heat of love. The whole cause of that suffering was that Jesus loved us and could not help us in any way except through his sacrifice. As a result, he rather gave himself up to the deep and heaviest suffering rather than to allow us to lose our salvation. . . . In the suffering of Christ, deep patience is seen not only as we have already pointed out toward his heavenly Father in that he did not oppose his will, but also toward men in that he did not oppose anyone who caused him suffering but willingly allowed himself to be treated as others would treat him. . . . Moreover, one is particularly to note the meekness which the Lord presented to all his enemies in his suffering. . . . And finally we see in Christ a glorious humility. . . .

We have thus seen what kind of a splendid example for virtue is to be found and to be meditated upon in the sufferings of Christ and thus we are consistently to consider not that this example of Christ's is something beautiful, which would be a fine thing to follow, and to continue in if one could, but we are to assure ourselves that we are simply and basically bound to following this example. For it is written 1 Peter 2:21: "For to this you have been called, because Christ also suffered for us, leaving us an example, that we should follow in his steps." Such activity belongs to the goal and intention of Christ and to our calling. According to Philippians 2, 5, and 6, if we have heard, we are also to be of the same mind as Jesus Christ was. We are not only to so live and act as he did, but we are to be so minded in our souls. . . . (Eph. 5:2. . . .)

We must consider the matter further. Our dear Savior purchased us with his suffering as his own possession. This act binds us to him since we are no longer ourselves but are truly his; we may then no longer live according to our own will but must live completely for his pleasure. As a result, as often as we consider the suffering of Christ, we must remember his act which impels us to earnest godliness. (2 Cor. 5:14–15. . . .)

We must consider further that the suffering of Christ binds us to so much earnest practice of godliness, since through his suffering was won for us the power by which we are able to mortify our flesh and to conquer it; this power according to all our abilities we must then make use of . . . . (Rom. 6:5, 6–11. . . .)

This is the proper meditation on the sufferings of Christ; it encourages all to further a repentant knowledge of sin and to follow faith and godliness. The means to this are as follows: (1) The divine Word, for the Word does not only present to us the history and the fruit of the suffering of Christ, which we are to meditate on, but it

also has the power to impress into our souls what befits the meditation. As a result, where such a word considering the suffering of
Christ is zealously heard and meditated upon, we will create from it
the necessary power belonging to meditation.

(2) The second means of meditation on the suffering of Christ is
holy Baptism, in which we find the power itself. Thus Romans 4:3
says, "Do you not know that all who are baptized into Jesus Christ
are baptized into his death. . . . ?"

(3) Moreover, the Lord's Supper is a noble means for this meditation. Indeed, it is one with it because we in our eating of the sacraments, in which we always receive the power of the death of Christ,
are to stir up the sufferings of the Lord within ourselves. (1 Cor.
11:25–26. . . .)

The fourth means is prayer. . . . Fasting and prayer are placed together in the Scriptures and, thus, fasting is also an external but necessary practice along with prayer for a fruitful meditation on the
sufferings of Christ. Because of this, the ancient Christian church at a
very early period and before the time of the Pope, began the custom
of fasting at the time of meditation on the sufferings of Christ, although it did not make such a practice a requirement but allowed one
to choose it freely. Some would be accustomed to practice for more
days, others for fewer days, until finally they decided on forty days,
but unfortunately, such fasts in different ways soon became corrupted; they were required and considered meritorious and, instead of a
fast, a mere human practice of the flesh was brought in and free
choice was left out. We still see such abuse and superstition practiced
among the Papists, who are responsible for bringing questionable
practices out of initially good practices. As a result the Reformation
because of the misuse of fasts completely set them aside. . . .

The hindrances to such meditation cannot be lifted in a short
time but chief among them is worldly joy . . . and particularly the
practice of holding carnivals [on the Tuesday before Ash Wednes-
day]. Such a practice, which is still called a Bacchanalia from the heathen idol Bacchus, had its beginning among the heathen nations who
let the Devil come in among them, and slipped in along with other
heathen practices during the time of the Pope. . . .

We have now heard, my beloved brethren, how meditation on
the sufferings of Christ is to be carried out. Let us not continue to
talk but let us enter into the practice itself. We know that our blessed-

ness rests in repentance, faith, and following Christ, and to this meditation on the suffering of Christ gives great aid; therefore, we ought to turn faithfully to our Savior to honor him for the good of our souls. Let us then not leave one another until we agree together to truly turn the present time to such a godly goal and work to heartily call to God for His grace. . . .

Philipp Jakob Spener

RESIGNATION*

Lord, if you will make me pure
Matt. 12:2

INTRODUCTION
It is the chief glory of man that as he was created, God was united with him and thus wished to work all things in him; just as man's nature was an image of divine holiness, so all his actions were the working of divine power.

Man wished to become God and thereby tore himself away from this dependence. He wished to be his own Lord, to act and not to act according to his own pleasure. In this wish consists his greatest corruption and misfortune, for he is ignorant and weak and his will is in every way evil.

If he is to be helped, he must come again to the place of giving himself over to God and allowing God according to God's pleasure to do with him what he will and to rule over him.

This state we call resignation; it is the chief virtue of the first commandment.

For no good reason some theologians have questioned the use of this Word. There is nothing wrong with it in itself and the concept is strongly emphasized in other languages. Not only did Arndt use this word, but likewise did many other holy men and contemporary theologians. Luther writes in the hymn: We resign ourselves to you totally and completely. Indeed, in the German bible, at the beginning of the register, there is a title concerning resignation and beneath it many verses and citations are indicated as belonging to it.

---

*Translated from Philipp Jakob Spener, *Die Evangelische Lebens Pflichten In einem Jahrgang der Predigten . . .* (Franckfurt am Main, 1715), pp. 557–561.

Ah great God, you who alone are worthy for us to resign ourselves to your working and purification, teach us now to know correctly this virtue in the light of your Spirit. Grant that we resign ourselves so immediately to the work of your Spirit that I might now say nothing nor my hearers hear anything and that we might not contemplate on anything except what you yourself work in us through Jesus Christ, Amen.

[The basis and method of resignation: The basis of resignation is the great power of God himself and his might. The mode of resignation: It desires help; it places itself and its own will completely under the divine will; since it does not know what it will have or what is fitting for it to will, it does not know clearly what to ask for, but it resigns itself simply to God. This mode seems to be opposed to the mode of faith, which should be a certain trust in God's grace. Note that faith is clearly a certain trust in God's grace and that it does not know if such grace will be given to this or that person, but resigns itself to Godly wisdom and pleasure and is satisfied in all things.]

CHIEF POINTS

The virtue of resignation: Partly a fruit of faith, partly a piece of the divine order to faith.

1. It requires a denial of everything which a person can have in the world and on which his heart can hang. Note Matthew 10:37 and particularly Luke 14:26, 33.

2. The denial of one's own will. This is true denial of one's self, without which we are not able to be the disciples of the Lord (Matt. 16:24). To this belongs the crucifying of the flesh (Gal. 5:24; Rom. 8:13) and the denial of the desire for one's own honor, value, pleasure, and freedom to which we are naturally inclined.

3. Giving ourselves over to the divine will so that we desire nothing other than what will come to us will be pleasing to the Lord. This is as we pray in the third petition: Thy will be done. This virtue must be practiced at all times.

4. The understanding that God will work in us what is pleasing to him without opposition, that is, that no place will be given in us to Satan and the world. We wish that we will be able to do nothing for ourselves, but that the Lord is to do with us as he pleases.

5. Patient waiting that God will bring about his will in us, and that we will be satisfied that if that which we otherwise would desire

does not come about, we will accept the circumstances without great sorrow. See the example of David in 2 Samuel 15:25–26.

6. Where we discover and feel divine movement and stirring in us, that we follow it obediently and that we do that to which we are directed. At the same time to resign to God our understanding, will, affections, and members so that he may use them as he wishes. We see an example of this in the prophets and ancient heros; his Spirit spoke to them and directed them that they do not oppose it but resign themselves and follow. (Judges 14:6, 19, 15:14; 1 Samuel 10:6, 10, 11:6, 16:13.) In the same way the holy men of God did what they had been told to do, directed by the Holy Spirit. 2 Peter 1:21. Likewise, Paul said nothing except what Christ worked in him. Romans 15:18; 2 Corinthians 11:3. Such persons who were directly impelled provide an example of resignation. They resign themselves to the Holy Spirit to do the works which would come forth through them as the Spirit willed, and not to hinder the Spirit. Resignation must likewise also exist among all Christians, in that they resign themselves to the Holy Spirit that he may work in and through them what is pleasing to him. They say what he gives them to say in each situation from his own word; that is, he points out what is necessary to do for the honor of God and the good of one's neighbor and they do what he directs them to do. Romans 8:14. We must give ourselves to the Holy Spirit as an empty canvas on which he is to paint.

The means are: (1) The divine Word which gives us this commandment and provides us an example. Christ completely gave himself over and resigned himself to his heavenly Father. He did not say his own words but the words which the Father had given him. John 12:49, 50. He did not seek his own honor but the honor of the Father. John 7:18, 8:50. He did not do his own will but the will of the Father. John 4:34, 6:38. Likewise he did not wish to be freed of suffering other than according to the Father's will. Matthew 26:39, 42.

(2) The Holy Sacraments. In baptism the old man dies so that thereby we testify that we no longer live but that the Lord lives and that the new man is hereafter to live and work in us. In the Holy Communion we eat the body and blood of the Lord so that he is ever closer and increasingly united with us, and that he lives in us much more so than we live in ourselves. Galations 2:20. Thus we are not only bound but are given power. Prayer, that God himself will take us and work in us what is pleasing to him, indeed that his will will be allowed to be done in and by us. The Cross is a means which com-

pletely weakens self-will and brings it about, Romans 5:4, that we resign ourselves to the Lord more willingly, as we have often sensed and experienced his grace. 2 Corinthians 4:16. The denial of the exterior man renews the interior. It is a piece of the fruit of peace. Hebrews 12:11.

The special means for help. (1) Meditation on how important it is that we resign ourselves to the Lord since he is the highest and we are but poor earthworms; he the wisest but we ourselves are foolish. Is the servant to direct the will of the Lord? (2) Meditation on how much better and more useful it would be to us to be ruled by God than to rule ourselves since we would always corrupt what we do. He understands everything better and loves us better than we love ourselves. . . .

(3) Meditation on how things must occur according to the Lord's will, and how it can only happen if we will resign ourselves with love to the Lord, or if the Lord must tear us apart with power. . . .

Hindrances. (1) The natural inherited self-will of all men by which one desires to be one's own ruler and to rule God. This is the poison of our first parents. We must always crucify and kill this evil for it remains as a piece of the sin of our first parents.

(2) The fantasy that when we do not consider our own situation and look after ourselves by our own will, that it is a great evil. This is pure unbelief, for we have always to set our foolishness against God's wisdom, goodness, and promise. I will not leave you nor forsake you. Hebrews 13:5.

Ah, that we learn this virtue properly!

(1) Our own blessedness depends on it. If we do not give ourselves over to the work of God the Holy Spirit, who himself will bring about repentance and faith in us, we will remain without repentance or faith and without any blessedness. The one who is damned will be damned because he has not resigned himself to the divine work of grace but has stood against it. Acts 7:51.

(2) It is the rule of our prayer that we do not pray for anything except resignation to the divine will, when this will is not clearly revealed to us. Therefore in physical and also in spiritual matters which are not solely necessary for the honor of God and our own salvation, we are not to pray for anything except the divine will. 1 John 5:14. When we pray according to his will and the Lord points out what is not his will we must remain satisfied. 2 Corinthians 12:9.

(3) This is the rule of our life. Without resignation we are not

able to love either God or our neighbor. Thus we must follow and be obedient to divine movement if anything good is to be done by us.

(4) This is the proper ground for patience and suffering. In suffering we learn to resign ourselves completely to the will of the Lord. The consolation for suffering is that in it is the greatest assurance of our salvation, because we ourselves are not ruling but resign all to the Lord, and thus are free of all sorrow, disease, dread, and fear. All these things arise because we do not will to leave everything over to the Lord without exception. A resigned mind is capable of copying all divine activity, and in God we find more than we have given up in all creatures.

Ah great God, heavenly Father, allow us rightly to believe that in us and in our will, everything which is of us is corrupted and that in your will and rule our only salvation stands. Blot out in us all self-will and dependence on everything which you yourself are not, so that we may stand resigned to you alone and that you may then work without our opposition and do everything in, for and concerning us what is pleasing to you in time and eternity for Jesus Christ's sake, Amen.

Philipp Jakob Spener

GOD-PLEASING PRAYER*
John 16:23–30

Explanation of the Gospel

So as to understand the basis of the material in the gospel we wish to observe the basis, method, and fruit of prayer.

If we wish to understand the continuing base of prayer on which it rests so that we can pray and also be certain that our prayers are heard, we have to consider a threefold basis. (1) We pray because the Father loved us and he is the same to whom we call. It states in the text: "if you ask for anything from the Father." There is no one from whom a child has more right to ask for something than from his Father. Nor is there anyone other than his Father from whom a child can be more certain that he will receive that for which he asks. Because we have the heavenly Father as our Father, who is also Christ's Father, we come before him as children before their father and receive everything, as well as trust that we will receive everything, according to our prayer because we are his children. And we do so much more because the Lord expressly said that the Father's love must be directed toward us. . . .

(2) The second basis on which we pray is that we pray in Christ's name: "in my name." This means that we pray according to his commandment, because Christ ordered us to do this, and gave us an example of how to do it, because of his heavenly Father. We pray according to his promise because he said that we will certainly be heard and we pray according to his merit by which he purchased in

*Translated from Philipp Jakob Spener, *Die Evangelische Lebens Pflichten In einem Jahrgang der Predigten* . . . (Franckfurt am Main, 1715), pp. 621–644.

88

the most powerful way the grace and love of the Father for us. Thus prayer rests on a firm ground. . . .

(3) Associated with this is the third basis for prayer, which rests upon the second. This basis is faith which holds to the grace of the Father and the name of Christ. In the passage he does not only say that he gives them the testimony that they believe, but that whatever they pray or do in Christ's name contains faith in it and that no one can pray in his name who does not believe that the Father has required his prayer, that assurance is promised, and that his Savior has truly purchased him. If this faith and knowledge is not present one does not pray in Christ's name. . . .

We wish now to make a few comments on the method of prayer. This will be more fully explained in the doctrinal section of the sermon. (1) Prayer must be directed to the heavenly Father by locking out all creatures. The Lord said "whatever you ask of the Father." In this statement Christ does not separate out himself and the Holy Spirit as if he were saying that we dare not direct our prayer to these two for as the three persons are one being and God they are all three to be prayed to together. . . .

(2) In prayer there is not one certain thing indicated to us by God for which we are alone to pray casting aside everything else because it says "whatever you ask from the Father." Since it says "whatever" there is no narrowing of the request, as long as it is useful to us and not mispleasing to God in itself. God is a great God seeking his honor not in giving this or that but in giving everything in itself just as he is the only being who can give us everything.

(3) All prayer is to be given in a humble cry whenever you ask something from the Father. The Greek says *aitein*, that is, a prayer as a beggar prays. By this it pointed out that praying is not speaking certain words alone but must include a desire for those things for which we pray; they must first be in our heart before we bring the word of them to our mouth, just as a beggar is truly in earnest desiring alms. . . .

(4) The fruit of prayer is twofold: 1. Being heard; "it will be given to you." This is a certain and unfailing promise and, therefore, he says for our assurance "amen amen" or "truly truly I say to you. . . ." 2. The second fruit is complete joy: "Pray so that your joy might be perfect." That is, that you will experience joy in your soul as you rejoice inwardly over the reception of that for which you prayed, indeed over the assurance of divine grace which you gained from your

prayer having been heard. Thus it will be as perfect as it can be in this world, until finally it will be perfected in a super abundant way in the life to come.

CHIEF POINTS

Concerning the chief doctrines, we observe that the prayer be pleasing to God.

The foundation of all that which belongs to prayer which ought to be and is to be pleasing to God can be described in various ways. (1) Because prayer is to be worship and because in it one is dealing with the highest, it is required that one bring service before him which is pleasing to him. The greater a Lord is in this world, the more care one must take in dealing with him in varying words and deeds. . . .

(2) The second foundation is that prayer always occurs before those to whom the basis of our heart is open. Prayer is not only heard by those to whom we speak with our mouths, but also those to whom we open our hearts (Ps. 19:15). . . . Whenever we pray with our mouths God looks at the same time not only upon our tongues but also on the base of our hearts out of which the tongue speaks. All this demonstrates that for prayer, it is not only necessary to take great care concerning the high majesty of God, but also that care be directed toward the interior life so that one appear interiorly before God as is pleasing to him because only by so doing can one please him in all externals.

(3) The third ground on which prayer rests is that in prayer one must take care how one pleases God because prayer is a means to attain all our needs. . . .

How then is prayer to be carried out if it is to be pleasing to God? (1) Prayer must occur from a repented heart. . . . (2) Prayer must also occur in faith. . . . (3) Prayer must occur with great humility on our part and with a heart inclined to great reverence toward God. . . . (4) Prayer must occur with reflection, that is, with zealous concern and thought toward that concerning which we pray; thus we must understand the words we pray and we must thus pray in a language which we understand. . . . (5) Prayer must occur with zeal and true desire for that for which we pray. . . . (6) Prayer must occur with fitting modesty and discretion. . . . (7) Prayer must occur in a fitting order; this consists in that we pray for spiritual things, that is, things which belong immediately to the honor of God and thereafter for things which concern our own blessedness ... and only finally for physical things. ... (8) Prayer must occur out of a heartfelt love for one's neighbor. ... (9) Prayer must be continual and unceasing. ... One is not speaking here of an external prayer, as anyone can easily understand, for one could not in a natural way carry out such a prayer day and night without ceasing to speak ... but what is intended by without ceasing and at all times to pray ... is particularly meant that a pious Christian must accustom his life so that at all times he will desire nothing from his heart other than that in everything we do in living, eating, drinking, working, sorrowing, and whatever comes that God's honor be raised, his kingdom made firm, and his will be done. These desires must be so deeply impressed into us that they are in us without ceasing not only when we expressly think on them but at all times. ... (10) The last thing that is necessary for prayer is that we give it in thanksgiving.

We now look further to the fruits of prayer. (1) God hears our prayers. ... (2) Through it we practice faith, love, hope, and patience. ... (3) The chief use is that through it God's honor is made great and he is glorified. ...

The means of carrying out this kind of prayer are as follows.

A. The general means are (1) the word of God. In this we find how God understands prayer, how he describes it, and in it we find very good examples of God-pleasing prayers in various formulas of prayer, particularly in the psalms of David. ... And the example of the Lord Jesus who zealously and deeply prayed and also taught his disciples to pray along with us the *Our Father*. ... (2) Meditation on holy Baptism helps prayer. ... (3) Likewise does meditation on the Holy Communion, which feeds us in a spiritual way so that our whole inner man is strengthened through the life-giving flesh and blood of Jesus Christ which has the Holy Spirit with it. ... (4) The practice of prayer itself. ... (5) A particular help and means is the cross [or suffering] by which Christ often increases our prayer and purifies it. ...

B. There are other specific means to bring about God-pleasing prayer. (1) A zealous preparation of the heart. Whenever we wish to pray, we should not simply begin but, for a short time, we should consider what we are doing in quiet (even if it is only a short period of quiet). We should consider what we have before us, how great and majestic a God into whose presence we are about to proceed and what we are about to state to him. We must consider the kind of witness our heart will present before him, how we stand with him, if we have looked toward him as good, or if we stand outside of a state of grace. We have to consider what we wish to pray for, whether it is pleasing to God or not. Wherever one considers such things, the required reverence and humility before God and care in reflection will be brought about.... (2) It is particularly useful if one is accustomed to pray out of one's own heart. Certainly it is not improper if one reads prayers from books or prays by means of such prayers which he has learned by memory wherever they fit his own situation and himself specifically; indeed even a practice prayer often at times needs such encouragement. But there is a particular advantage if the Christian is accustomed to pray out of his own soul before God for the most part without particular formulas, for, since in memorized prayers thoughts can more easily stray, meditation can be far better integrated where one must give attention to the thoughts and words which one is to speak. Moreover, no one finds in one book at all times the prayers which fit particularly his own situation and position in the same way as one does from those prayers which are poured out before God. And simple people are not to think that it is difficult for them to find the words with which to speak to God for they must know that they have a position before God and are to speak to him as a child does with a physical father....

(3) A special means for meditative prayer is fasting. Just as a body which has eaten much is weary and sleepy, so in most cases is a sober soul much more vigorous to deal with spiritual things and also to pray....

(4) There is another good means to prayer. At times some holy Christians should come together eagerly for prayer so that they can pray with one another for their own needs and the needs of others....

Finally we must discuss hindrances to God-pleasing prayer. (1) The chief of these is a Godless life.... (2) Among such hindrances as well is far too much distraction in worldly activities....

Now then, my beloved, let us take on this duty of prayer heartily. We often complain that we lack much. Why this is so the apostle teaches us in James 4:2, 3: "You have nothing because you have not asked me for it." Thus, whenever we pray zealously, we will have much more which is necessary for our salvation. Someone might say: One prays a great deal in the church and at home and yet has nothing or lacks a great deal. The apostle goes on: "saying you pray and do not gain anything because your prayer is evil." Thus it is not enough that one pray but one must so pray as we have above pointed out. . . .

Alas, how many are lacking in this duty? There are many who forget to practice prayer at a good time and their souls die spiritually because of it. . . . There are others who pray but pray merely of the custom without consideration, saying the words which they have learned or which they read from a book and not thinking about them . . . others pray but pray solely alone and thereby their prayer is hindered because the Lord desires, as he indicates to us in the Our Father, that we continually think upon our brothers. . . .

Let us then be zealous in our practice of prayer for there is certainly no more useful practice for the Christian man than prayer. Let us pray at all times and in all places so that the Lord may also be hallowed in all places. Let us pray with our mouths and with our hearts and if there is no opportunity to do so with our mouths let us at least do so with our hearts. Let us pray for ourselves but particularly for others and let us be assured that God will hear our prayer, to a greater or lesser degree, the more zealously we include others in our prayer or not. . . .

There is great consolation in this matter of prayer when we consider how great an honor and use it is for us that we appear day and night at all hours before the face of our heavenly Father and that in what we desire and pray for we can be assured that we have his hearing. . . . The pious also have the consolation that God will eagerly give to them his spirit through which they pray. . . .

Philipp Jakob Spener

CHRISTIAN JOY*
John 20:19–31

CHIEF POINTS

The Spiritual Joy of Christians.
I. The basis of joy.
    1. The assurance of divine grace. Joy is not without peace; it follows upon justification that is upon forgiveness of sins. Romans 5:1; 1 John 3:21.
    2. True faith takes on such assurance; insofar as we are joyous insofar do we believe. . . . Psalm 73:18. This faith brings it about that we know the proper good because we have and have grasped it as a present reality; since it cannot hereafter fail we must rejoice because of it. Acts 16:34; Romans 15:13; Ephesians 3:12. . . .
    3. Christ's appearance which does not come visibly but through a powerful working of his Holy Spirit in us so that he allows us to know and taste his being in a special manner in our souls.

II. The mode of Christian joy.
    1. It is the fruit of the Holy Spirit. Galatians 5:22; . . . .
    2. It is a sensible working felt by the soul as such and indeed in the higher grades of love it is itself experienced as a power. Psalm 94:3.
    3. It has different grades and each is stronger than the one before. Indeed it can properly grasp a loving foretaste of eternal life in itself. Hebrews 6:5. It can come to such a grade that it truly extends beyond human conception and thought. Philippians 4:7. . . .

---
*Translated from Philipp Jakob Spener, *Die Evangelische Lebens Pflichten In einem Jahrgang der Predigten* . . . (Franckfurt am Main, 1715), pp. 582–586.

4. Such joy comes at times into a person who is experiencing great sadness to console and uplift him. God also allows it to come to beginners in true Christianity so that by it they might be enticed to give themselves wholly over to the Lord. Often the joy passes quickly. It appears as a lightning bolt; indeed, it is often followed by the greatest desolation and sorrow, a thorn in the flesh. 2 Corinthians 12:7. . . . Thus it is often given to prepare men for difficult battle which the Lord wishes them to undertake. See Matthew 17:1ff. . . . It is very difficult in this world for anyone to have joy without ceasing but it shines above our present circumstances. The sad, however, are at all times joyous. 2 Corinthians 6:10, 7:4–5. . . . The basis of joy remains at all times undisturbed in the heart but internal and external sufferings hinder at all times the breaking out of joy into the exterior of man.

III. The fruit of joy.
    1. It brings forth a natural fruit.
    2. It makes men eager and ready to do good. What one does with joy one does much more easily and better. Matthew 13:44. . . .
    3. It incites man particularly to the praise and honor of God in singing.
    4. In particular it makes a person joyous in suffering and enlightens him. Matthew 5:12. . . .

IV. The means of joy: in general:
    1. The word of God. This brings the Holy Spirit, the spirit of joy, along with itself. Through the preaching of the gospel we receive this. Galatians 3:2. . . .
    2. The holy sacraments. (1) Holy Baptism: In it we are given the most precious of goods and reflection on this is the most glorious means to spiritual joy. Any person in temptation will often be able to grasp consolation and joy if he has not earlier by a reflection on the presence of the holy baptismal act. . . . Acts 8:39. (2) The Holy Communion: Since Christ comes to us in it he is often a special sweetness and joy which worthy communicants are allowed to sense. The body and blood which now are in eternal joy we taste and they bring with themselves something of that sweetness. As a result they are the most precious goods, namely the whole service of Christ in the Holy Communion, and therefore it does not remain without joy.
    3. Prayer: The Holy Spirit who is the spirit of joy we must come to through prayer. Luke 11:13. . . .

4. The Cross: This is seldom mentioned in that it often brings more sorrow than joy but the more it dampens the joys of the flesh the more capable it makes the soul of gaining spiritual joy. (Heb. 12:11. . . .) Under the yolk you will find peace for your soul. The Cross is often the chief means for joy. 1 Corinthians 1:5. . . .

V. Particularly must be noted:

1. Zealous meditation on the divine good deeds and promises, particularly on the good deeds of Christ. Luke 2:10. . . .

2. Godly life and the good conscience arising out of it. Although the chief basis of joy is the assurance of divine grace and forgiveness, the complaints of the conscience can be a great hindrance but the joy of the conscience can be a particular aid. John 15:11. . . .

VI. The hindrances:

1. Unbelief. All sadness comes from a mode of unbelief or from the lack of a feeling of faith and the weakness that arises from this.

2. A godless life: That brings an evil conscience and also sets joy aside. Where the holy spirit is not, there can be no joy, for he does not live with evil.

3. The joys of the world hinder spiritual joy to the greatest degree and make minds incapable of it. Worldly joy is gross, spiritual joy is subtle. Worldly joy draws man into the flesh, spiritual joy lifts him. Worldly joy puts him ill at ease, spiritual joy gives him peace. Ecclesiastes 2:2. . . .

4. Sorrow for earthly things and for things of the world which bring death. 2 Corinthians 7:10. . . . These are so far away from spiritual joy that in time they also make the heart incapable of receiving it. . . .

August Hermann Francke
1663–1727
&
the Halle School

August Hermann Francke

FROM THE
AUTOBIOGRAPHY*
1692

As far as my Christianity was concerned, particularly during my first years in Leipzig, it was very bad and gross. My intention was to be an eminent and learned man to gain wealth and to live in good days. . . . The surges of my heart were vain and were directed to future things which I did not have in my hand. I was more concerned to please men and to place myself in their favor than I was for the living God in Heaven. In external matters as well, I copied the world in superfluous clothing and other vanity. In short, inwardly and outwardly I was a man of the world and did not remove myself from evil but drew evil to myself. My knowledge increased but because of it I was ever more pompous. I have no cause to complain to God because of this situation, for God did not cease often very strongly to stir up my conscience and to call me to repentance through his Word. I was truly convinced that I was not in the proper state. I often cast myself down upon my knees and asked God for improvement. The result, however, demonstrated that my actions were of passing intensity. I knew very well how to justify myself before men, but the Lord knew my heart. I was in great unrest and in great misery, yet I did not give God the honor to acknowledge the basis for my dis-ease nor did I seek in him alone the true ease. I saw clearly that I could not acquiesce in such principles on which I based my activities, yet nevertheless I allowed myself to be ever more enmeshed in them through my corrupted nature, and I pushed off my repentance from one day to the next.

I can say only that for twenty-four years I was nothing better than an unfruitful tree which bears much foliage but for the most

*Translated from Marianne Beyer-Fröhlich, hrsg., *Pietismus und Rationalismus* (Leipzig, 1933), pp. 19–29.

part evil fruit. In such circumstances my life pleased the world to such a degree that we were able to get along very well together, for I loved the world and the world loved me. I was therefore very free from persecution because among the pious I had the appearance of being pious, and among the evil I was truly evil; I had learned to let my cloak blow in the direction the wind was blowing. No one hated me for the sake of truth because I did not eagerly make people my enemy, nor could they say anything against me truly because I did not live in opposition to them. Nevertheless such a peace with the world was not able to bring any rest to my heart. But concern for the future, desire for position, the desire to know everything, the search for human favor and friendship and other similar things flowing from the evils of worldly love (in particular, however, the continual secret nagging worm of an evil conscience that I was not in the right state), drove my heart as a stormy sea now to one side, now to the other, even though I often presented an external joyousness before others. I spent most of the time in Leipzig in these circumstances and I cannot recall having taken up a truly earnest and basic concern for improvement until 1687.

But in the twenty-fourth year of my life I began to take up this serious question in myself, to acknowledge more deeply my wretched state and to look upon myself with greater earnestness, desiring that my soul might be freed from this state. If I were to say what first gave me the opportunity to come to this, I know of nothing outside of the continual prevenient grace of God, externally indicated by nothing more certain than my theological study, which I grasped only in knowledge and in reason alone. As a result I thought I could deceive people, hold a public office, and tell people what I myself was not convinced of in my heart. In the meantime I lived in a worldly society and was surrounded with attractions to sin. This was the result of long custom, but completely unnoticed, my heart was stirred by the highest God to humble myself before him, to pray to him for grace, and often to weep upon my knees, asking him to place me in a different life situation and to make me a justified child of God. The words of Hebrews 5:12 related to me: For though by this time you ought to be teachers, you need someone to teach you again the first principles of God's word. You need milk, not solid food. I had studied theology for almost seven years and I knew what our basic principle was, how to uphold it, what the opponents said against it, and I had read the Scripture through and through again, indeed I was not lacking in the other practical books but since all this was grasped by me only in my reason and in my thought and since the Word of God was not changed in my case into light but I had strangled the living seed of the Word of God and allowed it to be unfruitful, I had to make a beginning anew to become a Christian. I found my state in this matter so constricted, however, and was so wrapped up with many hindrances and stoppages of the world that I was as one who is in a deep quagmire and reaches forth an arm but does not find the power to tear himself loose, or as one who is bound with bonds and chains in hands and feet and in his whole body, and tears a small cord loose but looks forward with heartfelt concern that he might be freed from the others also.

God however, the faithful and true one, came to me at all times with his grace, and prepared for me at the same time the way to live more pleasing to him day by day. With his strong hands he soon lifted the external hindrances so that I was freed of them without expectation, and because he changed my heart at the same time, I grasped in my desire every opportunity to serve him more zealously. In such circumstances I was in semi-darkness; it was as if I had a gauze over my eyes. At the same time I had set my feet upon the foothold of the temple and yet was held back by the worldly love which was so deeply rooted in me and thus not able to move ahead fully. My heart was very greatly convinced, but old customs brought so many surprises in words and deeds that I was very troubled. There was yet a base in my heart that I very much loved Godliness and spoke about it earnestly without falsity as well as convincing good friends of my intentions hereafter to live a life honorable to God. As a result I was held a zealous Christian by some and after a time good friends told me that they had noticed a remarkable change in me immediately at that time. I knew, however, and it is not unknown to the Lord God, that the thought of this world still had the upper hand in me and that Evil was still as strong in me as a giant beside whom a child is placed.

Who is more wretched than I, had I remained in such circumstances, since I grasped heaven with one hand and the earth with the other, wished to enjoy God and the friendship of the world at the same time, or fought first against the one, then against the other, and could hold neither properly. But oh, how great is the love of God, which he manifested to the human race in Christ Jesus! God did not cast me aside because of my deep corruption in which I stood fast, but he had patience with me and helped me in my weakness, since I could not find the courage but only always hoped that I might break through into a true light which is from God. I experienced in myself that one does not have cause to complain about God, but that he always opens door and gate where he finds a heart that honestly looks to him and seeks his presence earnestly. God always went before me and lifted the blocks and difficulties out of the way so that I was convinced that my conversion was not mine but his work. God took me at the same time by his hand and led me as a mother leads her weak child, and so great and overpowering was his love that he always grasped me once again when I tore loose from his hand, and allowed me to sense the rod of his discipline. Finally, he heard my prayer and set me in a free and unbound state. . . .

For God brought it about that I had to leave Leipzig, where there were still hindrances holding me in capture. He stirred the heart of a relation of mine, a Doctor Gloxini, to offer me a stipend. This person desired with great earnestness that I should pursue exegetical studies above all things and invited me to travel to Lü Neburg. . . . I went in the fall of 1687 with great joy, since I hoped to achieve perfectly my chief task by doing so, namely to become a justified Christian. The external hindrances were now taken away at once by the dear God. I had a room to myself in which I could not be disturbed or distracted from good thoughts by anyone, and I took my meals with Christian and godly people.

I had hardly arrived when I was asked to present a sermon in the church of St. John, and I was asked to do so a good time before the sermon was to be presented. My mind was in such a state that I was not only concerned with the mere preaching of a sermon but chiefly with the upbuilding of the congregation. Thinking on this, the text came to me; "this is written that you may believe that Jesus is the Christ, the Son of God, and that believing, you may have life in his name" (John 20:31). With this text I had particular opportunity to discuss true living faith, and how this faith is distinguished from a mere human and imaginary foolish faith. Earnestly considering this matter, the thought came to me that I did not find the faith in myself that I was to demand in the sermon. I therefore left off meditation on the sermon and found enough to meditate on in myself. The fact that I had no true belief troubled me in an ever more serious way. I wished to justify myself and to drive the sad thoughts away but they remained.

Up to this point I was accustomed to convince my reason on

good grounds, because I had experienced little of the new being of the Spirit. Therefore I thought I could help myself through such a way, but the more I wished to help myself the greater I fell into unrest and doubt. I took to hand Johann Musäus's book, which I had earlier made known to others, but I had to lay it aside again and did not find anything in it to which I could hold myself. I thought that I could hold to the Holy Scriptures but as soon as this came into my mind I wondered, who knows if the Holy Scripture is God's Word; the Turks have their Koran and the Jews their Talmud, and who is to say which one of the three is correct. Such thoughts always took the upper hand until finally there remained not the least thing which I believed from my heart, which I had learned throughout my life and particularly throughout the eight years of theological study concerning God and his revealed will and essence. I no longer believed in a God in Heaven and therefore I could not hold either to God or to man's word, and I found as little strength in the one as in the other. For me it was not that kind of wickedness which drives the truth of God into the wind out of worldly minded hearts. How eagerly would I have believed everything, but I could not. I sought in this way and that to help myself but it did not work.

In the meantime, God did not cease to bear witness to my conscience. In such an actual denial of God which was in my heart, nevertheless my whole earlier life came before my eyes; I was as one who looked over a whole town from a high tower. First I could count the sins but then the chief source opened itself, namely unbelief or mere false belief with which I had so long deceived myself. And there my whole life and everything which I had done, said, and thought was presented before me as sin and a great abomination before God. My heart was put in great dread that it had one as an enemy whom it denied and in whom it could not believe. This sorrow brought much weeping to me and I am not generally accustomed to weep. Sometimes I went to one place and wept and at other times I went here and there in great mental disturbance, and at other times I fell upon my knees and cried to the one whom I nevertheless did not know. However, I said that if God is true he may have mercy upon me. This I did often.

When I was among people I covered up my inner misery as much as I could. Once, when I had finished eating, I wished to go with a friend to the superintendent who lived in the area. I took along the Greek New Testament to read. When I opened it up my friend said, "Truly we have in this book a great treasure." I looked about and asked him if he saw what passage I had opened the testament up to. He said no. I told him to look at the answer: We have our treasure in earthly vessels (2 Cor. 4). As soon as he had said these words they struck me in the face. They entered into my heart a little and I thought that it was really not strange that this should thus happen—it seemed thus that a hidden consolation sank into my heart but my atheistic mind immediately brought forth corrupted reason as its instrument to tear the power of the godly word once again out of my heart. I went on the way with my friend and came to the house of the superintendent. He directed us into a room and had us sit down. Hardly had we sat down but the superintendent began to discuss the question "how one should know if he had faith or not." He said different things about this question, so that a believer might be strengthened. I sat there, however, and initially wondered if such a highly necessary discourse had come to me merely by chance, since no one knew for certain of my state. I listened carefully to him but my heart would not be still. Rather, I was by his words much more convinced that I had no faith because I knew in myself the opposite of this mark of faith which is cited from Scripture.

When we said goodbye and I went again with my friend into the city, I revealed my heart to him, saying that if he knew in what state I was, he would wonder how we ever came to discuss such a matter. And he asked, "In what state are you?" I answered "I have no faith." He was frightened by this and sought to do everything he could to correct me. I opposed him and finally said that I could give him good reasons for what he stated, but it would not help me. Would that I had also been able to wish that I might preserve it in myself. In the meantime, I continued in my earlier activities, in zealous prayer and in great denial of my own heart.

On the following day, which was Sunday, I thought that I would likely lie again in my bed in my earlier unrest. I was also thinking that if no change arose I would not preach the sermon since I could not preach in unbelief and against my own heart and so deceive the people. I did not even know if it would be possible for me to do so. I felt very deeply what it is to have no God to whom the heart can hold, to whom it can confess its sins while not knowing where or who he was who brought forth tears, or if there truly was a God whom man had stirred to wrath. I also knew what it was to see the heart's misery and great sorrow daily, and yet not know or understand any savior or any refuge. In such great dread I went once more upon my knees on the evening before the Sunday on which I was to preach. I cried to God, whom I still did not know nor trust, for salvation from such a miserable state [asking him to save me], if indeed he was a true God. The Lord, the living God, heard me from his throne while I yet knelt. So great was his fatherly love that he wished to take me finally, after such doubts and unrest of my heart, so that I might be more convinced that he could satisfy me well, and that my erring reason might be tamed, so as not to move against his power and faithfulness. He immediately heard me. My doubt vanished as quickly as one turns one's hand; I was assured in my heart of the grace of God in Christ Jesus and I knew God not only as God but as my Father. All sadness and unrest of my heart was taken away at once, and I was immediately overwhelmed as with a stream of joy so that with full joy I praised and gave honor to God who had shown me such great grace. I arose a completely different person from the one who had knelt down.

With great care and doubt I had fallen to my knees but with an unspeakable joy and a great certainty I stood up again. When I knelt down I did not believe that there was a God but when I stood up I believed it to the point of giving up my blood without fear or doubt. I then went to bed, but because of the great joy I could not sleep and if I closed my eyes for a few minutes I woke up again and began anew to praise, give honor, and acknowledge the living God who had given himself to be known by my soul. It was as if I had spent my whole life in a deep sleep, and everything to this point had only been a dream and I had just woken up. No one can tell me what a difference there is between the natural life of a natural man and the life which is from God. It was as if I had been dead and now saw that I was alive. I could not stay in my bed that night but I leapt from it for joy and praised the Lord my God. I wished that everything might praise the name of the Lord with me. "You angels in heaven," I cried. "Praise the name of the Lord with me, the Lord who has shown me such mercy." Reason stood away; victory was torn from its hands, for the power of God had made it subservient to faith.

Nevertheless, the thought came to me that this experience could be natural, that one could also experience such great joy naturally, but I was completely and totally convinced that this was false and that all the world with all its joy and glory could not awaken such sweetness in the human heart as the sweetness I had, and I saw in faith that after such a foretaste of grace and the goodness of God, the world with its attractions to worldly joys would have little more hold on me. The streams of the living water were so lovely for me that I could easily forget the stinking swamps of this world. Oh, how pleasing to me was this first milk with which God feeds his weak children! How precious is your steadfast love, oh God! The children of men take refuge in the shadow of your wings. They feast on the abundance of your house, and you give them drink from the river of your delight. For with you is the fountain of life; in your light do we see light (Ps. 36:7–9). Now I experience that it was true what Luther had said in his preface to the epistle to the Romans: "Faith is a divine word in us that changes us and gives us new birth from God (John 1:12) and kills the old Adam, makes us completely other men in our hearts, minds, thoughts and all our powers and brings the Holy Spirit with it." And "faith is a living, moving trust in God's grace, so certain that one would die for it a thousand times. And such trust and knowledge in divine grace makes one joyous, bold and delighting in God and all creatures; this the Lord God does in faith." God now filled my heart with love for him; he gave me to know the highest and only precious good.

On the following day I was able to tell my friend, to whom I had declared my wretched state on the evening before, about my redemption, but not without the tears, and he rejoiced with me. By the middle of the week I returned once again to the sermon I was to preach, with great joy of heart and out of true divine conviction concerning John 20:21, and I could say with truth the words of 2 Corinthians 4:13: "since we have the same spirit of faith; as it is written: I believe and therefore I speak, so we believe and so we speak."

And this is the period to which I can point as that of my true conversion. From this time on my Christianity had a place to stand and it was easier for me to deny the ungodly ways and the worldly lust and to live chastely, righteously, and godly in this world. From this time on I held continuously to God, and I cared nothing for promotion, honor, and visibility in the world, riches, good days, and exterior worldly pomp. Whereas earlier I had made an idol out of learning, I now saw that faith as a mustard seed counts for more than a hundred sacks full of learning and that all the knowledge learned at the feet of Gamaliel is to be considered dirt beside the superabundant knowledge of Jesus Christ our Lord. From then on I also knew for the first time properly what the world is and how it is distinguished from [the life of] the children of God. From then on the world began immediately to hate me and to build up enmity against me. . . . Nevertheless, in this I must praise the great faithfulness and wisdom of God, who did not allow a weak child to be corrupted through strong food, or a pliant plant through an all too chilly wind, but he knew what was best, and in what degree he should give something to his children and through this he tested and guided their faith. Thus, I was not lacking in testings but in them God at all times watched over my weakness, and first give me only a little suffering but later a greater amount of suffering; according to the divine power which I received from him the last and greater sufferings were much easier to bear than the first and smaller ones.

August Hermann Francke

RULES FOR THE PROTECTION OF CONSCIENCE AND FOR GOOD ORDER IN CONVERSATION OR IN SOCIETY*
1689

1. Society gives many opportunities to sin. If you wish to protect your conscience, consider carefully that the great and majestic God, according to his omnipresence, is of highest rank in society. In the presence of so great a Lord a person ought to have the greatest fear.

2. In whatever you do, see to it that no one (and particularly yourself) disturbs your inner peace and rest in God.

3. Speak of your enemies only out of love, honor for God, and for their best.

4. Do not endeavor to speak too much. However, if God gives you the opportunity to speak, speak with reverence, good thought, gentleness, and insofar as you have certain knowledge with loving earnestness, with precise clear words, orderly and with good discretion, without hastening to speak much, without repetition wherever necessity does not demand it.

5. Do not let yourself be moved to speak of the things of this world unless by such speech God will be honored, your neighbor aided, and your own need provided. There is a word of the Lord: "Everything which you do in word or deed, do in the name of the Lord Jesus and thank the Father through him" (Gal. 3:17).

6. See to it that your speech is not biting or sarcastic. Shun all

---

*Translated from Gustav Kramer, *August Hermann Francke: Ein Lebensbild* (Halle, 1880), vol. 1, pp. 270–272.

abusive and senseless words and manners of speech which can bring about contention. Ask others if you use such words, for habit makes one unaware that one does so. Cursing is the gravest sin. The person who curses, curses himself and all that belongs to him.

7. If you would speak about God and your Savior, speak with great humility and reverence. Do so as if you were in his presence. Be ashamed to make the name of Jesus a commonplace.

8. In giving account of yourself or a situation, be very careful, since the spirit of the lie rules in such a time. If one does not fully remember, one establishes the circumstances at one's own devising. A person ought, therefore, to test himself if he is telling a story, to be certain that he is not speaking in one or another case uncertainly. No Christian should listen to comic or wanton stories since they are either not true or at least uncertain, or they are told without love of neighbor, or they result in a misuse of spiritual things, or they awake in other people the belief that by telling such stories an individual intends or requires that more of the same and worse stories are to be told. Do not forget examples of virtue, divine providence, power, goodness, and justice for on such examples one can build a great deal. But if you are telling such, do so out of firm conviction, clearly and in a very orderly manner, without digressions. If you forget something do not be ashamed, but confess it.

9. If you are speaking about yourself, see to it that no self-love lies under your statements.

10. Do not go from one good conversation immediately to another. By doing so many people find themselves incapable of knowing how to speak about a matter fully, but begin one conversation and, immediately after, another. Remain in your conversation as long as it is not problematic for the other person. You will thus overcome many misunderstandings, edify yourself and others, and gather together for yourself a good treasure of important matters and good and precise thoughts for further speech when it is necessary.

11. Consider that in yourself there are evil words, cursings, unnecessary oaths, and gross, unchaste language. Such are useless words which serve no purpose and have no proper end. Such too are good words, directed to the honor of an individual who already knows the word before it has come from the tongue. Shun evil and unnecessary words, for you must give an account of each of them. Endeavor to speak good words.

12. Hold all conversations either out of necessity or out of the

hope of improvement, or choose them carefully. One cannot shun external relationships with the godless, but enter into their society only as is necessary. It is more likely that you will be led astray than that you will win them for the Lord. If you must associate with them, however, protect yourself greatly.

13. Many conversations are good, but they are not carried out in proper society or in the proper place. In church, even the best statements can be an offense to the weak.

14. Do not speak secretly or whisper into the ear or in a foreign language in the presence of others. Such an act raises contention, and the other person will think that you do not trust him.

15. When others are speaking who wish generally to be heard, do not begin to speak to another person alone, for this results in disorder and ill-will.

16. If you raise an issue which you know from someone else or have heard from someone else, consider carefully before you raise it if the person from whom you have heard it will be satisfied with your repeating it. If you have any question in the matter, be silent.

17. If someone begins to speak while you are speaking, be silent, for such a person wishes others to hear him. If you continue to speak, he will, of course, not understand you properly, for he is thinking on what he himself wishes to say.

18. If someone else is speaking, do not begin to speak yourself because everyone is offended if one does not hear him out. You may for a time think that you have fully understood what is being said and yet you will not properly have grasped the meaning. The other person will be secretly offended if you do not hear him out. You would not commit such an act if it were done before a great lord whom you wished to honor. If you break into someone else's conversation, consider what you have done and you will discover that your mouth has stepped out without thinking first. You will more easily win love with each person if you listen with great patience to each person.

19. If someone contradicts you, be well on your guard for this is a real opportunity for you to sin in society. Unless the honor of God and the good of a noble suffers because of such a contradiction, let it go by. People often struggle, but when the struggle is over, neither side has any more certainty regarding the matter than they had before. If someone opposes the truth, guard yourself from any sort of impetuous mental turmoil. Such turmoil is only carnal zeal. Be satisfied if you have articulately presented the truth and good reasons for

it. You will accomplish nothing further with antagonism. Your opponent will consider the matter if he sees that you are certain regarding your position and do not wish strife. If he learns nothing else from you he will learn gentleness and modesty from your example.

20. Games and other pastimes such as dancing, jumping, and so forth, arise from an improper and empty manner of life, and common and unchaste postures in speech are associated with them. If you begin to take part in such activities, so that no other greater sins follow, consider well if it would not be wiser for you to leave them than to remain with them, since they provide an opportunity for you to become enmeshed in a disorderly way of life, or at least make it very difficult for you to preserve the peace of God in your soul.

21. If you must rebuke others for their sins, do not put off the unpleasant moments because of fear or shyness. Fear or shyness must be conquered just as other evil mental turmoil must be. But before you chastise another, chastise yourself so that your reproof will arise out of empathy. Rebuke with love and great foresight and modesty so that the other person might be convinced in his conscience in whatever manner that he has not done right. Christ rebuked Peter with a glance when Peter denied him, and Peter began to weep bitterly. But Christ also rebuked with expressive, harsh words. In this, love must be your teacher. Only do not make yourself a participator in others' sins.

22. At mealtime be temperate in eating and drinking. If someone insists that you surfeit, know that it is a temptation to make you sin against your God. Do not let yourself be led to follow the pleasures of good eating and the need to fill your stomach to the fullest. It would be better for you if you ate often but ate little, so that in sobriety of mind and in the proper manner you would remain able to do something good rather than filling your stomach and being placed outside of a sober soul's loving and joyous manner of life. By much eating and drinking, body and soul are weighed down. Continual temperance will be a great test for your spiritual intelligence. If your tongue is so delicate as to choose only the finest food for yourself and thus to satisfy the lowly needs of taste, and to eat and to drink in a disorderly manner without proper hunger and thirst, you are not yet temperate.

23. At all times and in all societies guard yourself against indecent demeanor and activity and disorderly posture of the body. These give witness to disorder in the mind and testify to your secret mental turmoil. Your beloved Jesus, who is among the lowest, does not wish

you to do such things. Why then do you not follow him in his external life? Let a good friend tell you about your actions, for you are not able to come to self-knowledge about these.

24. Guard yourself from unnecessary laughter. All laughter is forbidden. It is fitting that the most pious person rejoices inwardly not over earthly but rather over divine things, and his mouth gives witness with the circumspect laughter of loving kindness which arises in his mind. One can fall into sin very quickly by the use of the tongue, and the way is thus prepared for a dangerous dissipation of the senses (Wisd. 9:15). How frivolous such action is becomes clear when a person wishes to draw near to the ever-present God once again in deep humility. In particular, if others are laughing over jokes or frivolities, guard yourself that you do not laugh with them. Joking does not please God; why then should it please you? If it does not please you, why do you laugh over it? If you laugh, you have sinned as well. By remaining sober you reprove your sins in the consciences of these senseless talkers.

25. If others are mistaken in what they say or wander from the correct path, endeavor to bring the conversation in time back into a reasonable order. By doing this, you will avoid much perplexity. Very few use this gift, and thus it is very necessary.

26. Do not strive to precede another. Do not endeavor to reach a position of superiority. For the sake of good order you must remain in your position. You are dust and the other person is ashes. Before God you are both alike. As a result, as is insofar possible, do not concern yourself whether you stand or move. Love is humble and through its humility it awakens love in others. A proud man burdens every man.

27. Honor each person in society, but fear none. God is greater than you and he; fear only God.

28. Do not be sad and melancholy among people, but joyous and loving for joy and love enliven everyone.

29. If you see that it is not necessary for you to be in society, that the honor of God might be better increased in some other ways, or that love does not press you to serve your neighbor in your neighbor's presence, then do not wish to remain in society. You must not be present in society for one moment, if you have no other purpose to be there than to pass the time in a useless manner. If the time a Christian spends with his God is tedious, it is a mark of that Christian's shortcomings. Even pious people find themselves in this difficulty

and because of it fall into the trap of speaking many useless words and undertaking useless activities which later trouble their souls.

30. See to it that your heart be evenly disposed whether it be solitary or in society. If you do not find it so, you have a great reason to spend more time by yourself than in society so that you can bring your heart into correct order as it once was. If you do find your heart evenly disposed, see to it that it remains so and that you do not fall from that state.

August Hermann Francke

ON CHRISTIAN PERFECTION*
1690

1. We are justified only by faith in the Lord Jesus without merit or the addition of work in that the Heavenly Father because of the perfect satisfaction and the precious merit of his Son judges us free and liberated from all our sins.

2. Through this justification, which occurs through faith, the justified person becomes completely and totally perfect; indeed, it is seen as the justification of God himself, as St. Paul writes: God made him who knew no sin to be sin for us so that in him we might become the justification of God [2 Cor. 5:21]. Just as God looks upon the Lord Christ as sin (because our sins were reckoned to him), so he sees the sinner as just and completely perfect because he gives to the sinner as the sinner's own the innocence and righteousness of Christ.

3. He who does not have this perfection cannot become holy. Perfection is nothing other than faith in the Lord Jesus and is not in us or ours but in Christ or of Christ for whose sake we are considered perfect before God and thus his perfection is ours by ascription.

4. However, if a person is justified he can be completely certain of his blessedness. Nevertheless he immediately discovers the weakness of the flesh and inherited sinful behavior. He desires in the depth of his heart nothing other than God and eternal life and he looks upon everything which is in the world as the lust of the eye, the lust of the flesh and the pride of life as dirt and harm. Nevertheless, he discovers that original sin stirs in his flesh and causes in him all kinds of doubts and evil thoughts, at times evil inclinations of the will. Likewise he discovers that because of the great and long habit of

---

*Translated from Gustav Kramer, *August Hermann Francke: Ein Lebensbild* (Halle, 1880), pp. 273–275.

114

sinning he often hastens into this or that external activity with words or deeds.

5. Such remaining disorderly patterns and activities, however, are not reckoned to the justified man. There is no condemnation for those who are in Christ Jesus, namely, those who do not walk according to the flesh although the flesh attracts them but according to the spirit. Thus as soon as the newborn man recognizes his error which does not proceed out of his own intentions, he turns in true faith to the grace of Jesus Christ and is in his heart an enemy of sin.

6. If the newborn Christian acknowledges such sins of the flesh, he strives with all earnestness against the evil which arises in his flesh. And he does so not through his own power and strength, but he destroys the works of the flesh through the spirit and he depends on the power of Jesus Christ which is made sanctification for him from God and conquers the evil in him.

7. In such sinful habits and crimes the justified man remains, however, never standing in one position, but through the grace of God he sets aside ever more and more the evil, and day to day grows in faith and in love just as in one's physical life one is first a child then a youth then finally a man.

8. In such growth however a person can never get as far as he wishes. He is never completely perfect but he can grow and increase in good works as long as he lives. One who prides himself in an understanding of perfection deceives himself and others.

9. Nevertheless it cannot be denied that in the understanding, in a certain way, a perfection is attributed to man according to the Holy Scripture, namely, I can call someone a master in an art even if he has not completely learned that art and has other masters over him. Thus the Scripture does not wish to teach that a person can be completely perfect in his life, that he can be without sin or the attraction to sin, but that a person can come to a human strength in Christianity so as to kill the old habits in himself and to conquer his flesh and blood, and that one person is always more perfect than the other. Thus the epistle to the Hebrews [5:12–14] says that for the perfect there is strong food and it describes the perfect as those who have, because of practice, a practiced sense of distinguishing good and evil, but they are not those who are no longer inclined to evil through sinful lust.

10. From this it follows that both the following statements are true in a certain sense: We are perfect, and we are not perfect. Name-

ly, we are perfect through Christ and in Christ through our justification and according to the righteousness of Jesus Christ ascribed to us. However, we are not and will not be completely perfect in the sense that we will nevermore be able to grow, to set aside evil and to take on good toward sanctification.

11. The one who does not wish to err in this matter must distinguish well the article concerning justification and that concerning renovation or sanctification. Otherwise he will increasingly become entangled in controversy.

12. From this it follows that a justified man has no sin, namely, after justification, and he has sin after renovation, for that which still clings to a man is not reckoned to him because of Christ's sake.

13. If the person who is justified prays or goes to confession, he prays that for Christ's sake God will forgive the sins which are still in him and not ascribe them to him. He knows and is assured that as one who is in Christ Jesus there is no damnation for him.

14. As a result the justified man eats the sacrament for the strengthening of his faith and for the improvement of his life.

15. In all this, however, one has to be careful that his repentance is not hypocritical, but that he works out his salvation with fear and trembling. Otherwise the consolation from the grace of Christ can easily become willful and the person who has love for the world will speak as if the love of God is in him. Such an act is a deception and makes Hell rejoice.

August Hermann Francke

A LETTER TO A FRIEND CONCERNING THE MOST USEFUL WAY OF PREACHING*
1725

Honored and Dear Friend,

In answer to the question which you have proposed to me, namely how a faithful minister, who earnestly desires to save and to edify the souls of his hearers, to gain sinners unto Christ, and to inflame their hearts with a growing love to their Savior, may best adapt his preaching to these excellent purposes? I can at present only suggest a few things briefly; if I had more leisure, I would choose to write more copiously on so weighty a subject.

I must take it for granted that a minister who sincerely desires and who is likely to do good by his preaching is a minister both in heart and in life, as St. Paul describes in 2 Tim. 1:13, 14: one who holds fast the form of found words (or the pure apostolic doctrine) which he has heard, in faith and love which is in Christ Jesus; and who keeps that good thing which has been committed to him by the Holy Ghost which dwelleth in him.

It will not a little serve the good ends proposed in the question for a minister, very frequently, to lay down in his sermons the distinguishing marks and characters both of the converted and of the unconverted, and that with all possible plainness so that every one of his hearers may be able to judge his own state, and may know to which of these two classes he belongs. But then great care must be taken that

---

*Revised and modernized from *A Letter to a Friend*, trans. David Jennings (London, 1754).

those distinguishing characters are correctly drawn, for it may easily happen, because of a preacher's unskillfulness in this affair, that the unconverted, on the one hand, may be deceived into a good opinion of their present state, and may grow thereupon more secure and careless; and that some converted persons, on the other hand, may be unreasonably disturbed and filled with groundless and fruitless fears. However, a prudent minister, who has experienced a work of grace upon his own heart, will have no great difficulty in describing it to others, so as to guard sufficiently against the mistakes on both sides, and to lead both one and the other, by the unerring light of Scripture, into the knowledge of the true state of their own souls.

For the purpose also let a minister carefully and clearly distinguish in his preaching between mere morality and true religion, between the moral honest man and the believer who, from a deep conviction of the depravity of his nature and the errors of his life, has learned to hate sin from his heart and lives by the faith of the Son of God. For it is hardly credible what multitudes of persons there are even in Christian countries, where the gospel is publicly and faithfully preached, who, though they are wise enough in other matters, yet in this they are greatly ignorant, and thereby miserably deceive their own souls.

And, because this kind of self-deceit is so very common, it is very necessary for a minister to instruct his hearers with all possible plainness in the duty of self-examination, and very often to exhort them to it; more especially to enquire if ever they were awakened from their natural sleep in sin; if they have escaped out of the snare of the devil; if they have ever had a lively and affecting sense of the corruption of their own hearts, and of the misery of their natural state; and, in short, whether they have good and solid reasons to conclude that they are regenerate persons: Whether they can find in themselves the genuine marks of a true conversion to God, and a living faith in Christ, or whether, on the other hand, they do not conclude that they are true Christians and in a state of salvation, different from being merely moral honest men, and not living in any gross and scandalous sin; and, perhaps too, from their saying prayers, hearing sermons, and frequenting the places of public worship, and from their practicing such outward duties of religion? Or again, whether they do not flatter themselves that their eternal state is safe, merely because their lives are not altogether so bad as the lives of some others.

It would also be of very considerable use for a minister often to explain, and to show the difference between a legal and an evangelical frame and principle of religion or between that slavish fear by which alone it is that some persons, even of a serious turn of mind, are forced and dragged as it were to their duty, and that evangelical newness of spirit, that filial love to God and delight in his service, which usually grows and flourishes in the soul where it is once planted, and which produces a free, unconstrained, and acceptable religion. This would be an excellent means, not only of awakening sinners out of their carnal security, but of turning them thoroughly unto God, to a holy walk and to a pleasurable conversation with him, one which becomes his children. And for this end it is of very great importance that a minister not only instruct his hearers what they must do, and how they ought to act, but that he also labor fully to apprise and to convince them, by the evidence of Scripture, of their own natural weakness and impotency for all that is spiritually good, and that he further show them, by the same word of truth, where they must look for, and from whom they may hope to receive, all grace and strength, not only to renew their souls in their first conversion, but also afterward to enable them to perform every duty, as well of outward as of inward religion. They must be told that they can do nothing without Christ, according as he has assured us, in John 15:5: Without me ye can do nothing. And again, that by the help of his grace they may do all things, according to St. Paul in Philippians 4:13: I can do all things through Christ which strengtheneth me.

Thus gospel ministers should constantly make it the aim and direction of their preaching to lead their hearers to Christ and to his grace—to him by whose stripes we are healed [Isa. 53:5] and whose blood takes away all the sins of all that truly repent and believe in the Lord Jesus; and to him by whose divine power all things are given to us that pertain both to life and godliness (2 Pet. 1:3). Thus the holy apostles preached; these were the topics which they insisted upon, and if their example is not followed in this matter, it will be no wonder if our modern preaching comes vastly short of their success. By this means some of our hearers will be in danger of sinking into a mere legal frame and spirit of bondage, while they are pressed to duty and works, but not encouraged by the grace of Christ nor directed where to look for strength to perform it, and others of them will take up with a false peace, a carnal security, for want of being directed to Christ, who is the only foundation of the sinner's reasonable hope and solid comfort. But on the other hand, when both these points are well explained and duly insisted on, no other means are so powerful to awaken secure sinners, to bring them to Christ, and to settle their souls in solid peace and comfort. Hereby, under the influence of the Spirit of Christ, they find themselves transported as it were into a new life, and now they go on with vigor and pleasure in the practice of universal piety.

It would further be useful, and it is highly necessary, that ministers should not only preach of the necessity of conversion, and instruct their hearers to depend on the grace of Christ for it, but also that they should, very frequently, in their sermons explain the nature and the whole progress of conversion, sometimes extensively and distinctly, and at other times more briefly, endeavoring thereby to lead their hearers into a true knowledge of the state of their souls, and showing them how they must repent of their sins, what they must do to be saved from their natural misery and, in short, how they may obtain the full salvation of the gospel, so that every one may be able to give an answer to that most important question: What must I do that I may be a child of God and inherit eternal life? For let a minister entertain his hearers with the sublimest doctrines of Christianity, let him also declaim against sin and exhort them to their various duties in the most earnest and pathetic manner, and let all be adorned with the finest beauties of wit and eloquence; yet, after all, if his sermons are not so contrived and framed as, at the same time, to inform the ignorant how they may obtain an interest in the gospel salvation for themselves, and what means and methods God has appointed for that purpose, what will it profit them? No more than a parcel of shreds of cloth of various dyes, though they were of the finest thread and liveliest colors, would serve the purpose of a man who wants a handsome garment; whereas a sermon that informs the ignorant sinner, not only of the necessity of conversion, but also how that happy change may certainly be effected in his own soul, may not be unfitly compared, in respect to its usefulness, to a complete garment, made all of a piece, well fitted to the man's shape that wants it, and which he may therefore put on and wear with honor and pleasure.

But now in order to do all this, a minister must take pains with his own heart, as well as in composing his sermons. He must have a zeal for Christ, and must aim at nothing so much as to bring sinners to him. This should be in some measure the design and drift of every sermon that he preaches, so that if a person should happen to hear him only once in his whole life, he might, even by means of that one sermon, get some notion of the one thing needful, and be properly entered at least into the way of salvation. For this should every minister study and strive, and for this should he continually pray that God would fill his heart with pious zeal and holy wisdom, so that he may rightly divide the word of truth aright, and minister grace to his hearers.

It might probably make some good impressions on the minds of the people if a minister was often to inculcate, with great plainness and seriousness, the necessity of prayer; and more particularly what need they have to pray very earnestly to the God of grace that he set his word upon their hearts, that he bring the good seed to perfection in their full and blessed conformity to himself. And further, so great is the ignorance of many persons concerning the duty of prayer that they seem to have no notion of it other than merely reading some forms out of a prayer book. This makes it as necessary, as it would probably be a useful thing for a minister to lead them, as it were by the hand, into this path of their duty, that is, to explain it to them in a most easy and familiar manner, to show them that it requires no great art and skill to pray acceptably to God, for they are to speak to him as children to a loving father, they are to spread before him their sorrows and complaints, they are to tell him of the state and condition of their souls, just as they find and feel it. And they need not be at all solicitous about propriety of expression and elegant phrases in their secret prayers, for God regards the sense of the heart rather than the language of the lips. The Scriptures themselves furnish us with several examples of such artless and yet acceptable prayers. Let a minister then diligently instruct his hearers how they are, in the first place, to get their hearts disposed for prayer, and it may be of use too to assist and furnish the more ignorant with words and fit expressions. But at the same time let him inform them that they need not tie themselves to use those very words nor any form whatever, but that they should learn to pour out their hearts unto God, in such words by which they can best express the real sentiments and affections of their own souls, according to the Psalmist (Psalm 62:8): Ye people, pour out your hearts before him.

It is further extremely necessary that ministers should very often take occasion to explain in their sermons that renewing or change of the mind which is so essential to all true religion, and which yet, alas! very few persons seem to understand, or indeed to have almost any notion of. Nor is it enough to explain that first and mighty change, which is at once made in a sinner at his conversion, when he comes to love that good which before he hated, and to hate that evil which he before loved, when from being an unbeliever he becomes a believer, or when his false and dead faith is changed into a true and saving one. But that further progressive change should also be greatly recommended in which the Christian must be improving to the very end of his life, which St. Paul refers to in 2 Cor. 3:18: But now (the veil which was upon the heart being taken away, and the Spirit of the Lord having taken up his dwelling in it, 16, 17) we all with open face beholding as in a glass the glory of the Lord, are changed into the same image from glory to glory, even by the Spirit of the Lord. Hereby the mind is more and more renewed, the Christian grows up in the spirit and temper of Christ, and his lovely image is drawn upon the soul in fairer lines every day.

It is of considerable importance also that the whole faith and duty of a Christian be represented in its most amiable and attractive light, so that sinners may be won to religion upon a full conviction that if they would do well for themselves and obtain true peace and comfort, the shortest, the surest, and indeed the only way is to turn in good earnestness from sin to God and holiness, and that religion is by no means a grievous and melancholy thing, which any man need be afraid of, but full of pleasure and greatly desirable even for its own sake. And though it calls us, indeed, to a present combat, and requires us to fight and strive against sin, yet this is but in order to peace and to a certain victory, which will much more than recompense the toils of the war.

It is much to be desired that ministers not take up more of their sermons than needed to explain their text, but rather, after as short an explication of it as is sufficient to lead their hearers into the true sense and meaning (which must by no means be neglected), hasten to the application. And in that, let a minister address himself to his hearers with a becoming seriousness and earnestness; let him apply his subject both to saints and sinners, to the converted and to the unconverted, in order to awaken the secure and careless, and to build up true believers in their faith and holiness. Experience would soon show that this is by far the more profitable way than to spend almost the whole discourse, as some do, in explaining their text and subject, and then close with a very short application, because the time is gone.

It is also greatly to be desired that those under-shepherds of the flock of Christ would make it more designedly and zealously the purpose of their preaching to bring sinners to him, who is the great shepherd of the sheep, that they would strive by the most winning arguments they can possibly use, and especially by such as the grace of the gospel will naturally suggest, to persuade and even to compel them to come to him, as the hen when she sees a few crumbs or grains of corn earnestly invites her brood to come and share the treasure with her! She will by no means be satisfied nor leave off calling them till they come. Thus did our blessed Savior. How graciously did he call and invite sinners to come to him in the days of his personal ministry upon earth! As Matt. 11:28: Come unto me all ye that labor and are heavy laden, and I will give you rest. Again in John 7:37, 38: If any man thirst, let him come to me and drink: He that believeth on me, as the Scripture faith, out of his belly shall flow rivers of living water. And much to the same purpose we find him speaking in several other places. Thus also we hear the prophet Isaiah, in the Old Testament, inviting sinners to Christ (Isa. 55:1): Lo, every one that thirsteth, come ye to the waters, and thus St. Paul, in the New Testament (2 Cor. 5:11): We beseech you in Christ's stead be ye reconciled to God. And thus does the Apostle John speak over and over in his divine writings. Remarkable to this purpose also are the words of our blessed Savior concerning Jerusalem (Matt. 23:37): How often would I have gathered thy children, even as a hen gathereth her chickens under her wing! Christ called sinners to come to himself, as their proper Lord and master, as their only Redeemer and Savior. We, says St. Paul, preach not ourselves, but Christ Jesus the Lord (2 Cor. 4:5), and therefore we endeavor to bring sinners not to ourselves, but to him. But now in order to do this, and that a minister may be thus happily successful in his preaching, he must not only sincerely love his people and have an affectionate concern for their salvation, but he must be an ardent lover of Christ too. He must wish and desire and covet nothing so much as to bring all that hear him to Christ, to deliver every one of them, as it were, into his gracious arms, if he could but persuade them to be so happy, so that thus they may learn, even by the example of their minister, to love the Lord Jesus.

For this purpose it is further requisite that a minister should very often take occasion to display, in the most lively colors that he can, the excellency and glory of Christ's person, the kindness of his heart and the exceeding riches of his grace, both as he is God and man, as he is now a glorious triumphant Savior, as well as once he sustained and executed the same office in a humbled and suffering state. And that he further inform his hearers what excellent blessings are treasured up in Christ to be bestowed on all his friends and people, so that they may be drawn to him by a principle of desire and love, that they may most willingly give him their hearts, and so that it may be the breathing of their souls and the matter of their most earnest prayer to Christ that he would be pleased to manifest his love to them, that he would shed it abroad in their hearts by his holy Spirit (Rom. 5:5), that he would more and more reveal to them the glory of his majesty, that he would impress and affect their minds with a lively sense of it, so that they may yet more and more love and honor him their heavenly spouse, by whom it is that they have, and that they further hope for access to and acceptance with the Father, with whom they also hope to dwell forever and ever.

The love of Christ ought to be much more insisted on by preachers than is commonly done, because when we apply to ourselves in a right manner his passion, death, and atonement, his merits, and that purchase of salvation which he has made for us, the knowledge of his love to us, and of our pardon and justification through faith in his blood, is the truest spring and most powerful attractor of our love to him. Now the more we love Christ, because he first loved us (1 John 4:19), the better will every other branch of our religion flourish. Every other grace and every duty will then flow from its proper fountain. Therefore the more a minister endeavors to instill this principle of sacred love into the hearts of his hearers, the more comfortable success will he probably see of his labors, in their spiritual improvement and growing obedience to the gospel.

But especially, and in the first place, let every minister look to his own heart, and see to it that he himself loves Christ fervently, lest he be as the sounding brass and as the tinkling cymbal, which the Apostle speaks of in 1 Corinthians 13:1. And besides, without a sincere love to Christ in his soul, there will be little probability of his recommending him effectually to the love of others. It is not enough for him to preach a great many sermons on the love of Christ, and to exhort his hearers to love him, for if his own heart is not warmed with this sacred love, his discourses on that subject will be apt to be cold and lifeless, and therefore unprofitable and fruitless. Nothing could be more pertinently answered in a few words, to one that asked another how he might learn to be a good and a useful preacher, than this: *Si multum ames Christum*, You must learn to be a zealous lover of Christ.

But then let it be further noted that sincere love to Christ will always express itself not only in words, but by suitable or correspondent actions. Thus our Savior has taught us (John 15:14): Ye are my friends, said he, if ye do whatsoever I command you, that is, this is the best and most substantial evidence of your sincere friendship, that you truly love me.

I consider also the duties of self-denial and putting off of the world and its carnal pleasures, and, in short, from all the present things of sense and time, to be among those more important and necessary subjects which ministers should often preach on, oftener indeed than most of them do. These are subjects which our Savior Christ, when he was a preacher upon earth, very much insisted on in his sermons, as you may see particularly in Matthew 16:24, 25, 26: If any man will come after me, let him deny himself, and take up his cross and follow me, and Luke 14:26: If any man come to me, and hate not his father and mother, yea and his own life also, that is, in comparison to me, he cannot be my disciple. And how needful are these subjects now. For alas! how many persons there are who can talk well about Christ and religion, who carry a fair appearance of virtue and godliness, and who perform many outward duties with reputation and honor, and yet not having learned to deny themselves; their love of the world not being sufficiently mortified, they are easily overcome in a day of trial, and sacrifice their religion and their souls to their worldly interest. Let self-denial then be earnestly recommended, and that, not merely as a moral virtue or philosophical attainment, I mean not upon such principles only as the heathen moralists used to insist upon; but let it be recommended and urged as a Christian grace, as that which flows chiefly from love to Christ, even such a love as will make us ready to deny ourselves the pleasures, riches and honors of this world, all manner of sensual gratifications, and our very lives themselves, for his sake, as Christ not only expects but requires of us (Matt. 16:25).

Though the diligent reading of the Scriptures themselves, even the inspired writings of the prophets and apostles, and the very words of our Savior Christ, should be chiefly recommended, as they are undoubtedly far preferable to any other books of mere human composition, yet besides these a minister may very profitably recommend to his hearers some other good books of religion, both ancient and modern, to be read by them at home in their own closets or families. Such books I mean as are written in a truly evangelical strain, and with a spirit of lively devotion and piety, which would be no inconsiderable means both of preserving and nourishing the fire of divine love in their hearts. I might mention by way of instance Martin Statius's [d. 1655] *Lutherus Redevivus,* which is nothing else but an abridgment of Luther's works, in which the most important passages are collected into a narrow room, and such passages more especially as have the most direct and powerful tendency to awaken and excite the minds of men to lively practical religion. However, I mention this but as one instance, out of a great many very excellent and useful books which the providence of God has now furnished his church withal, and which we ought to account as a precious treasure to it. And further, let not any minister think that it is the people only who are to be profited in their souls by reading such good books, while all the use that he is concerned to make of them for himself is only to form his style by reading them, or to borrow thoughts from them, or it may be to steal sermons out of them (which is shamefully the practice of too many preachers), but he should read them, chiefly and in the first place, with a view to his own spiritual edification. He should endeavor so to use and improve the gifts which God has bestowed on other men that his own soul may be the better for them, as well as the souls of the people to whom he preaches.

Once more, let faithful ministers by no means forget to recommend it to their hearers that they would familiarly acquaint themselves and converse with serious, lively, and growing Christians, and with those more especially who excel in the gift and spirit of prayer; for as a live coal kindles another that is cold and dead, so will the savory discourse, the fervent prayers, and the holy conversation of warm and lively Christians be a probable means of kindling the same fire of divine love in the souls of dead sinners, or at least of nourishing and improving the sacred flame in the hearts of their most intimate Christian friends. Ministers should therefore do all they can to promote such Christian conversation among the more serious of their hearers, observing however the rules of necessary prudence, particularly that of the Apostle (1 Cor. 14:40): Let all things be done decently and in order. They should exhort them as St. Paul does the Colossians (Col. 3:16): Let the word of Christ dwell in you richly in all wisdom, teaching and admonishing one another in psalms and hymns and spiritual songs, singing with grace in your hearts unto the Lord. To this pious purpose that large and rich treasure of sacred hymns, both ancient and modern, with which God has graciously blessed his church, is not a little help; for this therefore we are bound to render him immortal praises.

Thus I have briefly answered your question, and given you my thoughts on the most useful way of preaching. May God, for Christ's sake, attend what I have written with his effectual blessing. To him I would now humbly offer up the following prayer:

O Lord God! give, I beseech you, both now and at all times hereafter to your church pastors and teachers after your own heart, even such as shall bring the sheep of Christ into his fold, and who, through the influence of your good Spirit, shall feed them with saving knowledge and under-standing. Make every preacher of your Word know and always remember that neither is he that planteth any thing, neither he that watereth, but you are all in all, who alone can give the increase. Let none of them vainly presume on their skill and ability to do any good by their preaching, and obtain any good success, but let them all humbly wait upon you, and by fervent daily prayer let them seek for and obtain the aids of your grace, to enable them to dispense the word of life, and let your blessing render their preaching happily successful to the souls of those that hear them. Amen.
May 25, 1725.

August Hermann Francke

ON THE RESURRECTION
OF OUR LORD*

Jesus said unto her:
I am the Resurrection, and the Life.
John 11:25

It may seem unnecessary to do that which is the common business of sermons on this day, namely, to prove the truth of our Lord's resurrection, and that which is the sure consequence of it, the certainty of our resurrection. It appears superfluous to multiply arguments to support an article of faith, into which we were all initiated in our baptism, which we still profess to believe, which we affirm daily in repeating the creeds, and which, on the yearly return of this season, we assemble to commemorate.

But when we consider the lives of those who profess this truth, who received the sacramental tokens of it in their Baptism, who repeat it daily in their creeds, and meet here yearly for the solemn celebration of it, as a fundamental article of their faith: when, I say, we consider the lives of these professors, there seems but too much reason to suspect that notwithstanding all our professions, many among us are not heartily convinced of it. For after all the elaborate discourses upon this subject, where is that indifference for the things of the world? Where is that spiritual joy, that purity, that heavenly mindedness, which the resurrection of our Lord should inspire? Where is that self-denial, that watchfulness over our own hearts and

---

*Revised and modernized from August Hermann Francke, *A Sermon on the Resurrection of Our Lord Preached on Easter Sunday* (London, 1732).

128

attention to the omnipresence of God, that exact justice in our deal-ing, that warm benevolence toward all men, and, in a word, that zeal-ous preparation against the Day of Judgment which an effectual assurance of our own resurrection would certainly oblige us to? I might ask how they would live if they did not believe any resurrec-tion? What alteration would there be in their manners? Would they be more addicted to pleasure, more intent upon their temporal inter-est, or less concerned for the good of others if they had never heard the truths of the gospel? Yet they lay claim to the venerable name of Christians, and assemble here to celebrate the triumphs of our Lord's resurrection. I dare not therefore say of them that they do not believe it, but I fear they have not duly thought about it. They do not suffi-ciently understand the wondrous effects and consequences of this great mystery. It is not enough that we know it by name and by hear-say. All saving knowledge is experiential. And it is not enough that we know the history, but we must also feel the power of our Lord's resurrection, not only that he is risen, but also that he is the resurrec-tion. As the sun is light to itself, and the great source of day to all the worlds around it, so is our Lord resurrection to himself, and the source and author of resurrection in all others.

Leaving therefore the history of our Lord's rising from the dead, as an established and acknowledged truth, and presuming, I hope not without good reason, upon your constant and open profession of it, I shall at present consider our Lord as he is the resurrection, not only in himself, whereby he raised his own most holy humanity, but as he works this great work in us, as I said, the immediate cause and author of our resurrection. This is what he plainly affirms of himself in the text, I am the Resurrection and the Life, which St. Paul clearly ex-plains in 1 Corinthians 15. Since by man came also the resurrection of the dead: for as in Adam all die, even so in Christ shall all be made alive.

This resurrection to be wrought in us by Christ is twofold, relat-ing to the two constituent parts of man, the body and the soul, for to these two belong two distinct resurrections, very different from each other.

The first resurrection, that of the soul I mean, is of a moral and spiritual nature. It is the rising of the soul from the death of sin, unto the life of righteousness, states more different, and infinitely more important, than those of natural life and death. It is peculiar to the saints of God. It requires our concurrence with the operations of grace, to which alone it is to be imputed: and this blessed and holy is he that hath part in this first resurrection (Rev. 20:6).

The second resurrection is that of the body, after our natural death. It does not take place till the Day of Judgment. It is common to all men; it is necessary and inevitable, and is the effect of the justice rather than of the grace of almighty God.

Of both these resurrections, Jesus Christ is the immediate cause and author. Of the first, as he is Savior of the world, and of the second, as he is the judge of it, for it is a prerogative very properly annexed to his office of universal judge that he should, by his own power, summon all mankind to his tribunal.

The power of this second resurrection from the state of natural death seems to have been principally intended in the literal sense of the text, which was spoken on the account of Lazarus, whom our Lord was then about to raise from the dead. I know, said Martha, that he shall rise again at the resurrection of the Last Day. Jesus said unto her, "I am the Resurrection and the Life" (John 11:23–25). I have the power of raising all men, and therefore I can raise any of them, how, or at what time, I think fit.

This resurrection from a natural death is, I think, well enough understood. We can all by a faith in the omnipotence of God form sufficient notions of our being raised again at the Last Day without bodies, so that the whole man, which acted in this life, may be qualified for the rewards or punishments of the next. There is, I suppose, little difficulty in understanding this, feeling the experience we now have, of the union of soul and body, may inform us, in a good degree, of what shall come to pass at the resurrection of the dead, when they shall be reunited.

But the spiritual resurrection of our souls in this life is a thing less thought of, and less understood by most men. This is one of those things of God, whereof the natural or animal man is ignorant. It requires a spiritual discernment, and some spiritual experience for proper apprehension. The Holy Scriptures treat of it very frequently, but nowhere more largely and clearly than in the second lesson of the morning service for this day (Rom. 6). I shall read the whole passage, only premising that the Apostle here treats of the death to sin, as well as the spiritual resurrection. The former is always necessary to the latter and is so connected and implied in it that they cannot be easily considered separately. But hear St. Paul: Know ye not that so many of us were baptized into Jesus Christ, into his death, that is, into an obligation, to be made comformable to it by dying to sin? Therefore we are buried with him by Baptism into death, that like as Jesus Christ was raised up from the dead, by the glory of the Father, even so we also should walk in newness of life. For if we have been planted together in the likeness of his death we shall be also in the likeness of his resurrection, knowing this, that our old man is crucified with him, that the body of sin might be destroyed, that henceforth we should not serve sin: for he that is dead with Christ, we believe that we shall also live with him. Let not sin therefore reign in your mortal body, that ye should obey it in the lust thereof (Rom. 6:3–12). You observe here that the death to sin is joined with the spiritual resurrection, as a circumstance indispensably requisite to and implied in it, for no person is capable of a resurrection till he is once dead. It is necessary therefore that we consider this death, that we enquire what the old life is and how it is extinguished, before we can understand anything of the spiritual resurrection that follows it, and the new life to be confessed. The life to be lost by this death is said to be that of our old man, which is a Scriptural phrase signifying that nature, temper, or disposition of mind with which we are born, as we are the sons of Adam, and heirs of original corruption, whereby, as the Scripture assures, and even our Catechism instructs us, we are the children of wrath. It is this innate depravation which makes us ignorant of God, blind and stupid to all spiritual things, selfish, covetous, unjust, deceitful. Hence arise that pride and arrogance, that envy, malice, and detraction, which make men grievous to themselves and one another. Hence also all other works of the flesh take their origin: our sloth, intemperance, and all other evil lusts, which make us odious in the sight of God, and utterly incapable of those pure and heavenly delights of piety, which constitute the proper happiness of our nature.

Besides those greater acts of sin, which fall under common observation, there is a depth of subtlety and wickedness, an endless train of vanity and self-deceit, which cannot be well described nor properly understood by any whose minds are not enlightened by grace, for as it is difficult to make a blind man understand what darkness is, at least, to give him such a notion of it as we have, even though he lives in it continually, so it is similarly difficult to give unconverted sinners a right notion of what is here meant by the old man, because this, as most other things, is best if not only known by its contrary. But in general we are to know, that whatever tendency there is in our

131

nature to commit sin, it is a part or member of the old man. It is the hereditary distemper of our souls, derived from Adam, the corrupt source of our race. While we are yet in our natural state, unreformed by divine grace, this lives, this reigns in our mortal bodies. Why is this man a drunkard, that one malicious, and a third unjust in his dealings? The reason is that, because the resurrection of Christ has not had its due effect, the mind is not renewed, and the old man of sin remains unmortified. That corrupt nature, which we received from Adam, is still active and vigorous, the nature, I say, we received from Adam, which therefore is called the old Adam, bearing his name from whom it is derived. It is also called the old leaven, because it has infected the whole race of mankind. It is also called flesh, and the body of sin, which are different terms for the same thing, the principle of corruption which is in our nature.

This, as I said, lives and reigns in the hearts of unregenerate men, and would ever reign there, for we can do nothing to hinder it, if Jesus Christ did not intercede and by the virtue of his sufferings and death communicate to believers such powers of grace which are sufficient to destroy this root of evil in their souls. I say that this corruption of our nature is such that we cannot possibly resist it by our strength. It is too hard for our most serious purposes. It bears down our feeble resolutions like a torrent, and renders all our opposition fruitless and ineffectual. In vain does the law encounter it with her impotent discipline. In vain does she set before us her rigorous commands and prohibitions. In vain does she display her rewards and punishments. These all serve only to show us our guilt and danger, but cannot work our deliverance. The rod of Moses cannot so expel the nature, but it will still recur, it will still return to us, and take its old courses. We are still the same men, and all our struggles after virtue are like the motion of a door upon its hinges, still fixed to the same place.

But, behold, a greater than Moses is come in the gospel dispensation, even our Lord Jesus Christ; and what the law could not do, in that it was weak through the flesh (Rom. 8:3), that is, our corrupt nature, which is too violent to be controlled by the dead letter of written precepts—what this law could not do, that St. Paul says has God done for us, by sending his own son in the likeness of sinful flesh (Rom. 8:3). He has for and through him granted us new powers and abilities, whereby we are enabled to mortify, that is, to kill and destroy our corrupt nature. Our old man is crucified with him (Paul says) that the body of sin might be destroyed, that henceforth we should not serve sin (Rom. 6:6). But this is still insufficient to make us either holy or happy. It is at best only a negative goodness. There is more required of us than a mere abstinence from vice. For example, it is not enough that we do not hate our neighbor, but we must actually love him with a sincere affection. We must, in a word, not only cease to do evil, but also learn to do well: and as the old man of sin is to be destroyed, so the new man is to be raised up in us.

But this is a natural consequence of the former: If we be dead with Christ, we believe also that we shall be raised up with him. If we have been planted together in the likeness of his death, we shall also grow up in the likeness of his resurrection (Rom. 6:4–5). This is the language of the Holy Ghost; and the best interpretation I can give you of it is to be deduced from the following principle, namely, "that every act or suffering of Christ, as is meritorious of grace, is also expressive of it. It represents that very sort, or kind of grace, which it obtains for us." Thus by his death he put off all that mortal corruptible nature which he had received from Adam. He destroyed that body, which was liable to pain, sickness, death, and all other infirmities, touching the fallen state of mankind, and thereby he purchased for us those graces which are effectual for the destruction in each of us the old Adam, the corrupt principles of sin inherited by us from the guilt of our first parents. And likewise, at his resurrection he resumed a new nature; his body was raised incorruptible, impassible, and glorious as it now resides at the right hand of the Father. And thereby has he obtained for us also a new nature, a new life, and such a frame and disposition of soul as will effectively produce all kinds of virtue, and richly abound in good works.

This is the great and unspeakable advantage which comes to us from our Lord's resurrection. But how few are there that rightly value it? It produces everything that is truly great and glorious. It confers a divine life. It makes us partakers of the divine nature—strong, by the strength, wise, by the wisdom, holy, by the holiness of God. But the men of the world enjoy none of these things. They have no eyes to see the beauty of holiness. Almost all their imaginations and desires run in direct opposition to it. They fear that thoughts of it should make them melancholy. All their concern is about the animal life; all their care is for the old man, for his maintenance and support, and how they may make provision for the flesh, to fulfill the lusts thereof. No wonder then that they feel no joy arise in their hearts at the news of our Lord's resurrection, or his assuring us that he is the resurrection, and that he will raise us up, as he did himself. They have no interest in it. They are not likely to gain by it, and therefore they see no glories in the gospel that relates it. But St. Paul has taught us that if the gospel is hid, it is hid to those that are lost (2 Cor. 4:3).

Others again, who pretend to have a higher opinion of virtue, and believe, by their words at least, that it is the most noble acquisition our nature is capable of, still think that there is no such great difficulty in attaining it, that there is no need of such heavenly machinery (as they may lightly term the mysteries of our redemption). *Nec Deus interfit nifi dignus vindice nodus* [God does not enter in unless a worthy problem lays claim]. Good morality, they say, will carry us to heaven, but they cannot see much ground for believing all the abstruse revelations of Christianity, nor how we shall be made wiser or happier by such belief.

But let these men endeavor to live up even to their own notions of morality. Let them try to acquit themselves in the duties of temperance, meekness, universal benevolence, and a suitable homage to the supreme being, and then, if they do not willfully deceive themselves, they will learn by their own experience that they cannot do these things by their own strength, and that they need divine support and assistance, in the arduous task of virtue. Provided they be sincere, and consequently not indisposed to the illumination of God's Holy Spirit, the gospel will then appear to them in its proper beauty, and they will find it, according to its true interpretation, good news, showing them that Jesus Christ is ready to do that for them which they cannot do for themselves: that by the merits and power of his death, he will destroy their old man, the principle of evil, which now tyrannizes their souls, and by the power of his resurrection, work their spiritual resurrection to the new life of righteousness. Then shall be brought to pass the saying that is written, death is swallowed up in victory. The sting of death is sin, but thanks be to God, which giveth us the victory through our Lord Jesus Christ. Therefore, my beloved Brethren, be ye steadfast, unmovable, always abounding in the work of the Lord, for as much as ye know, that your labor shall not be in vain in the Lord (1 Cor. 15:54–58).

August Hermann Francke

FOLLOWING CHRIST*
1702

1 Peter 2:21–25

The grace of our Lord Jesus Christ and the love of God and the communion of the Holy Spirit be with you all, amen!

Beloved in Christ, Jesus our most worthy Savior, the only and the good shepherd of our souls, the only master and teacher, who with his works and words has illuminated the way, the truth, and the life for us, has brought us the only word which can satisfy us in time and in eternity so long as we give ear to it, namely follow me (Matt. 9:9). Among others, he spoke to Matthew who was sitting at a tax booth and said "follow me." The text then goes on to say "and he stood up and followed him." If we give ear to this one word and follow him who is the way, the truth, and the light, we cannot err. Would it not be a great mistake for us, after hearing so many long sermons in our lives, not to leave the tax booth of unbelief, of the lust of the eyes, the lusts of the flesh, and the pride of life, and follow after our master and Savior Jesus Christ?

Since today this Word is presented before us as our shepherd, it is necessary that we be sober today and consider the following: If he is the shepherd you must follow him, since you are his sheep. . . .

Now then let us consider this matter carefully so that we might properly learn to practice and to understand the words "follow me." These words are found in the epistle for today. But before we begin, let us call out together in prayer to the heavenly Father in the name

---

*Translated from August Hermann Francke, *Predigten Uber die Sonn und Fest-Tags Episteln* . . . (Halle, 1741), pp. 627–647.

of Jesus the Resurrected for the presence of the Holy Spirit. Let us do so together believing and considering the words of the Our Father. (Text 1 Peter 2:21–25)

On the basis of the words of this text, beloved in the Lord, we wish now to consider in all simplicity the concept of following Christ. So as to make it clearer and simpler to treat the matter, we wish to break it down into four questions: (1) What is following Christ? (2) Is it necessary that one follow Christ? (3) Is it possible for one to follow the Lord Jesus? (4) How does one take hold of this matter so that one is able to follow the Lord Jesus? . . .

PART ONE

We must first ask, beloved in the Lord, what is following Christ? It is a shame that one must begin with such a question. As will be made clear in the following, we cannot be Christians at all if we do not stand in the state of following Christ; the very need for the question, as a result, is a sign that there must still be people who are not Christians. Unfortunately, it is well known that if one establishes an examination not only for children but also for elderly persons or adults, not only among the common people, but also among the nobles and the upper classes, and if one should ask what is following Christ, a great many people would be without words to answer it. Therefore, let us take note all the more so so that we might learn and grasp this concept which we do not yet understand with our hearts so that we might properly understand it and that we might preserve it well in the base of our hearts, so that henceforth we will not excuse ourselves out of ignorance which has no excuse before the face of God.

What then is following Christ? The word *following* in its common meaning indicates going in the footsteps of another person as a servant walks after his Lord, or to change the metaphor, as a sheep follows after the shepherd. This is the way one describes the following in terms of normal life. The Holy Scripture, particularly the New Testament, is accustomed to use this word in Greek so that the specific meaning of the word emphasizes an exterior following as it says in our text, "you are to follow in his footsteps." In addition to this word, however, the Scripture is accustomed to use another word which Germans usually translate with the word "following" but which is more specifically intended to mean to imitate someone. One imitates another if one speaks or acts or seeks another so as to speak or act like him. This concept is also used by the Holy Scriptures when one is speaking of following Christ as Paul does in this manner in 1 Corinthians 11:1, where he says "Be followers or imitators of me as I am an imitator of Christ or as I seek to imitate him in all things." And Ephesians 5:1 says, "We are to be imitators of God to be God's followers."

Now from this external understanding we must move to the matter itself so that we might grasp and understand it in a much clearer way. Our Savior spoke to Matthew and to the other disciples saying "follow me" or follow after me. By this he then understood an external following as he was then accustomed, as their master and Lord, to go before them and they to follow him. Thus Mark 10:32 states, "And they were on the road going up to Jerusalem, and Jesus was walking ahead of them; and they were amazed and those who followed were afraid." Nevertheless, Jesus was not doing this so as to have hangers-on as great people in this world do. He did not desire to be looked up to nor did he desire that a great troup should follow behind him. But it was his intention that his disciples would believe in him as the Christ and the Savior of the world and take teaching from him, follow his example and image and imitate the same. This word is sometimes taken in a higher and wider meaning. Jesus sometimes said it to Peter among others as in John 21:22, "Follow thou me." He did not intend here external following or that Peter was to be his disciple, for Peter was already his disciple. But he intended to indicate to him how he was to follow in a like manner of death and to die on the cross just as our Savior preceded him with such a death. In other places as well our Savior took this word in a wider and higher sense. In sum, then, this word is not only to be applied to all those who had lived at the time of our Savior when he lived upon this earth in his weakness but it also relates to those who have come after and believe in him. . . .

More specifically, we may also say that following Christ also can be applied in every way to external matters, namely, one must follow in the whole walk of Christ our Savior. One must not make the beginning with the external following of Christ or with the imitation of his external work but the base must be laid in an inner following of Christ. To this Paul directs our attention in Philippians 2:5: "Have this mind among yourselves which you have in Jesus Christ." Note in this the base for following Christ is laid in that one is to have such a mind, such a phenomenon, such a thought as our dear Savior had (1 John 5:20 . . . Romans 8:9). . . . What is the base of following Jesus is also indicated to us in that the spirit of our Lord Jesus Christ is in us and that we are anointed with the same spirit with which Jesus Christ our Savior was anointed. In Romans 13:14, Paul states that we are to put on the Lord Jesus not externally but internally according to the new man and that Jesus Christ is to accomplish in us a morphen, a structure (Gal. 4:19), so that the same mode, the same thought, the same characteristics might be formed in us which were found in Christ Jesus, our Savior. . . .

Following Christ begins in an interior way and it moves out into the exterior and this can be understood in the similitude of a tree. A tree cannot bear external fruit, it cannot blossom, it cannot even set a bud if it does not have sap in its roots. Likewise, one cannot bring forth true fruit which is pleasing to God, one cannot allow true blossom of the grace of God to be seen in one nor can one bud in the power of God, if Christ's mind and spirit are not in him. Christ's mind and spirit are in man as sap is in the tree which makes the tree bud, blossom, and be fruitful (Ps. 52:10). . . .

These fruits, however, which are to be brought forth in following Christ, consist in part in one's doing good without ceasing and in part in one's enduring evil so as to do good and enduring evil willingly from the base of one's heart. This is presented to us in our text, for Peter says in verse 20, "But when you do right and suffer for it and take it patiently you have God's grace." Thus it can be seen in these two, namely in doing good and suffering, that this is chiefly an internal matter but also an external matter according to the authority and rule of God.

. . . Christ left us an image. This means a copy text, a *hupogrammon* and in fact the kind of copy text which one places beneath another piece of paper so that one can clearly see through it all the letters and marks and can learn to imitate these from the copy text just as they stand in the original. . . .

PART TWO

We must now ask the second question, if this following of Jesus Christ is necessary. The word of God answers that it is both in every way possible and necessary. This is established by our text in that it says that "following" is our calling. . . . If it is our calling it must be necessary. Men are accustomed to consider their vocations as matters of the utmost necessity. Now, following Christ is the true calling which is far nobler than any external calling. For the calling which we have received through the word of the gospel, or eternal life, certainly precedes any external calling. If you think that your external vocational position is necessary, know that following Christ is a thousand times more necessary. . . . Consider for a moment that following Christ must be understood according to the image of Christ as a shepherd and we the sheep. The close of our texts states, "You were once erring sheep but you are now converted to the shepherd and the bishop of your souls." Is it even worth asking the question if it is necessary that the sheep follow the shepherd? Will one not answer: If they do not wish to fall into misfortune, if they do not wish to be eaten by wolves, they must freely follow him. Who would indeed ask if it is necessary to follow Christ? One who would so ask would indicate by the very question that he is still not a Christian, not converted to the shepherd and bishop of his soul.

Let us look once again to the text, namely, that this is the goal for which God gave his son, for which Christ came into the world, for which he became a man, for which he suffered, for which he rose again from the dead, for which he ascended into heaven; indeed, this is the purpose of the whole redemptive process that we might also follow the Lord Jesus to whom we were reconciled with God. Note that man through original sin fell into such a deep corruption that all of Adam's children as branches of a tree arise from one root, are poisoned by one sin of poison from which inner corruption nothing other than evil fruit can grow. Therefore, already in paradise God promised Christ who would overcome the poison of sin. Since he gave Christ to us for this end, that is, as an antidote against the poison of sin, it would be most foolish and inconceivable for one not to make use of Christ for this purpose and thereby remain freely living in sin. Rather one ought to rejoice that he has a Savior whom he can follow with certainty.

We can understand this even more clearly in the words "Who offered himself in his body on the wood for our sins." In these words it is indicated how our dear Savior hanging naked and alone between heaven and earth was offered for our sins, bore sins in his body and was made a sign in which one should see how terrible sins are in the eyes of God and that because of them the son of God was hung up as a curse between heaven and earth. Thus our sins are now offered upon the wood or were lifted up upon the wood. Why? So that we might die of our sins and live for righteousness. In this we see why he allowed himself to be crucified; not so that we could thus freely sin but so that we might die to our sins and live for righteousness. It is therefore a horrible deception of Satan when one says that one can console oneself with the merits of Christ if he lives openly in him. Against this Paul gives witness in Romans 6:2 ... therefore following Jesus Christ is the highest necessity because this was the purpose for which Christ died for us. ...

The basis of the necessity of following Christ we can also see in that we are so strongly directed to it by God the Lord, by Jesus Christ our dearly beloved Savior, and by his holy apostles. Already at the beginning of this sermon, we heard that Christ himself indicated his teaching: "Follow me, follow me" ... (Matthew 16:24 ... John 12:35. ...)

PART THREE

Many more reasons could be given to demonstrate the necessity of following Christ but one must now ask further, is following Christ possible? There are enough lazy persons in Christianity who hold that following Christ is impossible and see the conception of following Christ as a seed of the devil which he scattered among men. Now if one does not believe that something is possible, one will never take it up. If I tell someone that he should push aside a house or a mountain with his hand he would tell me that it is impossible and because he would consider it impossible he would not even allow the thought of trying to do such a thing to enter his mind. Thus if one does not believe that it is possible to follow the Lord Jesus, one could preach on following Christ for a thousand years and he would never begin to undertake it but would always excuse himself by saying that it is impossible. Therefore let us ask this question properly: Is it possible for one to be able to follow Christ? We answer in every way, yes. Just as it was possible for Matthew when he sat in the tax booth and the Lord called to him "Follow me," to follow him, so also must each person who is here in the church know that if the Lord Jesus speaks to him and says "Follow me" it is possible for him to follow the Lord Jesus even as it was possible for Matthew.

This possibility, however, does not depend on one's own powers. If it did arise in such a way that one was able to be so-minded out of one's own powers, as Jesus Christ was minded, then it would be clearly necessary, if you looked toward your own corrupted flesh and blood, for you to say that it is impossible, but you have already learned from your catechism in which it says "I believe that I cannot believe in Jesus Christ my Lord, come to him, and follow him out of my own reason or power." Must one then say "I cannot"? No, but it states further, "The Holy Spirit has called me through the gospel, enlightened me with his gift, and keeps me and hallows me in proper faith" and thus makes me capable of following Christ. . . .

If one is considering the possibility of following Christ, one must note particularly that at its base must be placed a true understanding of our wretchedness, contrition and sorrow for sin, true faith in Jesus Christ, a new birth, a new will, which God the Lord can give, and the gift of the Holy Spirit. Most people when they hear that it is not possible for us by our powers to follow Christ, that man cannot from his own nature do so, use this masterfully as an excuse and if one admonishes them to follow Christ they say, "Yes we are poor weak men who can do nothing but sin; there is nothing in our own power able to bring forth or to even think of good." But listen, dear man, God the Lord will not accept this excuse. For because of this Christ has come that he might help us in our weakness, that he might raise us up through his divine power in our feebleness, that he might awaken us in a spiritual manner from death and make us alive. . . .

Therefore, one must earnestly resolve to turn to true Christianity and to following one's Savior, which is in every way possible for a person if he is born of God, if he looks to the son in true faith, and if he has received his spirit. But this happens by steps, since in the Holy Scriptures a distinction is made between children, youths, and men in Christ. By this, one can see that in following Christ there is always a growth so that one goes from one step to the next and does not remain one year after the next in the same place or secure his whole Christian life in the dear church, and when the quarter year comes around go to the Lord's Supper but remain as he has always been. But men must come to mature age in Christ so that they might become stronger in faith and through custom gain the ability to distinguish good and evil. Insofar as one continues, one indeed will be ever more and more confirmed in the following of our Savior. The fact nevertheless remains that our dear Savior is the most perfect copy and that a man, so long as he lives, has to learn from him and can never say he is as perfect as his Savior. . . .

141

PART FOUR

We come now to the final question: "How am I to lay hold of the matter so that I follow Christ?" We have heard what the following of Christ is: that it is most necessary and as well that it is possible, simple, and sweet. One must be stubborn and hardened, if one on hearing this does not ask "What shall I do? How shall I grasp hold of the matter? How shall I come to the place that I stand in the following of Christ? I hear that I cannot be a Christian if I do not follow Christ. I hear that I cannot console myself in the merits of Christ if I will not follow him. I hear that I have no hope of eternal life if I do not stand following the Lord Jesus. How am I then to come to it?" This is the question which now must be answered. And how eagerly does one wish to answer this when each and every heart is directed toward it and wishes to bring its desires by God's spirit to it so that it thinks, "Oh, that I might be a follower of the Lord!"

Those who think thus in their hearts may then take up this answer so that they will not twist the matter or begin in an improper way. It happens so very often. As men we are so rooted in self-love by nature that even if we are not Christians, we nevertheless eagerly desire to state that we are Christians and that our sins and vices which we have are only human weaknesses which the dear God will overlook. As long as a person will not allow himself to be saved from this self-deception, it is impossible for him to be helped. Each person must test himself in all things with the question "Whom have I followed to this point?" If he has followed flesh and blood, it attracts him to pride, to wrath, to lust, and to arrogance. He must consider what directions his attentions and attractions have been both day and night. He must consider what he has done with himself earlier and if he has banned all evil intentions from his heart to live in this or that sin, or if he has taken the freedom to continue to think about this or that sin. God the Lord will deal with him accordingly. He must test himself to see if he has earlier had such a mind in himself so that before he could give himself over to God and knowingly give up a sin, he would rather give up his life.

If one discovers in oneself (the conscience is a quick witness) that he has not earlier followed the Lord Jesus in such a way but has turned his thoughts to temporal, carnal, and vain things and has lived in pride and in lust and concern over his preservation, he ought nevertheless to give God honor and to acknowledge that he has not to this point followed Christ but Satan, the world, and his own flesh and blood. . . .

What is then necessary? The first thing that is necessary is true repentance. One cannot say "from now on I will follow the Lord Jesus." How soon does one come to the truth of the proverb: "No longer to act in such and such a way is the best repentance." No, that is not enough; one must not leap over the divine order. But it is necessary, dear man, that you lay out properly your earlier sinful way before God your Lord, acknowledge humbly and with repentance, give God honor and confess simply that you have been to this point in no God-pleasing situation, that you have not been to this point a child of God, have not been a disciple of Christ, and that all your Christianity is not worth anything. . . .

If you do this, dear man, you will be more closely prepared for following Christ. Thus will Jesus Christ, the sun of righteousness, shine lovingly and powerfully in you, a poor, troubled, sorrowful sinner. Thus you will discover how true repentance operates, how the heart of a sad sinner is consoled through the gospel. Thus you will rejoice that the Lamb of God, Jesus Christ, has taken away your sins in his body on the Cross. Then you will thank him properly for his act and properly praise him for such overwhelming grace. What then is further necessary to come into the state of following Jesus Christ? Further, dear man, you must learn to understand properly your Savior Jesus Christ from the Word of God. This is the swaddling clothes and the crib in which our Savior is brought to us. Oh, how great an effect would come about among you if proper love, desire, and joy for the Word of God existed, if you would take up the Bible and would use the time which was given to you for meditation on the Word of God. Such an action would have a great blessing in your hearts and souls. But one is not to seek Christ in the Scriptures in a pharisaic manner as the Pharisees searched the Scriptures but did not wish to come to him. Rather, one is to seek, according to the proper method of the New Testament, Jesus Christ as the proper way, truth, and life, powerfully in one's soul, and might come to him so as to have life in him.

But how does this occur? It is clearly enough stated by Peter, not only in our text for today, but also in his whole epistle, for he points out in all ways how we are to make use of the suffering and the death of our Savior in all things for ourselves. See Chapter 1:18 . . . Chapter 3:18 . . . Chapter 4:1. . . .

PIETISTS—SELECTED WRITINGS

If we thus wish to come to following the Lord Jesus we must first learn to know the heart of Jesus properly and his fervid love for us. The love with which Christ Jesus loved must be stirred up in your soul and poured out in your heart. Consider how the Son of God gave up his life for you, evil man and brand of Hell, poured out his blood for you and gave up his life for you so that he might make you a child of eternal blessedness. Look upon this, and in your soul, and the dear Jesus will become loving and sweet; it will warm your heart and will press you into following him. If you do not come out of the fountain of salvation, you will never receive the living water which can strengthen and refreshen you. . . .

If you thus give yourself over to following the Lord Jesus through the force of his love, you will need no further instruction other than that you give yourself over to the ruling of his Holy Spirit and the beautiful example of your Savior as it shines forth in his person and in the persons of those who follow him. Then the whole Holy Scripture will be a teacher which will instruct you and the love of Jesus will drive you to it. . . .

August Hermann Francke

IF AND HOW ONE
MAY BE CERTAIN
THAT ONE IS A CHILD OF GOD*
1707

1 John 3:13–18

The first question is if one can be certain or not certain that one is a child of God. In our text for today this question is answered positively; in every way one can have a certainty of this. There are also other Scriptural passages among which are to be noted 1 Corinthians 2:12 . . . 2 Timothy 1:12 . . . 1 John 1:2, 7. . . .

We must now secondly consider how or from what source one knows whether or not one is a child of God. It is above all things necessary that proper indicators are given to the children of God through which they can be properly assured of their adoption. Their knowledge that they have come from death into life is a most important and glorious knowledge, but in this life they not only experience the cross and temptation externally but also internally. Among the temptations which come to a person after he has turned to God is the experience of the bitter hatred on the part of the world. . . .

We know as Peter, in 1 Peter 4:12, that we have come from life into death. But from what source do we have such knowledge? Are we to have such knowledge because the world is our friend? Far be it! For the friendship of the world is enmity to God. But we have this knowledge in that we know that we love our brothers. Note: This is

---

*Translated from August Hermann Francke, *Sonn-Fest-und Apostel-Tags Predigten* (Halle, 1746), pp. 859–882.

145

the most significant indicator which John gives us in his whole epistle and with which we now hold alone even though there were many other indicators given in the Holy Scripture. . . .

Dear Brethren, the Scripture teaches us in all ways that we can know indeed that we ought to have a proper certainty whether we are in grace with God or not. But this must be known according to certain indicators. It is not my meaning that one is to only firmly imagine that he is a child of God and is only to believe in a blind way that he certainly stands with God in grace, that without doubt he will be eternally blessed and that throughout everything he will not doubt concerning his blessedness, but that everything which comes into his mind he is to hold as a demonic temptation and to firmly and continually believe that he is a child of God. This notion is in no way taught by God's word but God's word teaches us with great care that we are to distinguish properly between a state of grace and a state of wrath from the indicators of both. Therefore, let each person guard himself against misuse of the doctrine and take very great care that he follow through in the testing to see whether he is a Christian or not. Dear Brethren, I tell you the truth; do not imagine that I understand and hold all of you who are here as pure justified children of God. . . . Some among you are the children of God but others are not as their fruits indicate. As a result we must treat the matter of the application of the proper indicators. God's Word does not say, "You are a Christian and that person is not a Christian." God's Word does not name your name specifically but God's Word gives the indicators which you must grasp in your mind and by which you must examine, test, and search yourself to see if you find those indicators in yourself that you are a child of God or are not one.

First you must simply ask if your certainty which you earlier had stands on a firm base or not. Many persons initially think that they are without doubt Christians. But if someone comes and asks them, "I can't see you as a child of God since you do not stand in a good situation," they become completely disturbed in their minds. From such disturbance one must conclude that he has no true certainty, for where there is true certainty, one does not turn away even if the whole world says that one is no child of God but is a child of the Devil. . . .

You must go further and take the indicators carefully before yourself and examine and test yourself according to them. And, therefore, one must particularly defend oneself from self-love, which is very deeply impressed upon our corrupted nature. Self-love will always say to a person that he ought to think: "I do not hope that my situation is so bad; I am of course mature and am I then no Christian? Am I to be no child of God? Am I to doubt concerning my blessedness?" But no, dear man, you have not even begun to doubt; what has happened is that you have been certain concerning your situation and should now be protected from doubt.

Behold, this is the way that you can first fall into doubt if you say to yourself that you are a Christian and even if others say that matters are now correct concerning your situation with regard to Christianity, your heart nevertheless is hardened against them and says: "No, I will not doubt about my blessedness." However, should you later come to your deathbed, you will see the situation completely otherwise. Then your eyes will be opened and you will see that you must die and come before the Judgment. Then you will first know that you are poor, wretched, naked, blind, and empty. See then Satan will be able to come to you and trap you into doubt. So that you would not come into such a great danger for your soul earlier, statements were made to you so that you might achieve a better basis in your heart and not let it come into so great a hazard.

Thus you ought not to say: "I am baptized, I go to church, I am a Christian." The hypocrites do the same. There is many a person baptized who yet went back on his oath and was faithless and fell out of his baptismal covenant. Many people go to the Lord's Supper and misuse it and receive it to their judgment and death. You must make no decisions because you follow externals. The Scripture is directed to your heart and indicates to you how you must find proper certainty and be sealed by the Spirit of God. You must receive the Spirit of God from God and from it you must know how richly you are graced by God. See, there you are commanded, there you can gain so great a good, namely that you might know what happens in the heart of God for your sake, whether God loves you, whether you are his child. Do not consider such a thing paltry but pray heartily to God so that he might give you this certainty and that he might make you his child if you are not yet his child. Dear man, if you are not his child it is better that you know it and pray to God because of it and say, "Dear God I know it, I am not yet your child." See thus will God give you his adoption so that you will find the proper indicators of this. Thereafter you will have joy and pleasure from it when your certainty has a firm basis.

I must add something yet. Many men are greatly deceived into believing that if they listen to sermons and not only give attention to the words but are also stirred up by them and come to a good resolution because of them, that the thing itself has occurred and they thus hold the beginning of their conversion to be conversion itself. They have good sensations that the Spirit of God works in them to bring them to the proper victory of faith but they are still far distant from a full victory of the faith. Among such the final deception is worse than the first in that they enter into a false light and imagine that they have been converted when they have not in fact been converted. Do not err in such a way here, brothers. You have often heard how great a matter it is that one be converted and go from death into life, true enough. You must not only open yourself up to good sensations, but when you are moved by the Word of God you must develop that movement into prayer and in a heartfelt way pray to the dear God that he will allow it to develop as power in you. You must follow up on the stirrings which you have received from the Spirit of God and be faithful to them; thereafter it will soon be indicated to you that you have come to the proper power. . . .

August Hermann Francke

THE FORETASTE OF ETERNAL LIFE*
1689

Matthew 17:1–9

I will behold your face in righteousness, I will be satisfied if I awake according to your image. Thus, dearly beloved in Christ Jesus, David speaks in Psalm 17:15. He distinguishes the fortune of himself and other believers from the desires of the children of this world, who have their share in this life. The children of God know more of tribulation and the Cross. Therefore he states here, consoling them: "I will behold your face in righteousness; I will be satisfied if I awake according to your image." Literally translated from the Hebrew, these last words are: "If you image awakes." What does David mean by this? He wishes to say: "Because the image of God has faded through the fall in man, indeed is lost, one cannot have rest in anything as long as one remains in such misery and corruption and is not made upright once again. One's heart can never be satisfied with whatever one seeks only in this world. However, if the image of God toward which a person was initially created is awakened in him once again (which occurs if he is once again enlightened by the Holy Spirit so that his eyes are opened to see what kind of wretched state the whole of his life stands in, and how he is lacking the true way and can have this only in Christ Jesus), then he refreshes himself and experiences how joyous and gracious the Lord is.

From these words one can see how a person can find in a certain

*Translated from August Hermann Francke, *Sonn-Fest-und Apostel-Tags Predigten* (Halle, 1746), pp. 363–387.

way a true blessedness in this life, a true satisfaction for his soul, but not as long as he sticks with the filth of the world; it can occur only if he is converted to God from the world and from the darkness of dead works to the light of the living. Therefore it is said, "He who drinks of this water will never thirst and he who eats of this bread of life will nevermore hunger," for any other temporal or passing joy.

The image of God is awakened in resurrection from the dead into its full clarity (in which complete blessedness consists) and is to be followed by complete satisfaction. The faithful have yet to know that God will bless them richly in this life, that he will give them to drink joy as if from the stream from which they can understand how great a good is to be awaited in the future life where they will be completely satisfied if the image of God is awakened in them. Are the first fruits as lovely and pleasant as the whole harvest will be glorious? In this life a foretaste of eternal life is promised by God the Lord to his people. In the next life, however, they will not only have a near taste but all fullness, all richness, all satisfaction, and all completion. Here it must be exchanged with the Cross, suffering, and tribulation; there it will be had without change, without variation, without vexation, and without distaste. Thus one will taste in all eternity the sweetness and joy and will not surfeit of these, but the more he has of them the more will he be satisfied.

God's grace and mercy is great by which he gives at this time a foretaste of eternal life to his people. Yet we are certainly not to think that God the Lord has only a few elect whom he allows to receive so great a grace, whereas others who yearn for such a grace and cry to God for such a gift are not able to achieve it. According to his quality, each believer will experience this and can trust in the goodness of the New Testament that no one who turns his heart to Jesus Christ, the living source, is forbidden to experience a foretaste of eternal life. If we do not enjoy the foretaste of eternal life nor participate in it, the fault certainly lies with ourselves alone and the responsibility for it is our great unconcerned thoughtlessness, foolishness, and diffidence. As a result, we wish now to seek in the gospel which we have just read and to discuss the matter further so as to observe together the foretaste of eternal life.

We will have to consider:
1. Who is to await this foretaste of eternal life?
2. In what does the foretaste consist?
3. How one is to use the foretaste? . . .

150

PIETISTS—SELECTED WRITINGS

PART ONE

Dearly beloved in Christ Jesus, we wish first to know who is to await the foretaste of eternal life or to enjoy it. Note what is pointed out in our text where it says "and after six days Jesus took to himself Peter, and James and John his brother and led them up onto a high mountain." In these words is clearly indicated the proper state which we are to have, if we wish to be among those who are awaiting the foretaste of eternal life. It is stated in this text that the Lord Jesus took his disciples to himself; from this we are first to learn that one is not to experience eternal life nor a foretaste of eternal life by means of one's human will or the powers of nature—one cannot achieve this on one's own. If one is to come to a foretaste of divine goodness, the Lord Jesus must take him to himself and transfigure himself in him. To acknowledge this is grace and wisdom. . . .

If you wish to enjoy the foretaste of eternal life, you must believe above all that there is no power or ability in your own nature to gain it; God dwells in light to which no one can come . . . therefore you must take yourself to Jesus, pray to him, and desire eagerly from him that he might give you such a foretaste of eternal life. Now, dear man, for this reason he came to us, for this reason he became a Savior of man and therefore he is called Jesus Christ the Savior and anointed of God that he might give everything to us because we can do nothing without him, nor can we have anything, nor are we ever able to do anything. If you wish to enjoy this gift of God and be happy in it, you must first seek zealously this person who has come from God and desire from him to achieve what is needed for your soul. You must leave it to his good pleasure when and where he will take you to himself and give you a foretaste of eternal life. . . .

Note that Jesus took three disciples with him, as it is written in our text. If you consider the names which these three disciples had when they came to Jesus, you can understand from these names in what way you are lacking and why therefore you have still not come to the foretaste of eternal life. The first person was called Simon, that is, a listener. Likewise you must have ears to hear what the Spirit of God says. However, he was called Peter . . . if you wish to have a foretaste of eternal life you must be a true Peter, that is, an intelligent man who not only listens to the words of the Lord but also does them and builds his house on a rock (Matt. 7:24). . . .

Further you must be a James. James means a conqueror, that is, your faith must be victorious over the world, Satan, the lust of the flesh, old habits in which you stand. If you are such a James, that is, a conqueror, and thereafter also a true Israelite, one who fights and is victorious with God and man (Gen. 32:28), then you will experience according to your measure what is the foretaste of eternal life which remains hidden from all vain worldly hearted people.

Finally, you must be a true John. John means "one graced by God." Likewise, you must seek the grace of God alone and place it above all the grace and favor of men. If you, as John, give yourself over lovingly and kindly to the Lord and love him from your heart you will be loved in turn; indeed, if you draw close to him and lay your head on his breast, he will not hide his heart but will give you and offer to you one gift after the other, one foretaste of eternal life after the other.

The two disciples, however, James and John, were also called the boanerges of the Lord Jesus, that is, the sons of thunder (Mark 3:17). Likewise, you must also be newborn by the thunder of the power of God, or be reared by the word of truth and be prepared in the power of God to allow this selfsame thunder of his word to sound forth for the improvement of your neighbor.

The story tells us further that he led these at his side. In these words it is pointed out how you must be prepared if you wish to experience the foretaste of eternal life. You must be led away from the noise of the world and its distractions, so that you can achieve in your heart spiritual stillness, sabbath, and day of peace. Concerning this spiritual sabbath, all the fathers gave witness, noting that God the Lord first allowed man to properly taste his grace in the foretaste of eternal life if one had achieved through the grace of God a spiritual sabbath in his soul, allowed all earthly or shadow works to leave his heart, and no longer hung to them with his love and trust. Luther himself spoke of this in his beautiful little book on good works. . . .

If you wish to enjoy a foretaste of eternal life, guard yourself that you are not directed by the actions of other people. . . .

The disciples had to climb up onto a high mountain before they could see Christ transfigured before their eyes. Dear man, you must believe that if you wish to taste the goodness of eternal life as a foretaste you must also certainly climb onto a mountain, that is, you must not hesitate to undertake the work of true repentance and mortification of the flesh, to crucify all lusts, desires, love of the world, and all earthly creatures. The experience of the foretaste of eternal life depends on this alone, that one is truly converted and is thus capable of experiencing such a foretaste as lowly, humble, small, and weak. No arrogant person can experience this. Arrogance hinders man from all such good gifts which God wishes to give. I am not speaking here of external pride alone, but chiefly about internal pride, and indeed not only about worldly pride but also about spiritual pride. The grace of the Holy Spirit, in which the foretaste of eternal life is to be found, flows down into the valley and not up onto high rocks. Therefore you must be truly humble and bent low in your inner man so that you lie down with your heart before God, confess to him your misery, sorrow, and need, and do not look to other men but acknowledge your own need and your own wretchedness. . . .

Luke tells us that our Savior went up onto the mountain in order to pray. The Lord God is accustomed to give most of his goods to men in prayer. Prayer is both the root and the salt of all divine activities. Prayer may not be distant from anything one does and in prayer arises all union with the dear God. You are to know that there is no better way to achieve a foretaste of eternal life than for one to humble oneself before God and truly pray, to remain constant in prayer and to walk continually with the dear God. . . .

PART TWO

Let us now treat the second subject: In what does such a foretaste of eternal life consist? The gospel gives us an example but we are not to think that the foretaste of eternal life is only available in such circumstances as those described in the gospel. No. The Lord God can allow his children to experience this in a thousand different ways and he is not bound to one or another way.

We can, however, notice one thing in this example in particular, in which the foretaste of eternal life generally consists. It states, "And He was transfigured before them." This transfiguration is also described as "His presence shone forth as the sun, His cloak was white as a light." What here occurred before the physical eyes of the disciples is accustomed to occur in an internal way before the eyes of faith. The foretaste of eternal life chiefly consists in Christ's being transfigured in us and making himself glorious before the eyes of our faith. For the transfiguration is explained in this text indicating that the Lord Jesus did not manifest himself to his disciples in a wretched, miserable, and lowly state, but in a truly glorious, heavenly form and

153

divine clarity. In a similar manner, the spiritual transfiguration of
Christ occurs in us if we gain, by the enlightenment of the Holy Spir-
it, the supernatural knowledge of the clarity of God in the presence of
Jesus Christ (2 Cor. 4:6).

Furthermore, what the foretaste of eternal life consists is pointed
out to us when it is said, "While he was yet speaking behold a bright
cloud overshadowed them and a voice spoke from the clouds saying
'This is my beloved Son in whom I am well pleased; listen to Him.' "
Note that this is the most important point in the text; the heavenly
Father gave witness concerning his Son Jesus Christ, and of this Peter
spoke in 2 Peter 1:16–19, "You will do well to pay attention to this as
to a lamp shining in a dark place until the day dawns and the morning star rises in your hearts." This is then a foretaste of eternal life
when one not only hears the Word of God and grasps it in his mind,
but also knows in his heart those things which stand in God's Word
and were said by Jesus Christ, so that God gives in the heart of the
believer such a witness concerning His son that in this he has eternal
life according to 1 John 5:9, 11. And this can come about in many
ways. It can happen in prayer, it can happen in meditation on the
Word of God, it can happen during the praise of God, it can happen
in faith and its fruits, it can happen in love and its works, it can happen in the hope for future goods. For those who wish to know more
about the foretaste of the Word of the eternal light there is much by
Johann Arndt in the third book of his *True Christianity* and particularly the tract in the fifth book entitled *On the Union with God....*

PART THREE

We have yet finally to observe how one is to use such a foretaste
of eternal life. This is indicated to us in the words of the heavenly Father when he says, "You are to listen." The first, most important part
is that by the foretaste of eternal life we are to better know Christ as
our Savior, to give our whole heart to him alone, to love him truly
and to remain firm in our faith in him. In the second chapter of his
gospel, verse 11, John said, "Christ revealed his glory before his disciples and they believed in him." Obviously they had believed in him
before. They were at this point strengthened in faith so that it seemed
to them that their earlier faith had not yet been faith. Such a powerful working comes about with one taste, a foretaste, of eternal life.
The heart is then properly drawn to God and the Lord Jesus, and at

the same time bound to them with the bonds of love so that henceforth one does everything closer according to the Savior, loves everything which he loves, and pays attention to his word not only with external ears but also with the heart, grasping it more deeply than he has before and following in a completely willing manner. Hereafter, as we read, the disciples fell upon their faces and were afraid when they heard the word of the Father himself. From this we are to know that men are still too weak in their mortal lives to bear such a foretaste of eternal life. Therefore, if God allows us to enjoy such a single foretaste of eternal life, we are to allow such to bring us to a deep worship of God so that we learn to properly fall upon our faces to acknowledge our great unworthiness and to give him the honor as one who works and gives everything from grace. . . .

One must certainly make a distinction between extraordinary and ordinary gifts. In a certain book, the extraordinary gifts are explained as those for which one must wait . . . the ordinary gifts (necessary for salvation) are common, and among them are the virtue of true humility, mortification, crucifixion of the flesh and of sinful lusts and desires, meekness, patience, long-suffering, goodness, and so forth. For these gifts we may well ask God that they be given to us richly and fully. However, if we ask for the gift of extraordinary grace, particularly if we desire great sweetness, experience, taste, and other like things, natural pride and self-will can very easily be mixed in with them; indeed, Satan can present himself before us to our harm as an angel of light and this can happen very much easier if one does not remain in resignation but wishes to force God to give him what he prays for. . . .

It is stated further that the Lord Jesus stirred up his disciples and said to them, "Rise up and do not be afraid." From this one is to learn that although the human heart is so poor and cannot easily experience the gift of God, indeed is afraid, . . . nevertheless the Lord Jesus comes to it, stirs it up, and says, "Arise and do not be afraid." Jesus gives the heart his power to walk in his way, to make its steps certain by following him and to go forth in the right direction in that hereafter it can believe that God the heavenly Father has pleasure in it because he looks upon it in his Son. Ah, how dear and how sweet is this observation; wherever God gives man to taste his fatherly love which he bears toward man for the sake of the Savior; as a result one can speak of something greater than earthly fortune.

The evangelist adds: "However, when they raised up their eyes

155

they saw no one except Jesus." From this we are to note that by the words of the heavenly Father, "This is my beloved Son in whom I am well pleased; you are to listen to Him," no one other is meant than the Lord Jesus Christ.

The text goes on to say that Jesus forbade his disciples to tell of this occurrence to anyone until he had again risen from the dead. From this we learn that the foretaste of eternal life is to be used with very great care so that one does not cast one's pearls before swine nor holiness before dogs. These words are to be applied to the marriage and union with Christ and in the bride chamber itself where one learns to know one's bridegroom, Christ Jesus, in true inwardness and in proper joy and pleasure of the heart. If, dear man, you have been refreshed by his loving kiss, remain still and do not come out in misunderstanding, but give God thanks for the gift. It can easily occur that if you speak of it you will lift up your heart because of it and mock the name of God and of your Jesus. Therefore you are better to admonish others to repentance to awaken them to grasp the gift of God and to praise them because of this, but one ought to take very great care in discussing what one experiences in fact in the inner and holy communion with Christ.

. . . This foretaste of eternal life, this transfiguration which occurs through the Holy Spirit in the heart by faith in a spiritual manner, is far more necessary and useful than the transfiguration which is described in the gospel for today. For the disciples themselves, after they had seen this transfiguration, went once again into their old way of life as we read in Matthew 18 and 20. . . . From this we can see that the spiritual transfiguration of Christ is something far more glorious and great than the external transfiguration of Christ. We are not considering the transfiguration of the Lord before the physical eyes of the disciples as something paltry but as something glorious and great because in it God himself gave witness concerning his Son. But if we consider what is useful for our health, salvation, and blessedness we place much greater attention on the fact that the Holy Spirit transfigures Christ spiritually in our hearts rather than before the eyes of the body.

Note this then, you who pride yourself greatly as being of the Lord Christ, who speak a great deal about him in your life, who read many prayers about him and often sing "Jesus My Joy, My Heart's Desire," and so on, but have nevertheless little experience of him in your heart . . . note this: If you know Jesus as your joy, as your heart's

156

desire, as your treasure, as your richness, as your honor, and as all your desire, if you love him and taste of him truly, then you will enjoy a foretaste of eternal life and experience the first drop of living water which will become in you a fountain of water which will run forth into eternal life. Then will be filled in you the Spirit and the truth as it is written in the gospel: "His face shone as the sun."

What does this mean? It signifies the bright radiance and light of the knowledge of Jesus Christ in you which God orders to shine forth from the darkness so that you might see God's unspeakable love and joy in faith as it is mirrored in the face of Jesus Christ (2 Cor. 4:6). Then the clothing of the Lord Jesus became as bright as light, that is, the gospel, the joyous sweet message of Jesus Christ and his gracious treasure in which he was clothed, will become completely clear and open to you, it will be for you a true gospel, a proper joyous message so that you will then know what you have in this Savior. Then his goodness, his sweetness, his patience, his long-suffering, his humility, his infinite love which he bears for you, his suffering and death, will become so clear in your heart and such a great consolation and joy to you that it will be as if you saw it all with your eyes because you will fully know how useful and blessed all of this is for you. Earlier you had no joy in the Word of God, earlier when you read the Bible you were happy when the chapter had come to an end and if you were at a sermon you were happy when it was over, earlier when you attended Communion you were happy with the external work alone. Behold this is no longer so; since Jesus is transfigured in you, his clothing, his word, and his sacraments are as a light. All becomes bright and clear, living and powerful in your soul. Then you will understand fully, for example, what is meant when it is said, "The Lord is my shepherd, I shall not want; he makes me to lie down in green pastures, he guides me to fresh waters, he refreshes my soul, he guides me on the right paths, for his name's sake." These words you will not only say with your mouth, but they will be as the clothes of the Lord Jesus, clear as a light, so that you will not find a paltry foretaste of eternal life in such words.

In the text it says, "Behold, then Moses and Elias appeared to them and spoke with them." What does this mean? It means that if Jesus is transfigured in you, Moses and the prophets will be opened to you and will be lovely and pleasant for you. . . .

There are further indications of what the foretaste of eternal life consists of in the words: "Then Peter answered and spoke to Jesus—

Lord, it is good to be here. . . ." Peter here experienced the peace of God which is beyond reason (Phil. 4:7) in his heart and in his soul and out of this refreshment he broke into the words "it is good to be here" because he was so completely involved in his whole heart, body, and soul that he wished to say with David: "My body and my soul rejoice in the living God" (Ps. 84:3). As a result he said it is good to be here. . . . See, dear man, from this you can understand a little bit in what the foretaste of eternal life consists, namely in that the heart has a true rest and a proper divine peace. O precious gift! There is hardly one among a thousand who understands what the words with which sermons are often concluded signify: "The peace of God which is higher than all understanding, protect your hearts and minds in Christ Jesus." And this is because of the fact that as long as men are so drunken in earthly creatures of this world they can never have a true inner peace. They might well indeed have external rest and peace but the peace of God they never taste. In all external experiences of peace there is a biting worm in their consciences, but divine peace is above all reason. Concerning this peace Christ spoke in John 14:27, "My peace I give to you, my peace I leave you; I do not give it as the world gives it." Such a peace of God is indeed truly a noble and glorious thing, a precious treasure. Indeed, he gives it himself as a treasure after victory, as it says in Colossians 3:15 in our German Bibles, "May the peace of God rule in your hearts." For if one only goes before God in prayer and seeking, God will allow the dawn and the light of his grace and goodness to rise up in the heart and will bless him as he blessed Jacob. Therefore strive for that noble treasure of divine peace in which you can enjoy a true foretaste of eternal life. . . .

August Hermann Francke

PURE AND UNBLEMISHED WORSHIP*
1704

1 Peter 8–12

PART ONE

Beloved in the Lord, let us first consider the duty of pure and unblemished worship insofar as it relates to ourselves. The matter can
be treated with a very few words taken from the Apostle Peter who
says: "Be temperate and sober for prayer." By temperance we are accustomed to understand that virtue by which one guards oneself from
overeating and overdrinking. By soberness, or rather by wakefulness,
we are accustomed to understand the virtue through which one does
not become weary or tired in regard to what one is to do, but rather
breaks off from one's sleep insofar as one is required to fulfill the duties laid upon one and carries out one's occupation with a cheerfulness of mind. . . .

In a deeper sense the Apostle understands by temperance that divine virtue by which the person who believes in Christ Jesus seeks to
keep his heart in proper temperance by controlling and ruling his affections and desiring and guarding himself so that he does not become drunken in worldly love. Worldly love, if it fills the heart,
makes one incapable of the kingdom of God just as surfeiting in food
and drink makes one incapable of it. Therefore, he requires that each
person who calls himself a Christian must see to it that his heart,
mind, and spirit stand in a proper sobriety, in a proper divine under-

---

*Translated from August Hermann Francke, *Sonn-Fest-und Apostel-Tags Predigten*
(Halle, 1746), pp. 715–732.

standing and health belonging to it so as to love what serves to his eternal peace and so as to shun what might disturb that divine peace in his heart.

And when the Apostle speaks of sobriety or wakefulness, he understands by it that characteristic and virtue of a faithful Christian through which he keeps his heart properly awake and lively so that he can stand on his guard and look into eternity to see what is needed for the eternal salvation of his soul, to allow his light to shine and his loins to be girded, and to set his hope wholly upon that grace which is given to him. If God wishes to perfect his gracious visitation in a person's soul, that person must then not be dissolute or otherwise weary or sleepy in his thoughts, but must be prepared to experience the workings of the Spirit of God in his soul. As a result, Peter says very clearly: Be temperate and sober for prayer. He states this to point out that the Christian heart is to be that prayer-closet concerning which Christ speaks in Matthew 6:6 into which one is to go and where one is to lock oneself away from all other thoughts so that one can speak with one's Creator in hiddenness and so that the powers of one's soul can thereby be gathered together in such a way that the soul can flow into the love of its Redeemer and that, at the same time, the fire of the Holy Spirit which comes down from heaven and ignites the heart might burn as upon an altar. This is to be the purpose of temperance and sobriety.

From this it can easily be understood that the Apostle does not wish to signify only the external moral virtues of sobriety and liveliness in human life alone, but that he intends something much more glorious, higher, and precious. Through the fall man entered into such misery that his heart was filled with the love of creatures, was scattered among the thousand things of this world, and was made drunk through the poison of Satan which Satan brought into the human nature through the fall. One must therefore enter into oneself through the spirit of propriety and thoughtfulness so that through this spirit he might be disentangled from Satan's bonds, turn once again into his own heart, acknowledge what is needed for his eternal salvation, and thus be watchful over his own heart and guard it with all industry so that the Lord might perfect his work in his heart and destroy Satan's work and kingdom in it. Thereafter, he will be able to establish in it his own kingdom which is righteousness, peace, and joy in the Holy Spirit. This is the purity of heart to which Christ commands us in Matthew 5:8: "Blessed are the pure of heart, for they will see God."

And this is the duty which one is to follow in regard to oneself, namely, before everything else one must begin to change, to improve, and to renew oneself toward the image of God in Christ Jesus, whenever corruption has begun in one's heart so that, before everything else, it might be purified and presented again to God, the Lord, in true temperance and sobriety, truth and purity, joy and wakefulness. . . .

PART TWO

Let us now think about the second matter, and consider our duties toward neighbors as these duties are emphasized in the words of the text "Above all else have a fervid love among yourselves, for love covers a multitude of sins." In these words the matter is indicated in which every duty toward a neighbor consists, namely, in love. . . . The author here indicates [by fervid love] the kind of love we require; namely, one is not to have that kind of love toward one's neighbor that is merely natural, but that kind which is ignited in the heart by the fire of the Holy Spirit and is, therefore, neither cold nor warm but fervid. . . .

Peter further describes that manner in which love in truth is to be demonstrated: "And to serve one another, each with the gift which he has received as a good householder of the manifold grace of God." He indicates in this that each person is nothing other than a householder of the manifold gifts of God which he has received from God the Father to use properly as all physical and spiritual goods, not so as to seek his own pleasure with them as seems good to him, not to keep these for himself alone so that he could gain treasure from them or seek his own honor with them, but that he might turn them to God's honor and the service of his neighbor. . . .

Thus, the wealthy in the world err badly when they think that they are special people because they have great wealth, for they will have to account for each coin at the Judgment Day of our Lord God, explaining how it came to them. How are they to then stand if they gathered it in covetousness, if they used it in show and vanity, if they spent it in banqueting and game playing and other frivolous ways? . . .

PART THREE

Let us now consider duty toward God. The text states "so that in all things God might be praised to Jesus Christ to whom be honor and power, from eternity to eternity, Amen." This duty toward God is not to be distinguished from that toward ourselves or that toward our neighbor, nor is it to be so considered, but it must be continuous with the duty toward ourselves and with the duty toward our neighbor. Therefore, the verse says "so that in all things, whether it concerns ourselves and our own hearts or whether it concerns our neighbors, in all things God is to be praised." Thus, one must direct one's heart and mind, one's responses and obligations, toward this purpose, namely, the praise of God. For this reason man was created, for this reason Christ came into the world to redeem us, for this reason the Holy Spirit was sent down from Heaven and poured out into the hearts of man so that God might be given honor. To this end all physical, spiritual, natural, and supernatural gifts which God gives to men are directed, namely, that God be honored through them. Thus, this duty must be the preeminent duty and all other duties must be practiced in light of this duty. . . .

This then, beloved in the Lord Jesus, is the pure and unblemished worship in Jesus Christ and through Jesus Christ, considered according to a threefold duty toward oneself, toward one's neighbor, and toward God, and consisting in the practice of the same through the power of the Holy Spirit. Now enter into your hearts and observe there your circumstances in regard to this threefold duty. See how far you have progressed in them or how far you have not progressed. And if you do not wish to deceive yourself, you must admit that it is clear that your present Christian state does not yet merit the name of a righteous beginning.

What help is there for us, then, if we always consider our worship to consist in going to church together, listening to one sermon after the other, looking around in our prayer books at a certain time or praying some thoughts or other from our heart, and at a certain time going to confession and the Lord's Supper, and yet always living according to our old manner? What help would it be for us if we now hold ourselves here to be beloved children of God and on the final day be known as evildoers, if we always console ourselves, saying we believe in the Lord Jesus Christ, and if on that day our Savior says to us, "Turn from me, I never knew you as my followers"? Let us lay off this terrible self-deception. . . .

August Hermann Francke

Outline of All the Institutes at Glauch near Halle Which Provide Special Blessings Partially for the Education of Youth and Partially for the Maintenance of the Poor, as the Institutes Exist in December, 1698.*

1. An institution for the education of the sons of lords, nobles, and other important people.

2. An institution for the education of the daughters of lords, nobles, and otherwise important people.

3. A special institution for Silesian children.

4. A *Paedagogium* or institution for the education of children who are supported and educated by foreigners and partly by their parents in distant places.

5. A special *Paedagogium* for those children who are to have only elementary instruction in writing, arithmetic, Latin, French, and economics, and are not to continue study, but are to serve important people, as scribes for merchants, trustees for possessions and useful arts. It is for the most part tied to the *Paedagogium* noted in 4 above but will be separated from it in the future.

6. A school mainly for indigenous Burger's children who are to be educated. Not as expensive as the *Paedagogium*.

7. Another school for Burgers in which boys can be instructed in Christianity, reading, writing, arithmetic, music, and manual skills.

8. A similar school in which Burger daughters can be instructed in reading, writing, arithmetic, catechism, New Testament, and singing.

9. The orphanage concerning which with other similar institutions there is a printed description.

10. From the orphanage, the best and most intelligent *Ingenia* are

---

*Translated from Gustav Kramer, *August Hermann Francke: Ein Lebensbild* (Halle, 1880), vol. 1, pp. 275–276.

chosen and are educated best according to their capacity for study or to other good arts.

11. Six chosen boys are carefully led through a special *legatium* to study.

12. The rest of the boys are educated in a manual trade and well instructed in Christianity.

13. The orphan girls are educated with special oversight and are instructed in Christianity and in all kinds of feminine work.

14. Six tables for poor students (70 in all) are free of cost.

15. One table of boys in the orphanage is supported at one-half cost and is maintained for study in the *Paedagogium.*

16. A hospital with a special *legatium.*

17. A poorhouse for certain old men and women with a special *legatium.*

18. An institute for Burgers who in their youth were not taught reading or catechism.

19. An institution for indigenous poor, who are educated for one hour a day and receive alms.

20. An institution for all arriving foreign beggars and Exulites who come together for an allotted two hours a day, receive good instruction in Christianity, and alms.

21. A school for poor boys.

22. A school for poor girls who can go to it free and return to their homes again after their education.

23. A special institution for children who are to attend the Lord's Supper. They are instructed for one hour each day. In all there are 500 children and 27 classes.

Ah Lord help! Ah Lord may it be a success.

August Hermann Francke

ADMONITION TO THE TWELVE STUDENTS TRAVELING TO LAPLAND*
1722

Prayer during travel and at all times.

Abrahamitic walk before God.

Humility, modesty with decorous *Parrhesie* [openness] toward all men.

Edification of neighbors during travel and at other times.

Shunning all contention while traveling, according to the counsel of Joseph and his brothers.

No unnecessary curiosity, but necessary observation of necessary matters.

In the vocation: the *dic cur hic* [say: why am I here?]

True denial of self, in particular if one cannot have everything according to one's own *Commodität* [comfort] and otherwise according to one's wish. Again: if one notes that one will be loved and preserved. Again: if better *Conditiones* [conditions] and promotions are offered.

Shunning dangerous and idle conversation even if it has a good appearance and *Praetext* [pretext] so as not to be directed into great temptations, sins, and shame.

To shun the supposed *Indifferentismus* [indifferentism] of the world, if one is invited as a guest and dinner companion or in some other capacity.

No day without food from God's Word and pouring out the heart before God; both with constant observation of oneself.

---

*Translated from MS Halle a.S., Francke-Archiv, D 90, pp. 1194–1195.

To remain with pure *tigniden* [building] truths; to shun paradoxes, meanings strange and difficult to explain to others.

To fill the mouth with the pure truth, in which is sap, power, and life, from the gospel of Christ, for example, *Lutherus redivivus* of [Martin] Statius [d. 1655].

To attend to God's way, not to deny the opportunities to promote the good, and to arm oneself for this with firm faith.

To count each day as the last and, so far as possible, to keep a diary.

Johann Anastasius Freylinghausen

SPIRITUAL SONGBOOK*
1705

PREFACE

Dear Reader:

The Old and the New Testaments, all of church history, and experience itself testifies that it is always a mark of special grace by which God visits his people or promises to visit them in the future, when and wherever spiritual loving hymns flow out from the mouths of spiritual children in songs of praise. . . .

[This can be seen in the songs sung by the children of Israel, by David and Solomon, by the prophets, by the Magnificat of Mary, and the Benedictus of Zacharias, by the songs indicated in the New Testament as sung by the apostolic communities, and by the songs sung thereafter, in particular by the hymns gathered by the Bohemian brethren.]

All the examples given to this point demonstrate the truth of the proposition that God visits his people in song; this can be demonstrated even more strongly by the experience of our own times in which the good hand of God has led us. In the last few years he has allowed the preaching of repentance and of the gospel, in particular in Germany, to ring forth with new strength, and he has sealed this not insignificant fruit. Not to acknowledge this or not to wish to acknowledge this is an indication of the most dangerous blindness. Likewise God has placed a new song in the hearts and mouths of many of his children and servants so that they might praise him with this song and by it elevate both present and coming grace. [The results of these new songs can be seen in the many songbooks of our day.]

---

*Translated from *Geistreiches Gesangbuch* (Halle, 1705).

Just as one does with all other good things, so also in the appropriation and use of this gift one is not to remain hanging to the wretched and petty instruments of this world, but is to look up to God the Father of light from whom all good and all perfect gifts come from above and who grants through the one spirit the many gifts for the improvement and building up of the body of Jesus Christ. One is to acknowledge and praise this same wisdom and faithful concern which God demonstrates toward his congregation and to use it for teaching and instruction, particularly for daily encouragement and a walking in faith, love, and hope, as well as for consolation and all struggle and suffering in this short pilgrim journey. One is to do this in humility and out of a simple heart.

For this end the present new songbook of the saints, elect and beloved of God, has been published in the good hope that through the grace of the Lord this end will be reached. . . .

Not every song fits every singer in the same way. The unrepentant and carnal man is not in any way able to sing so that his song pleases God, as long as he does not desire to leave unrighteousness but prefers the darkness to the light. Because of this many have the idea that, this being the situation, it would be more reasonable . . . to completely do away with the use of Christian hymn singing in public gatherings and to direct attention only to the preaching of the divine Word. Now although it is true that the song of the carnal and unrepented man does not please God, nevertheless, one cannot deny that God the Lord according to his manifold wisdom and loving condescension also uses oftentimes Christian hymns and songs to stir people's hearts to convict them and to bring them to a better way of life. Although there is no doubt that many an evil man without the slightest intention of bettering himself sings along only out of custom, whether openly or quietly to himself, when a powerful and spiritual hymn is sung, such an action prods his conscience, and if it does not lead to his conversion, nevertheless it certainly serves as a testimony to the Judgment Day. As a result, the practice of public singing ought not to be set aside. True servants of God faithfully direct carnal men to God the truth, warn them of their irrational worship, and indicate to them how they are to sing in the spirit and in truth whenever they sing out with full voices. He who seeks God in truth, whether he is just beginning or has already prepared a righteous base for his action, can sing hymns which will be pleasing to God and be heard just as he can so pray. And such a person will find abundant material in this book by which he can refreshen, nourish, and strengthen his soul according to his heart's every desire. . . .

The order of the hymns in this book is based on the order required by the economy of our salvation. The first hymns treat the essential matters, and in them Christ, the ground of our salvation, with his gifts and goods is presented in the most loving way. . . . Then follow hymns concerning the kindness of God and of Christ as the source and fountain out of which all our salvation and blessedness flows. Then follow hymns which present the means through which God wishes to bring us into communion with him again; they present a ladder from the works of creation, divine concern, and providence, and, chiefly, the so-called works of grace of the Word and the sacraments of Baptism and the Lord's Supper. Then follow hymns which indicate the order to which one must give oneself if you wish to have part in Christ and the blessedness achieved by him. Concerning the demands of this order you, dear man, along with false Christians, are warned and are directed to a true and righteous Christianity. In particular, the human misery and corruption is presented so that you will allow yourself to be brought to true repentance and conversion and to true faith in Jesus, the Savior of the world. This faith, if it is a true faith, does not only take on justification in the blood of Christ, but also the Christian life, and a Godly walk leading to a proper fruit and result. If you wish to know more specifically what kind of practices and virtues the Christian life and the Godly walk contain in themselves, you must consider what you are directed to by prayer, spiritual watchfulness, spiritual war and victory, chastity, denial of oneself and the world, desire for God and Christ, love of Jesus, brotherly and universal love, following after Jesus, the mystery of the cross which is ordained for you, Christian resignation, patience, and endurance to which you are directed, and the giving of your heart over to God. All these matters are treated in Christian songs in this book. If you wish to be found faithful in all these, you will have as your reward divine peace and joy in the Holy Spirit and the true joy of faith. Indeed, your heart and mouth will then flow over daily with the praise of God, and the wisdom of the childlike way will protect you. And what is more, your bridegroom will betroth himself to you so that you will be able to have part in the highest nobility of believers who stand above all the height and glory of this world forever. In this state, all the blessedness of the kingdom of grace and the powerful tasting of the coming eternal life consist. However, because you have not yet come to your goal or grasped the treasure, you are further reminded that the life of believers is here hidden with Christ in God and that the spiritual Zion cannot yet do without songs of sorrow; but one does not have one's hope silenced, and by hope one is able to stand firm and upright under all sorrows in this vale of tears so that one need not become tired or give up. And this hope goes through death and the blessed resurrection into heaven where the eternal and complete blessedness and glory is to be revealed and where all the fullness of the divine kingdom will from one eternity into the next be poured out over the Lord's people. . . .

HYMNS FROM THE SPIRITUAL SONGBOOK

Who is like you
Jesus, sweet peace,
Chosen from many;
Life of those who are lost
Along with their light,
Jesus, sweet peace?

Life, which
To redeem me from all need
Has tasted death,
Covered my guilt,
And out of need
Led me to God.

Light of glory,
Before time

You were given to us as redeemer,
And entered our flesh
In the fullness of time,
Light of glory.

Great hero of victory;
Death, sin, hell, and the world,
All the powers of the great dragon,
You have brought to shame

By the ransom
Of your blood, O hero.

Highest majesty,
King and prophet,
I will kiss your scepter,
I will sit at your feet
As many did,
Highest majesty.

Let me know your honor
As your own,
Through the light of the Spirit,
Continually burning in your love
As your own
Most beautiful honor.

Draw me completely into yourself
So that I
Might completely pass away and melt because of love
And direct to you my wretchedness
Which presses me down continually.
Draw me completely into yourself.

Shield of your gentleness,
Image of your humility,
Lay upon me, stamp upon me,
So that no wrath nor pride stir in me.
Nothing counts for you
Except your own image.

Guide my thought
Which is directed to the world
So that I might not turn from you,
But remain in the closet.
Be my victory.
Give me your thought.

Awaken me
So that my path

I might direct unchanged to you,
And not remain in the net
Of Satan.
Direct my path.

The impulse of your Spirit,
Place in my soul
That I might keep vigil and pray,
Come into your presence joyously;
Untainted love
Place in my soul.

When the power of the waves
In the dark night
Wishes to cover the ship of my heart,
You are to reach out your hands,
Take care of me,
Guardian, in the night.

The heroic spirit
Which would leave goods and blood
For you,
And hate the lusts of the flesh,
Grant this to me, highest good,
By your precious blood.

When I must die,
You will stand by me,
Accompany me through the valley of death,
And prepare me for glory
That I might see myself
Upright.

(Freylinghausen, 66)

*   *   *

Praise God! one step toward eternity
Is once again completed.

PIETISTS—SELECTED WRITINGS

In the movement of this time
My heart ardently turns to you
O source, out of which my heart flows
And all grace flows
Into my soul as life.

I count the hours, days, and years,
And time seems never-ending
Until I completely
Embrace you, O life.
Then what is mortal in me
Will be completely swallowed up in you
And I will be immortal.

With the fire of love
My heart glows so that it ignites
What is in me, and my mind
Binds itself so to you
That you in me and I in you
And I yet always more
Will press nearer into you.

Oh, that you would come quickly;
I count the moments.
Ah, come, before my heart grows cold
And turns to death.
Come, in your glory.
Behold, your bride has prepared herself;
The loins are girded.

And since the oil of the Spirit
Is poured out upon me,
You are closer to me in my interior,
And I have flowed into you.
Thus, the light of life enlightens me,
And my lamp is prepared
To receive you joyously.

"Come" is the voice of your bride.
"Come" calls your pious beloved.

She calls and shouts loudly.
Come quickly, Jesus, come.
So come then, my bridegroom;
You know me, O lamb of God,
That I am betrothed to you.

But the proper time and hour
Are totally left to you.
I know that it is pleasing to you
That I with heart and tongue
Promise to come to you, and, therefore,
From now on direct my way
Toward you.

I am satisfied that nothing
Can separate me from your love
And that free before every man
I dare call you the bridegroom,
And you, O true prince of life,
will be wedded to me there
And give me your inheritance.

Therefore, I praise you with thanks
That the day (night, hour, year) is ended
And that from this time
one more step is completed.
I step forth again speedily
Until I come to the gate
Of Jerusalem above.

When hands are careless
And knees shake,
Offer me your hands quickly
In the chest of my faith
So that through your strength, my heart
Might be strengthened, and heavenwards
I might rise up without intermission.

Go, soul, fresh in faith
And be not now afraid.

PIETISTS—SELECTED WRITINGS

Do not be enticed from the true path
by the desires of the world.
If you think you are too slow,
Hasten, as the eagle flys
with wings of sweet love.

O Jesus, my soul has
Has already flown up to you.
You have, because you are totally love,
Completely exhausted me.
Leave off, what are times and hours,
I am already in eternity
Because I live in Jesus.

(Francke, 346)

*   *   *

The day is past;
My spirit and sense
Yearn for the day
Which will make us fully
Free of all troubles.

Night is here.
Be near to me,
Jesus, bright candle;
Drive the darkness of sin
Away from my heart.

The light of the sun
Breaks in us now.
O uncreated sun,
Break forth with your light
Upon me for joy and pleasure.

Moonlight
Falls here
To lessen the darkness.

Ah, that nothing changing
Might hinder my journey.

The host of stars
For the honor of God
Glitters in the blue heaven.
Well is he who in that world
Shimmers like the stars.

What earlier stirred
And moved,
Rests now from its work.
Leave me, O Lord, in quiet peace
To contemplate your work in me.

Each person
In such stillness
Will use the sweet peace.
Let the unrest of this time,
Jesus, soon come to an end.

I also,
According to my practice,
Will now go to my bed.
Let my heart incline
To you as to rest.

Keep watch
So that no concern
And pain will disturb the Spirit.
Send the host of your angels
Who adorn my bed.

But when shall
The change
Of day and night cease?
When the day breaks
With which no day is likened.

PIETISTS—SELECTED WRITINGS

In that world,
When this ceases
Which Zion still makes to weep,
The moon and stars
Shall shine seven times brighter.

Then Jerusalem
Will lose
None of the sun's light,
For the Lamb himself is the light
Which shall adore the city.

Hallelujah!
Were I but there,
Where all things lovingly sound,
Where without change,
We sing in holiness.

O Jesus,
My help and peace,
Let me arrive there
so that in your light
I may dwell resplendent before you eternally.

(Freylinghausen, 615)

*   *   *

Jesus is the most beautiful image
Which wisdom has illuminated
Which so pure, calm, and mild
Has been spun out by eternal love,
Which the highest power of heaven
Has ever brought forth.

It is full art and decor,
Enrapturing sense and heart.
It is the masterwork of divinity

In which it impresses itself immediately.
If you wish to see the form of God
Look to Jesus; you will see it immediately,

For the beam of glory
Streams from his presence,
And the lightening of eternity
Makes his body and soul light,
And the first gleam of beauty
Is seen completely in him.

The grace and light of all angels,
The splendor and glory of all saints,
Is met a thousandfold
Alone in this image.
Whatever one can think
Is all met in Jesus.

Indeed, God himself, the eternal light,
Has never seen anything more beautiful,
And can never turn
His presence from him;
Say what you always will,
Jesus is the most beautiful image.

(Freylinghausen, 689)

* * *

My sorrow, dread, and torment
With time will come to end.
All weeping and all mourning
Which the Lord alone knows
will, thank God, not be eternal.
After the rain, a brightness
Of many thousand sunbeams
Will enliven my dead spirit.

PIETISTS—SELECTED WRITINGS

The seed I sowed
Will grow to joy.
When the thorns are out,
One will bring fruit home.
When bad weather passes,
Heaven will be free.
After battles, after struggles,
Come times of new life.

If one wishes to break off roses
One must suffer in stillness;
The thorns prick us.
All happens as God wishes;
He has pointed out the goal for us
Which one reaches only in battle.
If one wishes to find the treasure here,
One must first be a conqueror.

Our path is toward the stars;
It is filled with crosses.
One must not stand back,
Even if covered with blood,
To the castle of eternity.
No one comes without struggle.
Those who live in the walls of Salem
Count their crowns of thorns.

Truely, all pious persons
Who see heaven's clarity
Arrive there out of many sorrows.
Therefore, one sees them standing
Before the seat and throne of the Lamb,
Gleaming in the crown of honor,
And decked with palms
Because they triumph in fortune.

God's order stands firm
And remains eternally unchanged.
His friends and wedding guests

Will be given fortune after struggle.
Israel had victory
After battle and war.
Canaan will not be found
Where one has not conquered.

Therefore bear your chains,
My soul, and suffer patiently;
God will certainly save you.
The bad weather will cease
After lightening and thunder;
A pleasant day will follow;
Morning follows on evening
And joy upon sorrow.

(Freylinghausen, 732)

Johann Friedrich Starck

FROM
DAILY HANDBOOK FOR
DAYS OF JOY AND SORROW*
1728

The Eve of the Sabbath
The Believer's Preparation for Worship

Immediately after the fall, God taught our first parents the worship of sacrifice, and they transmitted the injunction to their children, Cain and Abel, for the sacrifices made by the latter two are expressly mentioned in Genesis 4:3, 4. These offerings were not made in silence, but with a confession of sins, a prayer for God's forgiveness, and a declaration of faith in the coming Messiah, whose blood was shed, like that of the sacrifice, for the redemption of man. At such times they also praised the goodness of the Lord, and preached his name. For this worship was set apart the seventh day, which the Lord himself had hallowed as a day of rest, when, after having created the world in six days, he rested on the seventh. This was the kind of worship observed ever after by all the patriarchs, until God caused the Tabernacle in the wilderness to be established, over which Solomon subsequently built the Temple. Under the New Testament, Christians also consecrate one day out of seven, Sunday, to God, that being the day on which Christ rose from the dead, and the Holy Spirit was poured out. On the approach of this day, the true believer shall

    1. Lay down his work early on Saturday evening, and disentangle his mind from worldly cares and troubles.

    2. Prepare himself for the coming Sunday with prayer, and

---

*Reprinted and revised from John Frederick Starck, *Daily Handbook for Days of Rejoicing and of Sorrow* (Philadelphia, 1855).

181

praise God for the many mercies vouchsafed to him throughout the week.

3. Read the gospel or the epistle appointed to be read and expounded on the following day; reflect upon it, and thus prepare himself to a devout attention to the word of God.

4. Retire to rest betimes, with such good thoughts, so that he may be found punctually and with invigorated frame and active mind in the house of the Lord.

PRAYER

Gracious and merciful God! I come before thee this day with praise and thanksgiving that thou hast so kindly preserved me during the past six days, and so freely blessed the work of my hands. Thou hast preserved me in my going and my coming, and hast done great mercies to my body and my soul; wherefore I thank and praise thee in the fullness of my heart. Hence, ye cares! I am building a temple unto God in my heart! It shall be a house of prayer, wherein I will serve my God alone. I "forget the things which are behind," I lay down my labors and my handicraft, and direct my thoughts to heaven alone, to God, that I may rejoice in him. Oh, the unspeakable love of the great God, who has appointed unto men a day of rest from all their toils! This rest is a token vouchsafed unto us in remembrance of the rest of paradise, where our constant occupation would have been to serve God, without any grievous labor. This rest is an emblem of the rest in Heaven which is to come; for there is yet a perfect rest offered and promised unto the children of God, which will commence in the life that is to come; when they shall be free from all toil, all suffering, and all sorrow, and free from sin.

O gracious God! Let me spend the approaching Sunday in thy fear and favor. Preserve me from evil company, lest Satan, with his instruments, deter me from attendance upon the worship of thee, and if he send them, help me to refuse to follow them. Guard me, that the holy day which thou hast set apart for my edification in the teachings of the gospel, for thy praise and service, may not be spent in idleness, sloth, luxury, amusement, and sin, to the greatest damage of my soul; but give my thy Holy Spirit, that I may devote the whole day, from morning unto night, to thy service. Keep my heart in unceasing devotion, so that no worldly cares may steal their way into it; and if any obtrude themselves, that I may banish them by thy power; or, if Satan should send me a bad neighbor, who should offer to bring worldly gossip into thy house, give me strength to turn a deaf ear to what he says, and to arouse and encourage him to thy service by my attention and silence. When thy Word is preached, open thou my heart, that I may apprehend it; gather it into my heart, and preserve it as a precious treasure. Help me that upon this Sunday I may grow in the faith, and increase in the knowledge of the truth, that what is spoken and heard may alter, sanctify, convert, and make of me a new man, so that as my years increase, my inner man may likewise grow in faith and piety, and become as a new creature, yea, a living member of the body of my Lord. Let me devoutly end the worship, carefully keep what I have learned, and close the day with prayer and praises. Oh! let me ever remember the words I have heard, that my walk and conversation, my life and my actions, may accord with it, and prove me not a forgetful hearer, but a doer of the Word. Thus let me celebrate Sunday after Sunday and Sabbath after Sabbath, until thou shalt admit me, through Jesus, my only Savior and Preserver, to the unceasing joys of Heaven, the eternal sabbath.

I will to God's own house with God's own people go,
Before his altar stand, dressed in a robe of snow.
My heart beneath his will, shall nestle as a dove;
My hands shall nought essay, but works of need and love.

Enter into my heart this day, thou King of kings!
Thy blessing and thy peace, spread over me thy wings.
Let thy all-saving grace upon my soul alight,
That so the sabbath may find favor in thy sight.

Amen.

HYMN

1. How lovely is thy word! It fills my heart with joy,
   My soul draws from it still comfort without alloy.
   It is the dearest prize in all the world I have,
   It shall enrich me still, when I am in my grave.

2. Thy word is the light that shines upon my way,
   And warms me out of hand whene'er my foot would stray,

Unto this word I cling unto the bitter end,
I know 'twill guide me safe where all my wishes tend.

3. It is my honeycomb, with which I do regale me,
   Whene'er the bitter gall of trouble doth assail me;
   How sweet unto the soul, all loaded down with care,
   Is the consoling tale thy Word doth still declare!

4. Thy Word it is my hoard, more worth than earthly treasure,
   In life and death from this alone I draw my pleasure;
   This prize no thief shall steal, no cunning foe despoil,
   It lies too firmly locked within my spirit's coil.

5. Let folly love to search for silver and for gold,
   The souls that worship thee, thy Word more precious hold;
   If both thy Word and gold, be set before their eyes,
   They stretch their hands to reach thy Word, the gold despise.

6. Some go to seek advice, who stand in fear to err,
   Thy Word my counsel is, to which I still recur;
   I ask what shall I do, for better or for worse?
   And straight thy Word, the best advisement doth rehearse.

7. By this sweet word of life, I'll shape my travel here,
   It shall my lodestar be, by which alone I'll steer
   Fearless and prompt, whate'er it bids me shall be done,
   And all it doth forbid with jealous care I'll shun.

8. Oh, from my thirsty lips take not thy Word away
   Until my dying hour let it my woes allay;
   And when these earthly lips no more of food shall take,
   Like living water still thy Word my soul shall slake.

9. Thus am I well bethought both while on earth I stay,
   And when my spirit leaves its tenement of clay!
   And what thy covenant doth promise here below,
   Shall be most richly mine when unto Heaven I go.

EXHORTATION FOR PRAYER
ON SABBATH MORNING
(Ps. 5:2–4)

All our life is nothing but prayer and thanksgiving, that is to say, we should cry to God every day in our prayers for his blessing, assistance, comfort, and grace, and when these are obtained, we should give thanks unto him with all our hearts. Therefore, O believer, when thou dost awake in the morning from thy slumbers, let it be thy first care to raise thine eyes to Heaven, think not immediately of thy business and thy toils, plunge not at once into the search of gain, but fall upon thy knees, thank God, and command thyself to his gracious protection. Do not think it a loss of time to devote half an hour in the morning to prayer. Oh, no! The time consumed in prayer will return with usury a thousandfold in thy labors, and what thou readest will lie in thy mouth all the day like honeycomb. When thou awakest, therefore, and arisest in the morning, hale and strong, reflect:

1. How many a devout Christian, more faithful, perhaps, than thyself, has spent the past night in fear and sorrow, in sickness, in suffering, in terror and great anxiety, of which thou hast experienced nothing.

2. Consider that others in the world have fallen into misfortune, loss, danger, and trouble, which thou hast been spared, and thank God therefore.

3. Pray to God at daybreak to keep thee throughout the day in his grace, that thou mayest not sin against him nor against thy neighbor.

4. Pray God to guide thee throughout the day, to preserve thee, and to bless thee in thy business and occupation.

5. Yes, surrender thyself unto God, so that throughout the day thou mayest stand in his love, speak of him, think of him, and not offend him wittingly or willingly, and then doubt not that the Lord will be graciously pleased to hear thy sighs and prayers, and give and grant unto thee throughout the day the things that shall be profitable to thy body and thy soul.

PRAYER ON SABBATH MORNING

Lord, early wilt thou give ear unto my voice; early will I stand before thee. Almighty and most merciful God! Thou art worthy to receive praise, honor, and glory. Who would not fear thee, thou King of nations, who would not honor thee, most loving Father? At the dawn of morning I appear before thee with humble thanks that thou hast flung thy mantle over me and mine this night, and hast renewed again thy goodness and thy truth. Fare with me and protect me this day also in all my ways. Let this day be a day of edification and blessing to my soul. In thy loving kindness thou hast disentangled this day from bodily labor, that thou mightest have thy work in me. Oh, then, instruct, enlighten, and sanctify my soul, and help me to lay up treasures which may give joy unto my spirit in danger and in death, in sorrow and in tribulation, which neither moth nor rust shall corrupt, nor thieves dig up and steal. My God, this day it shall be my delight to hear thy word, to refresh myself in the thought of thee, to sing songs of praise to thy honor and glory, to pray fervently and to yield up my heart to thee. How amiable are thy tabernacles, O Lord of hosts! My soul rejoiceth in the living God. But let me not be a hearer only, deceiving myself, but a doer of the Word. Open thou my heart, like that of Lydia, that with joy I may receive the seed of thy word, and then do thou seal it up that Satan may not rob me of it again. May I this day lay a firm foundation in faith, in the knowledge of Jesus Christ, in love, in self-denial, in indifference, deadness to the world, and in every Christian grace; so that during the whole of the coming week I may meditate upon it, act up to it, and bear good fruit. Preserve me from temptation if Satan should send his emissaries, so that I may not give up to the world the hours sacred to thee, or sacrifice to its sinful intercourse the time I should devote to thy honor, and thus bring a curse upon my soul, which would weigh me down throughout the week. Oh, let my public and private worship—my prayers, reading, hearing, and singing be pleasing unto thee. Be thyself my teacher, Lord Jesus, that my inner man may thrive until I shall be united with thee inseparably in the realms above.

The Believer Spends the Sabbath in Devotion

EXHORTATION
(Ps. 84:1–2)

Amid the many blessings which God has bestowed upon man is this, that he has set apart one day of the week as a day of rest from all his labors, burdens, and cares. Yea, he has especially blessed it, of which blessing those become partakers who keep it holy. To realize this blessing, the true believer himself is on his guard.

1. Not to misspend it in sloth and idleness; for in this manner horses and oxen and other beasts of burden keep the sabbath.

2. Not to spend the Sunday in gluttony, drunkenness, or luxury; for what is sinful on any day is doubly so on Sunday.

3. Not to desecrate the day by labor, by worldly business, by taking rides, collecting debts, casting up accounts, engaging workmen, or the like; for such employments distract the mind. Those who do such things are not true believers. They are mere lip Christians, to whom, according to their own confession, no day is so long and tedious as the Sunday. The true Christian knows better how to improve this holy day to the honor and glory of God, and the good of his soul.

4. He improves it to the praise of God with praying, praising, singing, contemplation of the goodness and mercies of God, which he has experienced through the last week and during his lifetime.

5. To the good of his soul, in dedicating this day to the hearing of God's word, so that he may grow in the knowledge of God and in his Christian faith.

6. But all this he shall do, not for one hour merely, but for the whole day; for the third commandment speaks of the whole day. Oh, surely, the devout observance of the sabbath is of great importance; it is fraught with many blessings. Who knows why many men are weighed down as with a curse and the lack of blessings? The old saying runs,

Who bears God's holy word alway,
Shall never know what 'tis to say,
I have no bread to eat today.

7. Having heard the word of God, keep it diligently in a good heart, live up to it, collecting at the same time a story of consolations and pithy maxims, which will be of service in times of suffering and of death.

The Believer Meditates on the Threefold Sabbath

EXHORTATION
(Heb. 4:1)

If the true believer would spend a Sunday pleasing unto God, he must remember that there is a threefold sabbath.

1. A weekly sabbath, if he spends Sunday in contemplating the mercies of God.

2. A daily or spiritual sabbath does not consist in an entire cessation from labor, but in a daily laying aside of our sins. As he foregoes his handiwork on Sunday, so he daily foregoes wantonness and malice. He guards against speaking evil of God or his neighbor, against doing evil alone or in company with others, against being seduced by others, and strives to keep his soul undefiled of the world. He is at pains to think of God often while at his work, to pray to him for the assistance of his Holy Spirit.

3. Whoever has kept the weekly sabbath devoutly, and the daily one zealously, may be assured of the eternal sabbath in the life to come, when the faithful and elect children of God will repose from all bodily labor, from all trials and sorrows, and from all sin, and will see God face to face, praise him, and serve him unceasingly. A holy and glorious sabbath, which will never be disturbed!

PRAYER

Holy and merciful God, inasmuch as I this day observe the weekly Sabbath, which, according to thine own ordinance is a day of rest from labor, so that I may be edified by thy word and rejoice in thee, oh, grant me thy Holy Spirit that I may spend it in hearing, reading, and meditating thy word, and may avoid all sinful allurements, wantonness, evil company, and sin. This weekly sabbath also reminds me of that daily spiritual sabbath, on which I am to renounce all sin, and sanctify unto thee my body and my soul, my life and my death. Now, my God, this by thy grace shall be my daily task, hereafter to do thy will, not mine, to banish evil desires and thoughts by thy power, that thou alone mayest dwell in me, and enlighten and sanctify me more and more. Grant that this daily and spiritual sabbath of my heart may never be destroyed, and take me at last to thy eternal sabbath, where we shall in eternal rest and in heavenly, blissful joy forever praise thee to the temple of thy glory. There shall I utter the Holy, Holy, Holy, with all the angels and cherubim. O my God, let me in the end attain to this felicity!

The True Believer Gives Thanks unto the Lord, after Having Heard His Holy Word

EXHORTATION
(James 1:22)

As all the good gifts of God are abused by the children of this world, so is it also with the hearing of God's Word, wherein they differ greatly from the true children of God.

1. The world's people think the sabbath instituted for their luxury and amusement, in which, being free from labor, they shall seek the comforts of the flesh, which is manifestly wrong.

2. The world's people at best go to Church in the morning, but amuse themselves in the afternoon with hunting, gaming, and sinful recreations, and then come home, if not intoxicated, at least with silly thoughts, sinful distractions, and worldly follies.

3. The world's people give no heed to the word which is preached, and if they were to be asked on Monday what their going to church had profited them, and what they had heard and learned, they would not know; the devil has already snatched the word out of their hearts, to prevent them from believing and being saved. (Luke 8:12)

4. And if they do remember anything, they do not put it into practice.

But the true children of God, who have begun the day with God and with prayer, do otherwise.

1. They hear the Word of God with devout attention.

2. They repeat at home what they have heard, write it down, and rejoice over it, as over a great treasure.

3. They think of it all the week, and endeavor to practice it.

In the Old Testament the Lord had chosen those animals for sacrifice which chewed the cud; and those souls also are after his heart which ruminate on the word they have heard and read, and derive new nourishment from it, for the sustenance of eternal life.

The Devout Believer Commits His Ways to God
and Invokes a Blessing at the Beginning of the Week

EXHORTATION

(Col. 3:17)

If we have reason to pray at the beginning of each day, how much more reason has a true believer to lift up his heart and eyes to God at the commencement of the new week! How many pass the sabbath and commence the week in the enjoyment of health, who are already in their graves before the ensuing Saturday arrives? How many have begun the week happy and blessed, but before its close, misfortune has overwhelmed them like a storm, so that they have ended it in anguish and woe, with wailing, weeping, and wringing of hands? This, my dear fellow Christian, may also be your and my lot and hence we should always turn to God at the beginning of the week.

1. The true believer must call upon God for the Holy Spirit to sanctify his heart and guide it, so that he may not lapse into sin, offend God, damage his conscience, wrong his neighbor, and load a heavy responsibility upon his soul.

2. He must not forget to pray and worship God during the week, but faithfully attend meetings for prayer and spiritual improvement, not on Sunday only, but also during the week.

3. As success does not depend upon his incessant toils and overexertions, he ought constantly to think of God and implore his blessing, and think of God when engaged at his work, and begin and end his work with a prayer.

4. He must speak soberly, walk as a Christian should, have God before his eyes at all times, and remember that one week after another is gliding away, and that his dying week will soon come, when our souls must render their accounts unto God. He who does this may begin the week in grace and end it under God's protection; even if God should make it a week of trial for him, he will still be and remain his help, his preserver, and his stay.

PRAYER

O thou loving and merciful God, by thy assistance I commence this new week, but I do not know what may transpire before it closes. How great adversity and misfortune may overtake me in a single day—how much more in a whole week? Therefore at the commencement of this week, I come and commend myself wholly unto thee. O

190

my God, grant me thy Holy Spirit, to sanctify, lead, and govern me, and bear witness with my spirit that I am a child of God. Bless thou me this week in my going out and coming in, in my daily business and occupation, and in all my steps. I lift up my eyes unto the mountains whence my help cometh; my help cometh from the Lord, who made the heavens and the earth. So thou keep me I shall not fall, so thou lead me I shall not go astray; therefore, let thy loving kindness ever attend me. Bless all that is mine, and let it flourish under thy blessing. O my God and faithful Father, protect and defend me from all harm, dangers, loss, and misfortune; let me stand day and night under thy guidance and protection. Guard my house about like the house of Job, let the angels make a rampart around me and mine, then shall no mishap overwhelm us, how great soever it be. Hear my prayer when I call unto thee, and let me not go unheard from the throne of thy grace. Preserve me from grievous sins, and guide me by thy truth. Keep my heart to this one thing, that I fear thy name. Grant that this week I become more pious and godly, increasing in the knowledge and love of thee, and as I leave week after week behind me, so may my inward man grow that when the last week of my life arrives, I may be assured of thy grace. Should this week prove a week of crosses, strengthen me by thy Holy Spirit, that I may bear and overcome everything by thy powerful assistance. Be thyself my help and my preserver from all trouble. Now I commend myself, body and soul, to thy fatherly protection, as all Christians should.

Amen, I say, forever
  Believing in my soul,
God will with my endeavor
  Be pleased in the whole;
  Then with a lightened heart
Straight to the task I bend me
Which God was pleased to send me,
  My calling and my art. Amen.

The True Believer Rejoices That He Was Born Again

EXHORTATION
(1 Peter 3:4)

If any man glory, let him glory in the Lord; and if any rejoice, let it be over that which will make him eternally happy. Now if there is anything in which a true believer may glory and rejoice, it is this being born again, that he was baptized, and thereby became a child of God. We have obtained innumerable blessings by the rite of holy Baptism.

1. God is our Father, who will sustain, preserve, and care for me as for his children, and will not forsake us.

2. Jesus Christ. All that Jesus has earned by his sufferings and death, has been imparted to us as our own by holy Baptism.

3. The pouring out of the Holy Ghost, who will dwell in our hearts to enlighten, sanctify, and direct them. By such indwelling power of the Holy Spirit, we are daily removed farther from sin, and grow in faith, piety, and godliness, as a newborn babe increases in years and strength.

4. We shall have a part, after this life, in the bliss of Heaven. He who ponders these things must needs rejoice in God with all his heart. But let the believer also most carefully watch and pray

1. that he do not lose the grace bestowed upon him;

2. that he walk worthily in his calling;

3. that he do not again love the world, and that he sin not willfully with unregenerate and worldly people, and become like them;

4. that he be obedient unto God as a loving child, and follow the Lord Jesus, and withstand not the Baptism of the holy Spirit. Then he may rest assured that he will enjoy the love, favor, support, and assistance of the triune God here in time, and hereafter in eternity.

PRAYER

Great God, and dearly beloved Father, how can I love and praise thee enough, that thou hast had mercy upon my soul, that I might not perish! What honor hast thou shown me in imparting unto me the right of holy Baptism, wherein thou hast acknowledged me to be thy child! Do men boast the great happiness derived from their high birth, the possession of dignities, riches, and domains; much more do I prize my happiness in being thy child, for if we are children, we also are heirs, that is to say heirs of God, and brethren of Christ, provided we suffer with him, and are elevated to glory with him. If I am a child of God, my heavenly Father will preserve, govern, guard, and defend me; yea, he will never forsake me in the time of need. If I am a child of God, I have not only an unfailing stay in him in this life, but great cheerfulness in death, for he will refresh me as his child, love me, comfort me, and, after my departure from this world, he will lead me to the life of bliss to come. If I see anyone do evil, if I hear evil spoken, let me remember that I am a child of God, to whom such things are not becoming; let me joyfully say, in thy power: World, know that my birthright and my heritage in God are not to be sold for thy pleasures and thy vanities. Blessed Jesus, thou knowest that I love thee, and am greatly distressed when I do not always and in very truth love thee as I should. Oh, be graciously pleased to take my will for the deed and let me lead a life of faith and piety, holiness, purity, and childlike humility, let me love, honor, fear, and obey thee, that I may live and die as thy child, and attain everlasting joys in Heaven. I have put on Jesus long ago in holy Baptism, therefore did thou love me, and hast adopted me to be thy child, O God! I beg for the sake of the blood of Christ, let my end be well. Amen.

The True Believer Prays God to Continue and
Increase the Faith Awakened in Him

EXHORTATION
(Luke 17:5)

As unhappy as is an unbeliever, so happy is a soul which stands in the faith and true knowledge of God, of Jesus Christ, and of its own salvation. For an unbeliever is like a room in which there is no light, wherein it is dark and disagreeable, but a believing soul is like unto a room wherein it is light, and wherein a taper is lit, which taper is faith. This faith man cannot give unto himself, but it is God that lights it within us.

1. Therefore, a true believer shall thank God that he has brought him to the faith and to the knowledge of Jesus Christ, and thereby made him happy above Jews, Turks, or heathens.

2. He shall be mindful of his covenant of Baptism, and the glory thereby conferred upon him, and shall not wantonly transgress the covenant entered into with God.

3. He shall diligently and devoutly hear God's Word, that he may be constantly more enlightened, and brought to a better understanding of his will in his works.

4. Therefore, a true Christian must not be satisfied with saying, I believe, but he must also let the fruits of faith, as piety, charity, chastity, patience, meekness, and others, shine forth throughout his life.

Then he has the consolation that he will secure the end of his faith, eternal salvation.

The True Believer Prays That the Love of God May Be
Kindled in His Heart

EXHORTATION
(1 John 4:16, 19)

God is love, and because he is love, he wills that all his children and believers should stand in true love. Love is the tie which rivets our hearts to God, but also to the hearts of our neighbor.

1. A true believer prays to God that he will fill his heart with his holy love.

2. He must not despise the means whereby the love of God can be commenced and increased in him, devout attention to and reflection on the Word of God, and the proper use of the Communion.

3. If he stands in the love of God he must prove it by a holy Christian walk, becoming speech, and works well pleasing unto God.

4. But he must be well on his guard, lest, like Demas, he come to love the world again; for who so loves the world, the love of the father is not in him. Therefore, out of love to God, he must eschew the world, which would lead him away from God again.

5. In such love he must remain till death.

6. The love of God must increase constantly with increasing years; it is a shame to spend twenty, thirty, or forty years in the pleasures and follies of the world, forgetting the love of God.

The True Believer Prays God to Inspire Him with Love
to His Neighbor

EXHORTATION
(1 John 4:20, 21)

"A new commandment I give unto you, that ye love one another; by this shall all men know that ye are my disciples, if ye have love one to another." Thus does Christ designate the true mark of his disciples, in John 13:34. Let no one imagine that he may stand in the love of God, if he hate his neighbor. Oh, no!

1. Our neighbor means our friend, benefactor, or kinsman.

2. Also our neighbor, stranger, and fellow-citizen, even if he envies, overreaches, and hates us.

3. As against our enemies we should banish from our hearts all bitterness, implacability, hatred, or malice, and should prove by words and works that we have a loving heart toward them, and should do in deed and in truth what Christ says: "Love your enemies, bless them that curse you, do good to them that hate you, and pray for them which despitefully use you and persecute you, that ye may be the children of your Father which is in heaven." (Matthew 5:44, 45)

PRAYER

O thou loving God, who dearly lovest us but has also commanded us to regard our neighbor with the same love with which thou lovest us, oh, lament before thee that my heart has not yet surrendered itself to this sincere and perfect love to my neighbor. According to thy commandment I ought to love my neighbor as myself, I ought to rejoice when thou givest him happiness, health, and prosperity, as if the same had been accorded to me. I ought fervently to love my enemy, who hates, despitefully uses, persecutes, and oppresses me. I ought to wish him well, and to pray that thou wouldst grant every blessing to his body and his soul. But, omniscient God, thou seest and knowest how my heart is estranged from these duties, how, alas, when thou doest good unto my neighbor, when thou givest him happiness, honor, and benefits, and not to me, I am ill content that thou doest not the same to me. Thou seest how feeble and how tardy are my prayers for my enemies. O my God and Father, I recognize herein the sinful depravity of my heart, and how far I am from that true condition of a disciple of Jesus which is known by this, that they have love to one another; not only to their friends and benefactors, but also to those that envy them, to their enemies and persecutors. Therefore I beseech thee to change my revengeful and rebellious heart, that through thy favor I may love my neighbor heartily and sincerely, as myself. Give me strength to see with pleasure the good gifts thou vouchsafest unto my neighbor, and not to repine if thou dost not rejoice me with a like favor. Preserve me from being false, that I may not pretend to be his friend and kiss him, like Judas, and yet betray him, but that I may be sincere with him. And if I must experience the persecution, the spite, and the wrongs of enemies, give me strength to overcome with gentleness, not returning evil for evil, and revilement

195

for revilement, but wishing them prosperity and every happiness. Lord, my God, thou seest how hard this duty is to the flesh, but by thy favor and assistance I shall succeed. Amen.

The True Believer Resolves to Follow Christ

EXHORTATION
(Ps. 139:23, 24)

A careful traveler enquires frequently whether he is still in the right road; and so the Christian traveler often asks whether he is still in the path of Heaven. Many deceivers have gone out into the world, says St. John, and therefore we must constantly watch that we be not deceived.

1. A believer must not follow *the world*, which would entice him into its sinful ways and manners. Nor dare he follow the desires of his own sinful and corrupt heart. But whenever something presents itself to his mind, he asks himself, Is it right?

2. But he must follow the sacred Scriptures, which tell him what he must believe, experience, avoid, and do. This is his rule of faith and practice. What it forbids he carefully avoids.

3. He especially sets before him and labors to imitate the holy example of the blessed Savior, Lord Jesus, who hath set us an example, that we might follow in his footsteps. His footsteps are his benevolence, humility, patience, meekness, sincerity, friendship, purity, and zeal.

4. He also observes the pious example of other Christians. If he sees in them zeal, devotion, charity, and other virtues, he strives to imitate them.

5. He must follow Christ until death, and then he shall be taken to Heaven and numbered among those who follow the Lamb whithersoever he goeth. (Rev. 14:4)

The True Believer Meditates on the Coming Glory of the Children of God

EXHORTATION
(1 John 3:2, 3)

A true Christian should daily consider *three* things: what he is, what he *possesses* in God—a father, a benefactor, and the best of

196

friends, and what he has yet *to expect* at the hands of God, heavenly pleasures and bliss. Such contemplations tend to keep alive in his soul the flame of love to God, and cause sin to lose its charms and power over him.

1. True believers have great glory even in this life; they have the pardon of their sins, are the sons of God and heirs of Heaven, have peace with God, consolation in affliction, bliss of the soul, rest in God, and a Mediator; compared with this, silver, gold, money, and kingly crowns are as nothing.

2. They have great glory to expect in the life hereafter. They shall enter into Heaven, see the triune God, associate with the saints and angels, and, freed from all sin, sorrow, toil, and pain, rise in the body to eternal life.

3. The true believer anticipates this with joy, draws consolation from it in sorrow, and is assured that the time will come when all trouble will turn to endless rejoicing.

4. He must not forfeit this glory by a sinful life in this world's sins, but must consider that he is destined for something better.

5. He stands fast in faith and regards the things of earth as a fleeting show, which he must leave behind, but often sends his heart before to where he longs to dwell forevermore.

The True Believer Thanks God at the End of the Week

EXHORTATION
(Ps. 116:12)

One day and week after another passes away, and we are brought nearer and nearer to our graves; yet our God is still so merciful as to vouchsafe unto us many benefits in soul and body, and fill our hearts with gladness.

Such should be the reflections of the believer at the end of the week.

1. He thanks God for the blessings which he has received, for the care and protection exercised over him, for the help extended to him, and for all the tokens of his love given him in answer to his prayers. If he hears that others, during the week, have been overtaken by distress, he sympathizes with them, and thanks the Lord for having so mercifully preserved him.

2. He remembers that the goodness of God should lead him to

repentance; wherefore, on the last day of the week, he repents the evil he has done each day, and thus makes the last day of the week a day of confession of sin, humiliation, repentance, and prayer for pardon, as well as of thanksgiving.

3. He beseeches God for the continuance of his protection and care, his mercies and blessings during the coming week.

4. He ponders the fact that one week after another of his life is rapidly passing away, and that his dying week will soon come. For this he endeavors to prepare himself by a life of repentance, faith, and prayer. He constantly strives to become more holy and devoted to God. Such meditations ought to make us more pious, watchful, thankful, and zealous. They should lead us constantly to look up to God as the author and giver of every good and perfect gift, and to commit ourselves to the spirit of his grace, that we may continue in his love and live according to his will, and be ever ready to leave the world in peace when the dying hour, dying week, and dying year shall come.

PRAYER

The Lord hath done great things for me whereof I am glad. Hitherto the Lord hath helped me. Truly, my God and King, I may use this language now, since thou hast so mercifully brought me to the close of another week. "How excellent is thy loving kindness, O God! Therefore the children of men put their trust under the shadow of thy wings." Thou dost watch over, protect, and keep them, and every morning thy goodness is new to them. O my God, thou hast extended thy wings over me, and preserved me, guided me, protected me, hast done me great good in body and soul, and hast allowed me and mine to enjoy the comfort of thy grace. Wherefore "bless the Lord, O my soul, and all that is within me bless his holy name! Bless the Lord, O my soul, and forget not all his benefits." How many during the week have fallen, whilst I, by thy grace, yet stand! How many have passed this as a week of affliction, pain, and suffering, while I have enjoyed peace and happiness! How many have spent their days in trouble and distress, and moistened their pillows with tears of sorrow at night, while joy and gladness have filled my heart! For all this I would magnify and praise thy name from the bottom of my soul. Thanks to thee, O God, for thy protection and grace, thy assistance and love, and all the blessings bestowed upon my body and soul. O my God, forgive me also in mercy the wrong that I have done this week. For the sake of the bleeding wounds of Jesus Christ spare me, and do not deal with me according to my deserts. By the mighty assistance of thy Spirit, I will endeavor during the coming week to avoid all the sins of the one which is now past, and that in holiness and righteousness I may serve thee all the days of my life. Amen.

HYMN

1. Soul! another week behind thee
   Sinks into eternity!
Let reflection well remind thee
   Of thy God's benignity.
Still his open hand outpours
Wealth and happiness in stores;
Still his unremitting kindness
Guides thee in thy tottering blindness.

2. As the living water courses
   From new fountains forth with speed,
So the current of his mercies
   Brings thee all that thou dost need.
Who can tell, beneath the sun,
All the good that God hath done;
For his wealth is like a mountain.

3. Pray that like a failing ember,
   He may fan the flames afresh;
And that he will not remember
   The shortcomings of thy flesh.
Yea, my Father, do not think
Of the sins 'neath which I sink;
As the week is gone and vanished,
Let my sins be also banished.

4. May I further taste thy favor
   In the week that is to be;
Grant that the delightful savor
   Of thy grace may make me free
From the sin that bears me down,
From the cares that on me frown;

Ever let thy goodness aid me,
And thy mercy overshade me.

5. If it be thy will to send me
   Care and trouble in this week,
   Let it not too fiercely shend me,
   Let thy goodness for me speak;
   That this week should be my last,
   Let thy mercy not forsake me,
   I am safe if thou dost take me.

The Afflicted One Considers the Design
of God in His Afflictions

EXHORTATION
(Heb. 12:11)

When a child is punished, it weeps and thinks it is made to suffer too severely. Is it strange, then, that the afflicted are often at a loss to know how they should support their sorrows?

1. Let the afflicted believer therefore remember that God chastises him not to destroy, but to save him. When the surgeon cuts into a wound, and applies irritating liniments, it is done to heal it; and so God sends upon us sufferings and sorrows to wean us from the world and draw us nearer to himself and to Heaven.

2. When God sees that our hearts and affections are too much wedded to any earthly object or being, he often finds it necessary to remove the idol, so that he alone may have our supreme love, and that we are to seek and have our chief delight in him. It often happens that when uninterrupted health, happiness, and prosperity are granted to us for a length of time, we become weary in well-doing, and negligent in prayer. This is a very great evil, and God sends some calamity or affliction upon us to bring us back to him. In all this, however, he still remains a wise, gracious, and merciful Father, who loves us sincerely.

PRAYER

My God, thou hast plunged me into such sorrow and tribulation that my heart is disturbed, my lips full of sighs, and my eyes full of tears! What shall I do, or whither shall I flee? Was I not happy once?

Did I not enjoy peace and rest? Whence then come my present sorrows and sufferings? Oh, misery is great! But I will not therefore attempt to flee from thee, my Shepherd. Hast thou not cast me down with this heavy blow? Oh, raise me up again with thy mighty Word! I know full well that this affliction has been sent upon me, not for my misery and destruction, but that by putting me into this condition, thou wouldst prove my love, whether it is true, and will remain the same in adversity as in prosperity. Thou wouldst prove my faith, whether I truly believe that thou art an almighty, wise, and merciful God, capable alike of rescuing me from this trouble, and of leaving me in it. Thou wouldst prove my patience, whether I will honor thee by bearing the Cross without murmuring. Thou wouldst prove my confidence, whether it is ready to trust thee above all things, and count upon thy grace, love, and mercy. Thou wouldst prove my hope, whether it will continue even where there seems to be no ground for hope to trust thy word and promise; yea, my gracious God and Father, thou wouldst by this means draw me away from the world—its lusts, sins, and wicked ways, that I might fix my heart upon thee alone. Well, thou God of love, be it so. I will submit to thy will, and cheerfully bear whatsoever thou mayest see fit to lay upon me. May the Holy Spirit give me strength, power, and endurance. I will be patient, let it last as long as it will. I will break with the world and worldly company, and be one in spirit with thee. May this affliction purify me, and be profitable to my soul. Thy help will come in its own good time. God will not desert me; though I be deserted of all others, I will cling to God. My heart and mind shall be faithful to him and trust in him, and consign all things to the care of him who never will forsake me. Amen.

The Afflicted One Prays for Patience and Endurance

EXHORTATION
(Heb. 10:35, 26)

Patience is a fruit of the Spirit; it comes from God, and must be asked of him in prayer. An afflicted one must pray the more zealously and eagerly, the more his sufferings beset him, as it is written of Christ, "And being in any agony, he prayed more earnestly."

1. It is patience to remain quiet under affliction, and submit to all the ordinances of God. The believer knows that the evil comes

201

from God, who is able to again remove it. He knows that even while he smites him, God loves him, and that he has not ceased to be his heavenly Father, although he has imposed the yoke upon him.

2. Therefore the afflicted one must not murmur against God, how long or how severe soever his afflictions may become. On the contrary, he resolves to be silent and speak not, knowing that God will make all things well.

3. If perchance the violence of pain or the multiformity of sorrow should impair his trustfulness, he must implore the Lord to give him strength. God administers consolation in various ways; sometimes he awakes a consciousness in our hearts that our sufferings will shortly cease; sometimes he declares he will not forsake us; and occasionally he assuages and mitigates our woes.

4. This will invigorate the afflicted one, and once more imbue him with the vigor of the Lord.

PRAYER

Lord, my God, my sighs are not unknown to thee, and thou art well acquainted with my wretchedness and sorrow. My consolation is that I know it comes from beloved hands. I have not brought it upon myself, but thou hast imposed it, and wilt help me to bear it. And as patience is one of the good gifts which come from above, from the Father of light, oh, bestow it upon me according to thy mercy. If thou strengthen me, if thou help and bestead me, I can do anything, nothing will be impossible for me, nothing difficult; I can do all things by him who fortifies me, even Christ. And do not seize me too violently, so that I may endure it. Have patience with my weakness, strengthen my sinking hands, brace up my tottering knees, and say to my faint heart, "Thy Jesus is near thee; thy king cometh to thee, he is a righteous and an almighty deliverer." Yea, Lord, if thou dost help me, I am well helped; therefore, help me, O my salvation. Teach me to consider that it is thy holy will that I should suffer as I do. I will cheerfully acquiesce, and say, "Father, not my will, but thine, be done." Call to my mind thy love, that thou lovest me in suffering and affliction, that my griefs will last but a little while, and that the sufferings of this little span are nothing beside the glory which is to be made manifest in us. Help me to consider that thou art my gracious God and loving Father, and that this present cross is not a sign of thy wrath but of thy mercy. Remind me of the example of my dear Savior

Jesus Christ, who patiently bore all things. Grant that by thy grace I may follow him in this composure; let me suffer with him, that I may be also elevated to glory with him. Let my affliction not tear my word out of thy heart, nor impair my faith, nor prevent any prayers, but give me new power and courage, whenever I am called upon to weather another storm. Give me to think that thy help will soon make me glad, and thy strong assistance give me joy. Thou art my rock, my rampart, my fastness, my shield, my power; so says thy word, my help, my deliverance, my life; my almighty God, who can withstand thee? Amen.

The Afflicted One Complains of the Weakness of His Faith

EXHORTATION
(Luke 17:5)

If anything is capable of frightening the soul of a true believer, it is when he imagines that he does not pray in a proper manner, or that his faith is not a living faith, which leads to doubts of his salvation. In such cases, the following reflections may be of service.

1. Let the desponding Christian be assured that the prayer which is offered up in the name of Jesus, in reliance upon his blood and merits, is a prayer correctly spoken.

2. The fact that he has a desire to believe is an evidence that he has already believed; for this desire is a work of the Holy Ghost; a godless man does not desire to believe.

3. Satan cannot extinguish the light of faith in our hearts.

4. The fact that a believer does not at all times feel the same degree of happiness in prayer is no evidence that he has no faith, no more than coals concealed beneath the ashes prove the fire to be extinguished.

5. The best evidence that we have faith is the fact that we strive against sin, and that the fruits of the Spirit appear in our lives. But the fruit of the Spirit is love, joy, peace, long-suffering, gentleness, goodness, faith, meekness, temperance; against such there is no law. (Gal. 5:22, 23) For such frightened souls are afraid to speak or to do evil.

6. Our faith may be strengthened by prayer, reading God's word, patient continuance in well-doing, hope in God.

7. Christ has died for the weak in faith as well as for others, and

203

prays for them, that their faith fail not; and even if they should feel themselves unable to believe this, it is still true, because taught in God's holy word.

Part IV
Exhortations, Prayers, and Hymns for the Dying

The Dying One Appears before the Judgment Seat of God

EXHORTATION
(2 Cor. 5:10)

"If we would judge ourselves, we should not be judged," is the admonition of the Apostle Paul in 1 Corinthians 11:31; and truly the man who examines his own life, accuses himself, and prays for grace in the name of Jesus will not be condemned by God, but will experience his goodness and mercy; for he who acknowledges and renounces his trespass shall have mercy. This, therefore, should be the care of the dying.

1. He must remember that sooner or later he must appear before the judgment seat, for it is appointed for man once to die, and afterwards the Judgment.

2. Therefore a dying one will do well to be reconciled to God in time, to ask his forgiveness in the name of Jesus' blood, and thus attain unto grace; then he may rest assured, that, die when and as God will, quickly or slowly, God will graciously accept his soul, and that on the last day he will enter into life eternal, justified by the blood of Jesus.

PRAYER

I know, O God, that it is appointed for me once to die, and afterwards the Judgment. Therefore, I now appear before thy judgment seat, while yet I live; I would be reconciled to thee before I die. O righteous God, I know that I am a great sinner! I have broken all thy holy commandments, often designedly, I have not loved thee with all my heart, nor with all my soul, nor with all my might; I have not always followed in the footsteps of my Jesus, nor suffered the Holy Ghost to lead and guide me as I ought to have done. I remember that I was made thy child in holy Baptism, but that I have not always lived as a child of God, that in confession and at thy holy table I have made many promises of which I kept but few, and again associated myself with the world. Lord, I have done amiss; the load of my transgressions presses me down; I have not walked in the way pointed out by thee; my sins rise over my head, and like a weighty burden they have grown too heavy for me. O gracious God, thou who has declared that thou dost not seek the death of the sinner but that he should turn and live, behold, I come and desire to make my peace with thee. Oh, I repent of my sins, and fall down before thy judgment seat, and beseech thee, Lord God Father in Heaven, to have mercy upon me! Lord God Son, the Savior of the world, have mercy upon me! Lord God Holy Ghost, have mercy upon me! I invoke thy great mercy, O Father! I have sinned in heaven and before thee; I am not worthy to be called thy child, yet oh, be merciful unto thy child, and do not disown me! I fly unto thee, O Jesus, my Advocate! Oh, intercede for me, a sinner, now, and in the hour of my death! For the sake of thy precious blood, forgive my trespasses; for the sake of thy holy wounds, let me find grace before the austere judgment seat of God! Lord, be gracious unto me according to thy goodness, and wipe out my sins after thy great mercy. O most precious Holy Ghost! I pray to thee to create a new heart within me, sanctify and purify it, give me thy testimony that I am a child of God and in favor with God. Yea, work in me a true repentance, a living faith, and holy resolves to live only to thy honor, and to die in childlike obedience. Oh, produce in me holy thoughts, devout sighs, acceptable meditations on death, and give me a refreshing foretaste of Heaven and of the glory that is to come. Let me hear thy consoling words in my heart, "Be of good cheer, my son, thy sins are forgiven thee." O most Holy Trinity, have mercy upon me, let me find favor in thy sight when I leave this world, and do not take me into judgment for the evil I have done, but have mercy upon me according to thy love. Amen.

HYMN

1. "Rise from your graves, ye dead!" Thus shall
   the call be sounded,

Which on the latter day shall find us all astounded;
Which to the faithful flock promise rare
  delight,
And fill the trembling hearts of sinners with
  affright.

2. "Rise from your graves, ye dead!" Your sleep at
     last is over,
   Ye blessed of the Lord, no more without shall
     hover.
   The garments are prepared, the crowns are for you
     stored;
   Enter into the joy and comfort or your Lord!

3. "Rise from your graves, ye dead!" Come from
     your earthly cover;
   Ye wicked all the pangs of hell shall now discover
   Ye once rejected me, I hold you nothing worth;
   Wailing and gnashing teeth shall be your lo.
     henceforth.

4. "Rise from your graves, ye dead!" Lo, here are
     bone and tissue,
   Flesh, sinew, hand, eye, foot! from earth and air
     they issue.
   That wherewith you have served the Lord is glorified,
   That wherewith you have sinned, consumed and
     cast aside.

5. "Rise from your graves, ye dead." Ye faithful
     now shall glory
   In halos like the sun, undimmed, untransitory.
   Immortal bodies with immortal souls shall blend,
   Ye shall enjoy the rest of saints that hath . . . end.

At the Beginning of Holy Lent the Devout
Christian Meditates the Sufferings of Christ

EXHORTATION
(2 Cor. 5:21)

Among the early Christians the holy time of Lent was a time of devotion and prayer, spent in contemplating the sufferings of Jesus, as is the custom of all the true children of God to this day. Although Satan has brought the children of the world to such a pass that they begin the holy time of Lent, not with prayer and devotion, but with drinking, masquerades, gluttony, luxury, and ungodliness, testifying that they care nothing for the crucified Jesus, yet the true children of God think otherwise, and have a dread of such abominations.

1. They not only commence the season with prayer and singing, but unshackle their minds as much as possible of all earthly things, so that all their joy may be in the blood of Jesus.

2. They think over all the sufferings of Jesus, his agony in the garden of Gethsemane, his appearance before the judgment seat, at Golgotha, on the Cross, and in the grave, calling to mind at every scene that this was suffered for their salvation.

3. They do not allow their devotion to disappear with the season of Lent, but as they mean to be comforted all their lives by the blood of Jesus, so they remember, all their lives, the crucified Jesus, who rose again.

4. This remembrance impels them to crucify the desires of the flesh, no longer to live according to the course of this world, nor wantonly to sin, but to die to sin, and be born again in the spirit.

PRAYER

Jesus, my Jesus! How great is thy love, extended to me in thy bitter sufferings. Thou art the only-begotten Son of God, thou art the immaculate Lamb, the Lord of Glories, the Most Holy, who has never committed a sin; and behold, thou dost commit thyself to the most disgraceful death and unto the most cruel sufferings for me, an unjust one, a sinner, and a slave of death. How great is thy unspeakable mercy! The holy one takes away my unholiness, the pious one takes away my wickedness, the just one my injustice, the innocent one my guilt.

My sins are laid upon thee, so that thy righteousness may fall upon me. My Jesus, in thy sufferings I can see the wrath of God against sin, the abomination of sin, the punishment of sin. For it was in chastisement of the trespasses of others, and shifted sins, that God tortured thee, innocent Lamb, on the Mount of Olives, and suffered thee to be so wretchedly maltreated by the hands of thy foes. How severely then will those be punished hereafter who do not allow themselves to be moved by such sufferings to faith, to repentance, and to sanctification. Jesus, I approach thee, and believingly regard thy sufferings. Thou goest to the garden of Gethsemane, and bloody sweat drops from thee to the ground; alas! for me, that I may be delivered from the power of the Devil. Thou are brought to judgment, accused, and condemned to death; alas! for me, that I may be acquitted after death, and on the last day, before the judgment seat. Thou art scourged, and thy body seamed with blood, deep furrows are drawn upon thy back; alas! for me, that I may not be punished for my sins. Thou art led to death; alas! for me, that my death may be wholesome to me and a passage to Heaven, aye, a journey to the Father. Thou art crucified; alas, for me: Thou, the Lamb of God, has taken away all my sins. Thou diest upon the cross; alas! for me, that by thy death I may have life. Thou are buried; alas! for me, to sanctify my grave. Is not this love, is not this mercy, that by thy bitter suffering I am to attain life, grace, and the forgiveness of all my sins? The punishment of all my sins is upon thee, so that I may have peace, and be delivered from them. These sufferings I will have before my eyes wherever I am. Thy death and sufferings, until soul and body sever, shall dwell within my heart. If Israel was free from all guilt and punishment, upon believingly sacrificing a lamb to God, and seeing its hot blood flow: I know that because thou, O Jesus, thou innocent and immaculate Lamb of God, wert slaughtered for me, and thy hot blood was richly poured out for me, that, if I receive it in faith, I am reconciled with God through grace. Thy blood is the true sacrificial blood, the blood of atonement, the blood of purification, the blood with which to sprinkle our sills and doorposts. O Jesus, I will think of thy sufferings and of thy blood when my heart is tempted to sin, I will have before my eyes thy holy image on the Mount of Olives, when thou wert scourged, and at the Cross, whenever the world with its evil example would make me like itself. Into thy wounds will I flee when my sins oppress me, thy blood I will claim as my ransom when conscience besets me, aye, in my dying hour I will know nothing but Jesus; thy holy name shall be my latest word, thy bleeding form my latest thought, thy last word upon the Cross my expiring sigh, "Father, into thy hands I commend my spirit!" In that last hour, O Jesus, be my comfort, my joy, my refreshment, my assistance, and appear to me in thine image, a consolation in my need, how thou, Lord Christ, didst bleed to death. I will look toward thee, and in faith clasp thee to my heart. Who dies thus, dies well. Amen.

HYMN

1. My best of friends departs; my Jesus, my salvation,
   Already bows his head, and leaves his high vocation;
   His face is deadly pale; from the accursed tree
   He sinks into the grave; my bridegroom parts from me.

2. My best of friends departs that I may never perish,
   But in eternal bliss his loved remembrance cherish;
   For me, for me he dies, to clear my guilt and shame,
   To bring me to the grace of God, and end all blame.

3. My best of friends departs, yet is my life unsmitten,
   Deep in my soul the name of Jesus still is written;
   I love him while I live, I love him when I die,
   I love him on the Cross, and when he sits on high.

4. I follow when my friend in his dear grave they bury,
   See with believing eyes how they the ritual hurry.
   My friend, here is my heart! Oh, sink into it deep,
   Let it thy dwelling be, and bed where thou dost sleep.

5. I sacrifice my heart to thee alone forever,
   Thy precious death from mine no difference shall sever.
   Oh, while I live, live thou, friend of my soul, in me,
   And when I come to die, let me but die in thee.

Devotions for
Women with Child

The Woman with Child Offers Up Her
Morning Prayer

EXHORTATION

Every true Christian is bound, before going to his daily work, to commend himself to the divine protection and mercy, so that God may keep his body and his soul under his gracious care.

But if every man ought thus to commend himself to the care of God, how much more ought the pregnant to do so? They have much to pray for every morning.

1. To keep them throughout the day in good and holy thoughts, so that they may think of God, always have him in their hearts, and converse with him.

2. They must commend their life and their limbs to God, that God may guard their steps, preserving them from dangerous falls or other misfortunes.

3. They must also commit the fruit of their bodies to the holy providence of God, that it may grow strong and well formed, and may be filled with the gifts of the Holy Ghost.

4. They must guard, particularly, throughout the day, against anger, quarrels, and strife, must not take things amiss, or be unduly exacting, nor be too easily incensed, lest their obstinacy and passion bring misfortune, disease, or even death, upon their hidden pledge. If they thus surrender themselves to the goodness and mercy of God, they have the consolation of God that will set his angel over them, who will guard them in all their ways.

MORNING PRAYER

Lord God, the Father, what thou hast created; Lord God, the Son, what thou hast redeemed; Lord God, the Holy Ghost, what thou hast hallowed, I commend into thy hands. To thy holy name let honor, glory, praise, and thanks be given in the morning hour, and in all eternity. Amen.

O thou gracious, good, and merciful God, who art thyself the light before whom there is no change of the light and the darkness, I thank thee from the bottom of my soul that thou hast guarded me this night so mercifully, and hast suffered me again to behold the gladsome light of morning. O thou light of my soul! Shed a brighter radiance into my heart this morning, that it may strengthen my love of thee, and my hope and trust in thee. Sanctify my soul, that I may converse with thee this day; may think of thee, rejoice in thee, and enjoy the consolation of thy bounty. Grant that I may not willfully sin against thee this day, but may serve thee in holiness, and walk before thee in the righteousness of the children of God. Set thy most holy presence before my eyes, that I may be the more encouraged to persevere in sanctification, and not to offend thee. I commend to thee my life and limbs—my every step and tread. Thou, O God of all goodness and mercy, hast placed me in a peculiar condition, in which I need thy particular care and assistance. Therefore I humbly beg and pray, O thou protector of thy children, guard my going out and my coming in; let thy angel lead me by the hand, that I may not slip or fall, be wounded, or do harm to my limbs, and thereby also to the fruit of my body. Defend me, uphold me, preserve me. Drive away all that is hurtful to me, and may the good spirit guide me on even paths. Let me live to see the close of this day under thy protection, when I will joyfully thank thee for all the benefits thy mercy has vouchsafed unto my body and my soul. Now the Lord bless me, and preserve me; the Lord let his face shine upon me, and be gracious unto me; the Lord lift up his countenance over me, and give me peace. The grace of the Father protect me, the love of Jesus cover me, and the comfort of the Holy Spirit be with me now and at all times. Oh bless me in my sleep and waking. Oh, bless my every step and tread! Bless me in every undertaking. Pour every blessing on my head. Give me the experience of thy grace, and ne'er avert thy loving face. Amen.

HYMN

1. See the gladsome morn advances
   As the night retreats away,
And upon my inner senses
   Jesus brings returning day.
With him I have this night slept,
With him I have vigil kept,

With him I have borne all sadness,
With him I will share all gladness.

2. Guard my steps, where'er I travel,
   Jesus! send thy angels fleet—
Every danger to unravel,
   E'er it grapples with my feet.
What I bear beneath my heart
Thy great goodness did impart;
Let it thrive, what thou hast given,
As I would myself have thriven.

3. Keep me safe, serene, and quiet,
   Let no frights disturb my peace,
And no bitter passions riot
   Plunge me into fell disease.
Let thy lovely Jesus form
Comforter in every storm
Come, before my eyes to hover,
From my sight all ills to cover.

4. From my thoughts he shall not wander,
   Jesus still belongs to me.
On his grace I still shall ponder,
   He is mine, where'er I be.
From the morning to the night
Never will I leave his sight.
When again the evening closes,
My glad soul on him reposes.

The Woman with Child Offers
Up Her Evening Prayer

EXHORTATION

Oh, how great is God's bounty, whenever he permits a human being to reach the close of a day in safety; when he may say on retiring to his rest, I lie and sleep in peace! Oh, what a glorious rest it is to go to bed at peace with God, at peace with conscience, in peace and comfort of body! Then may a man say in praise of the triune God:

212

The Lord hath done great things with me, wherefore I rejoice. If he falls asleep with a grateful heart, and with the praise of God on his lips, his nightly rest will not lack God's blessing. In the same manner women with child, when they have safely completed the day, ought to raise their hearts, their eyes, and their lips to God, to thank God for their preservation, for his goodness and protection, and to recommend themselves to his continued care.

1. They must cry to God to preserve them from fright and accident, because sudden frights often expose pregnant women to great danger.

2. They must beseech him to guard them from sickness and pain.

3. They must pray to him to keep the wings of his mercy constantly extended over them and the fruit of their bodies.

EVENING PRAYER

Gracious, loving, and merciful God! I appear in thy most holy presence with a happy heart. Lord, how precious is thy goodness, that men rest trustfully under the shadow of thy wings: aye, under the shadow of thy wings have I gone in and out today; under them I have been preserved; no misfortune has approached me, but I have reached the evening in safety. Praised be the love of our heavenly Father, who has carried me in his arms as his child. Praised be Jesus Christ, my Savior, who has led me by the hand, so that no accident could overthrow me. Praised be God, the Holy Ghost, who has not departed from me. O thou Holy Trinity, Father, Son, and Holy Ghost, remain with me this night. Spread out thy goodness, Lord, Lord, over them that know thee, and thy righteousness over the pious. Guard my body and soul from all misfortune; let me converse constantly with thee in sleep, so that I may still be with thee when I awake. Behold, I know no help but in thee, thou God of Israel. Let thy angels watch beside and around my bed, so that nothing may be hurtful to me, and to what thou hast been pleased to bestow upon me. Drive out of my heart all sorrows, evil thoughts, and false imaginations; drive from my bed and from my house everything that can do me harm, or bring me suffering. Thus I lie down in the arms of my God—I sleep in the arms of my Jesus; his left hand is beneath my head, and his right hand covers me. O thou, my Creator, Redeemer, and Sanctifier, be and remain with me. Thou, triune God, art my light and my salvation; whom should I fear? Thou art the strength of my life, whom should I dread? I dread naught, because God is with me; I fear naught because I have Jesus near. When it is dark around me, Jesus is the light of my soul; if fear approaches, the Holy Ghost is my comfort and assistance. Let this night pass happily under thy protection, that I may see the lovely face of the sun, saved, happy, protected, and preserved! My mouth shall praise thee with joy, and thank thee for all the good thou hast done me. As often as my pulses beat this night, my spirit shall embrace thee; as often as my heart is moved, it shall be my desire to cry everywhere, with a loud voice: O Jesus, Jesus, thou art mine, and I am thine forever. Thus then will I fall asleep in thine arms, O Jesus! Thy providence shall be my covering, thy mercy my couch, thy breast my pillow, and my dreams the happiness flowing from the word of light, which thy spirit pours into my heart. Amen.

HYMN

1. Though the sun remains no longer
   On my path his rays to shed,
Jesus' light glows all the stronger,
   Which he casts upon my bed
Say am I not well bethought,
When around my midnight cot
Jesus' hands my slumbers lighten?
Now no harm my soul can frighten.

2. All myself will I surrender
   Jesus to thy guardian thought,
Bless the coming life so tender,
   Thy almighty hand has wrought.
All that is so dark to me
Thy prevailing eye can see
Thou thyself the gift hast granted
Do thou keep what thou hast planted.

3. Evening finds me very weary
   And I long for sweet repose;
Jesus' voice is soft and cheery,
   And his arms around me close.
Bless them all that share my home,
And the stranger soon to come;

Never, never let it perish,
In thy own fond bosom cherish.

4. Keep it safe from all disaster
    Till the day return again,
And from day to day, dear Master,
    Let it thrive, and know no pain.
While it rests beneath my heart
Never let thy love depart;
And if thou my love believest,
Let me see the gift thou givest!

Radical Pietism

Gottfried Arnold
1666–1714
&
Gerhard Tersteegen
1697–1769

Gottfried Arnold

FROM

THE MYSTERY OF THE DIVINE SOPHIA*

1700

On the Arrival and First Voice of Sophia in Man

Above all, O man, know and believe that this noble Sophia is not distant from you, but is able and wishes to be much closer to you than you are to yourself, if you do not drive her off. For, behold, the Lord drew her out upon all his works, upon all flesh, according to its measure.

Therefore, every spirit created according to God's image may find the divine virgin in himself and in his being. She is given once again after the fall to all men in a secret spiritual way and wishes to bring each person once again to his former life in her.

This virgin was in the first man, in his innocence, as a seed of his spiritual birth (as it is described), so closely bound and wedded to him that she dwelt in Adam in the breath or living spirit which God had blown into him (as into the divine image), and awakened in him all imaginable joy and desire. Adam should have been satisfied with this and willing to live with this pure bride in paradise; he ought also to have remained desirous only for God.

However, after he turned outward with doubt and desire toward creatures and became earthly, the divine Sophia turned away from

---

*Translated from Gottfried Arnold, *Das Geheimnis der göttlichen Sophia* (Leipzig, 1700).

him and from the whole of the earth, and instead of a heavenly bride he received an earthly carnal Eve which God created for him in his sleep (which was already an indication of his weakening) from a rib. . . .

Although this wisdom was taken away through sin and no longer dwelt in corrupted man in a paradisiacal manner, nevertheless she did not cease to speak to each child of Adam internally in their hearts and to bid them reestablish the lost treasure. She did this out of deep love for her ancient throne and place according to God's commandments.

This call came about through her secret moving, remembering, punishing, calling, and attracting activity in the soul which no man can deny nor completely rule out, but can hinder and can put out for a time. By this activity all blindness, error, and hardness arises. And since everything occurred in the soul, indeed, against human activity and intention, the divinity of this matter is more certain and its acceptance or rejection by each and every person must be considered more significantly and more carefully. For it is nothing other than a soft and loving breath and inner word in the soul which comes to the soul unlooked for and unsought if it is internally still. Indeed, it is so subtle and peaceful an inner word that it can be put out with the smallest outbreak of gross nature in word or works, indeed, even by thoughts which otherwise in themselves might not be evil. . . . In this first seeking [of Sophia in the soul], Sophia's proposal is nothing other than a divine call to obedience. . . . If anyone wishes to know when and at what age this hidden inner speech and seeking is accustomed to occur, the answer is to be found in the Scriptures in which it states that it occurs from youth on and that it remains with a person so long as the person does not oppose it. . . .

Concerning the General Means to Achieve Wisdom

All this happens to each soul in the world at certain times, almost without distinction. But men can be divided into two parties and groups, the first and largest group of which strives against the tug of wisdom; the second group, however, is obedient and therefore receives a special grace.

The person who wishes to belong to this second group has need of nothing more (to speak simply) than to be true and faithful through and in God and to do that which the spirit of wisdom indicates to him to do according to his living word. There are no further demands and commandments or running and walking in one's own powers and endeavors needed for those who search for wisdom in great earnestness and zeal. Nevertheless, it is not useless to note the thoughts of the early fathers concerning the means for achieving wisdom.

They warn, first of all, that one is not alone to seek wisdom in the dead letter and, therefore it also follows, not merely in this written account without active fighting and prayer for it. One ought not to strive for it outside of oneself but in the inner ground in which wisdom first testifies to itself. At the same time one is to step down with one's will and to sink into wisdom.

Perfect wisdom, the ancients say, God gives to each person as he wills.... For the man who wishes to receive wisdom, however, an open and prepared heart is required. Wisdom seeks only those who are worthy of her (Wis. 6:17), and thus she does not give herself to each person without distinction, and no unworthy person dare comfort himself in her, but only a newborn, pure, and holy spirit can endure and unite itself with this most subtle, pure, being.... The first and chiefest grade which leads us to wisdom is a pure heart free from all lower things....

This noble, loving being is very desirous and willing to meet a person in that person's simplest beginning of denial and to kiss him in his soul. However, if he does not, in a completely uncommon and heroic way, test his resignation from all creatures and especially lay aside his own self-love, he will not be able to experience any further and higher step in wisdom's glory.

What can come to you, O beloved spirit, from such a holy reflection and search other than a vision into wisdom's infinite glory and an experience of her love together with all necessary attractions of her glorious beauty? ... This desire and hunger of the soul's spirit is fate, by which it finally grasps hold and does not leave aside wisdom....

On the Special Means for Union with the Divine Sophia

When a fervid lover of his spiritual mother-bride, given to him by the Father, has begun, then the Holy Spirit who teaches truly will open one thing after another to him if he does not tire in prayer and obedience; these openings will occur in manifold circumstances, occurrences, temptations, and troubles. . . .

He who learns to know wisdom will first see and note that she is good and loving, an image of the goodness of God himself (Wis. 7:26). . . . The first and most necessary thing for such a soul is to duly hold to the Father and crawl to him in prayer. . . .

In such prayer the Holy Spirit will teach the soul to grasp and to draw nearer to the most gracious guide to the throne herself. . . .

[Also necessary is obedience toward wisdom, pious fear and pure love for her.]

On the First Activities of Wisdom in the Soul Particularly Its Working of Conviction and Its Discipline

. . . As soon as this beam of eternal glory enters the soul, or rather stirs itself up once again internally in the soul in which it lay hidden and extinguished as unfruitful, then it becomes active and endeavors to convince the person about his misery whereby it stirs up internally the following directives.

First, it punishes the person, makes him troubled and sorrowful internally concerning all that is evil as often as it finds him in such thoughts, words, or deeds. This the Scripture calls punishment or conviction, shame, and judgment. . . . Wisdom does not treat the soul other than in great earnestness and sharp strictness so that she can bring the soul to true changing of its mind or repentance (metanoia). . . . And after the mind is made pliant, docile, and obedient by this first tug of wisdom, wisdom moves on in a consoling way with its first faithful discipline. . . .

This discipline of wisdom is nothing other than the continual reminding, warning, admonishing, and calling in the mind; in her fervid endeavor for our salvation she moves continually in our soul as long as we do not hinder her. . . . Oh, how blessed, joyous, and peaceful is the spirit which continually holds this teacher in itself and renews obedience with its heartfelt thoughts. . . .

Concerning the General Teaching of Wisdom

After all this necessary discipline and first milk which the soul receives, Sophia takes up stronger nourishment to nourish the soul and to change it into a new life. After the internal ear through so much knocking has been opened and made ready to accept and the mind has been bowed by this and the will has been truly bound, wisdom is accustomed willingly to lay her treasure in a purified heart and to trust to it more and greater things than one could ever hope for. . . .

Therefore wisdom does not only call completely simple and foolish people to herself, but she also directs her children with her teaching. She has present with herself good counsel and knowledge (or according to the translation of the Septuagint, she harbors such) (Prov. 8:12) and she will allow the doctrine to shine forth yet more and make it to shine out afar as a morning light, and she will pour this out as prophesy (Ecclus. 24:32–33). . . .

The manner and fashion of this secret instruction is not to be expressed with words. This is especially so because it is a secret work. David himself said that God gives wisdom to be known in hidden ways (Ps. 51:7). . . . The ancients set forth this fact from experience: The soul as a spirit is enlightened by the spiritual light of the pure wisdom of God as the essence of air is enlightened by the moving light. Wisdom is an unblemished light as the clarity of the sun; thus it shines upon human hearts just as the sun shines upon the eyes.

From this it follows that wisdom comes inwardly in the soul and one must not look around for it with external eyes as a poor man in blindness is accustomed to do and to be deceived yet more by blind leaders. Wisdom is accustomed to give herself or to give her direction in holy souls so that they might receive her (Wis. 7:27, 8:17). . . .

Thus, an eager lover must seek her inwardly in his mind where alone is open to him the source of understanding, and what is divine and saving is to be revealed. For the spirit alone establishes a deep grounding and not only searches everything for itself but leads the new creature of man into itself as well and teaches it through its inner power and clarity.

A person visited by wisdom is able to find everything which is necessary for him, truthfully, purely, and exactly, and is to discover everything in her mirror concerning which one, except for wisdom, would never have known existed. . . .

The more that one follows in this light and grows further in the new birth through it, the more wisdom comes to him. A mind, newmade to all divine powers, sees in itself the character of the image of the divine form and knows its secret and the understanding beauty of

223

similitude with the Lord. It also achieves the treasures of the inner law and the wisdom which teaches for itself and learns from itself.

This is indeed spoken of a higher grade of the new birth, when the new light-body from the spirit of Jesus or of wisdom is formed essentially in man and is revealed as a fire-claiming, enlightening being out of which comes all glory, and thus the greatest enlightenment. . . .

On the Union of Wisdom and the Spiritual Birth of Her Children

Among the ancients, those who reached the first step of their glory described it in living color and testified with great joy concerning their union. They said that she takes up all those who seek her. The person who directs his soul to her will discover that she goes directly into the soul (Wis. 10:17) and establishes in it her inheritance (Ecclus. 24:7).

Indeed, in this she is very careful and concerned that the person does not embrace her light according to any as yet unmortified powers of his self-love and possession by which he might gain for himself more damage than good. As a result she gives herself to him with her holy loving power so that the soul will become a true dwelling place and seat of wisdom, as the ancients tell us.

One can never grasp her again according to his old birth and nature, but she only dwells in the new or reborn man in whom she shines and goes forth as a bright ray of light and yet may be so little grasped by nature or held in self, as the sun in a metal which it makes hot, melts, and changes, gives itself over to changing this.

As a result, wisdom remains eternally free in herself and an unbound being. She remains in herself and yet goes forth into holy souls (Wis. 7:27). The soul discovers her with its spiritual powers so essentially and truly in itself, as truly as the external, gross man feels visible food in himself when he has eaten it. At the same time one may not possess anything of her as his own, but she remains prepared and ready for his pure desire and love. If he clings to her in innocent purity and rejoices with his obedience, she remains and works her wonders.

Among these wonders one of the first is that she makes the soul a better form for purification and smelting. . . .

According to every opportunity the spirit moves forward so that that which expressed itself as false counsel in the mind of the old man is cast out. But, above all, he ceaselessly corrects at that time all thoughts, words, and deeds, sends out a burning zeal together with a painful biting sorrow over all the evil in his heart, lays the old Adam in death and dust after he with Christ has completely given up his blood and lost his powers on the cross. . . . Out of this arises a very remarkable change and improvement of man, and with joy he actively purifies his heart from the manifold evil crimes and sinful spots, and he looks toward a newly created divine will.

What can follow from this except the long-wished-for revelation and birth of the new creature in which wisdom as the only true mother brings forth her best? She comes down into the soul for no other end than to begin this, her spiritual birth-work, to give all the means for nourishment belonging to it and not to stop until Christ is formed in the heart according to his pure humanity.

At this, if one notes in his innermost being the firm movement of the Holy Spirit, one must give his faith purely over to the divine loving will, live closely according to all the directions given to him internally, and not neglect anything which is required for the development of the maturing new life which strives so fiercely with death and breaks forth in victory. In this resigned passiveness, Sophia gives herself to the soul with her life-water and love-water, and the spirit itself moves with soft workings in such a life-seed through an unspeakable pull of grace, and allows the soul no peace until it is born to its likeness in a spiritual way so that the dead image of God is once again reached and man is once again given his earlier heavenly being with all divine characteristics. . . .

Concerning the Spiritual Marriage with Sophia

I come now to a matter which is very weighty, certain and essential, but it is also too great for my understanding and sense and beyond words. . . . In the beginning or principles . . . Sophia is known inwardly in the soul under the image and the character of a worthy and earnestly loving mother. . . .

If the soul remains in all truth giving honor and obedience and has demonstrated and legitimated the honesty of its love through many hard battles against sin as through many actual tests, then Sophia immediately exchanges her earnest form with a more delightful one and takes up the soul as a wife of virginity (Ecclus. 15:2).

In every way she must proceed carefully and wisely after she was so tricked by the unfaithfulness of the first man and so shamefully troubled. For this reason she leaves only certain secrets, love-looks, kisses, and other vivifying marks of such protecting joy and pure virginal love-spirits as certain guides. The full marriage day, however, and the public consummation of such a marriage she keeps until man's full perfection. . . .

We are here speaking only of the first taste or pledge of the coming full marriage. . . . Only angelic tongues can describe the final marriage feast and only the spirits of perfect, righteous persons can enjoy it. However, the sweet beams of her love are also in the very first kiss and are experienced as so piercing that they set the soul-spirit in an undescribable joy.

In truth, all the desire of youth and all the supposed fulfillment of physical marriage are less than nothing with reckoned against this heavenly joy. It is an actual power of paradise when the most beautiful bride meets a spirit. It is a sweet transport and filling of all the powers of the soul and the sinking of all thoughts into the flood of love.

Whoever this dove takes into her lap she gives the oblation of an untroubled peace and of the certain hope of all certainty in the kiss of her mouth. She lets him experience all her freedom and supplies as much of her life-giving balm as he will have. One can then lay consoled on her breast and drink to satisfaction, and all her pure powers are open to draw one into a paradisiacal love-play in her.

In her full indwelling there is pure desire. Nevermore can an earthly bride be more lovely, adorned, and purer to a man than this greatly praised virgin. Indeed, there is not the least comparison between the two in this case. . . .

O pure joy, come and visit the soul which belongs to you more often, and let it no longer fail in your loving attraction, for although in your possession we dare neither desire anything of it nor speak of it, nevertheless you see yourself, O most beautiful among women, in our rude nature, in this troubled valley of our pilgrimage. Therefore, make us worthy evermore for your secret indwelling, my only and pure turtledove!

Gottfried Arnold

FROM

HISTORY AND THE DESCRIPTION OF MYSTICAL THEOLOGY OR OF THE MYSTICAL DOCTRINE OF GOD*

PREFACE TO THE NONPARTISAN READER

The material for this book I collected over a period of time with the material for my *Church History;* I had it at hand and as a result could more easily bring it into order. In the last number of years my intention has stood firm that I would no longer enmesh myself in purely historical and other similar matters or use my time up in such ways. An understanding reader will fully be able to know from this book that it leads more into a true knowledge and love of the invisible divinity than into a mere historical knowledge.

I will not make any excuses concerning the material itself or the method of expression and other matters because such excuses would be unnecessary for wise persons and those who fear God, whereas for erring persons and those of wordly learning such discussions would not be worthwhile since those people purposely do not wish to know anything better than their own traditions and rational conclusions.

There is only one thing I must not leave undone; I must endeavor earnestly to give nonpartisan references concerning the mystical material and persons. I have also noted necessarily the shortcomings of these. However, in mind I was continually held to a Christian

---

*Translated from Gottfried Arnold, *Historie und Beschreibung der Mystichen Theologie* (Franckfurt am Main, 1703).

moderation and discretion so that I would not become enmeshed in the horrid attacks which have, until this point, been poured out by many against mystical theology. I direct my attention much more to the good intention of those mystics, rather than reflect on any one of their shortcomings.

This is the reason why enlightened spirits will find in many passages of this book mellow and at the same time less strict judgments concerning specific matters or persons than often appears to be allowable by the narrow censoriousness of the pure spirit of Protestantism. However, I wish to state specifically and once and for all that I do not wish to give up in the least way the pure evangelical doctrine; I wish to teach the truth of Jesus Christ and not narrow it in the least. Rather, I desire to live, to teach, and to believe much more according to the one rule of the new creation in Christ, and I also wish that others will do likewise and I counsel them to do so in an earnest manner. Aside from this truth, I consider and always will consider all other human self-made and self-chosen things, be they ever so good and holy, to be dirt and falsity against the superabundant knowledge of the one master. For a nonpartisan student of Christ, each teacher must be and can be nothing other than beloved and held in honor in each part, but nevertheless for such a person the essential truth of Christ remains beloved alone and above all things.

The person who allows this one ground to be laid and made firm in his mind through the Scriptures of Christ will be able to use this material with profit. Without this and aside from it such persons will be able to have only images and conceptions in their brain rather than the truth and the light impressed in their hearts and wills. I must, however, leave all this to the wisdom and love of God which rules over everything and counsel the reader uprightly toward this. Written at Quedlinburg in the year 1701.

CHAPTER ONE
*Concerning True Theology or the Doctrine of God Held
among the First Christians Generally*

I call this book not only a history, that is, a mere recounting of things which are related to mystical theology at all times, but also a description. By a description is meant that the material and the essence itself of matters belonging to the subject are studies, and everything which serves the topic specifically is brought before the reader.

Every spirit loving the truth will immediately accept this and remember his duty, namely, that it is not enough to remain satisfied with the external history and mere knowledge as the chaff, but that one must seek and embrace the material itself and the kernel with one's interior powers and virtues in earnest fashion. And that he must use this material so as to taste the highest good as we will soon see.

It is known that the word *theology* chiefly and generally means speech or doctrine of God himself or from God himself. It comes from the Greek words *"theos"* and *"logos,"* a word or speech; it includes not only Christian doctrine generally as it does among the Latin fathers, and especially the doctrine of the trinity as it does among the Greek fathers, but also, more particularly, the doctrine of Jesus Christ and his divine nature.

In addition it is not unknown how the Apostle John in writing down the revelation which he had from Christ is particularly called "ho theologos" or the one taught by God, because he revealed and glorified in the most mighty manner the divine glory of the Son of God as a *theokērux* and *theophoros,* one who had the divinity living in him and therefore was able to proclaim it as the early fathers said.

And because the early fathers with their doctrine and theology say in particular how by it they were able to glorify the honor and majesty of God alone, they called those theologians, or speakers about God, who had been made powerful to do this by the Holy Spirit. Among others, Gregory Nazianzus held this title among the Greeks which they had otherwise generally given to all the prophets, apostles, and men of God as those who had been taught directly by God and were witnesses of teaching, and the Holy Scriptures themselves they called theology, or God-teaching.

Furthermore, because doctrine concerning God in himself is for the most part hidden to reason and too high for it, the truly learned of God cast aside the simplistic misuse of the carnal scholastic theologians and understood under the name of theology generally the secret wisdom of God revealed to the faithful alone. Thus a theologian was understood to be one who had his conversation with God or from God, and also a mystical teacher of hidden things who spoke the word of God himself. Again, he was understood to be one who saw the divine things, and theology was thus described as a power of God which is full of mystical life and nourishes the spirit with the Word of God, as well as betrothing an understanding soul by the holy prophets with the Word of God (Christ Jesus) to an unbreakable union by which one may finally be like God.

From this usage of the early fathers one can see further how a man, learned and enlightened by God, can be truly and must truly be called a theologian even if he is not a cleric or an academic school teacher, a doctor or a professor (according to the statements which arose during the fall of the church). Each true Christian or person anointed by the Spirit of God must learn and thus be a theologian if he wishes to know what is given to him by God and will again make him holy (1 Thess. 4:9, 1 John 2:20, 27). In this the special duty of the servants of the word is not set aside or weakened, but is rather made strong and upright if the whole people prophesy and all Christians are true Christian theologians, persons taught by God, the friends of God and the ones known of my God.

Like this true understanding of the word *theology*, similarly *theosophy* signifies wisdom of God or from God, because the mystical doctrine of God is a gift of the Holy Spirit, stirred up by God himself, goes with God, and is common to God himself and his saints as this word declares. Therefore Dionysius [the Areopagite] at the beginning of his writing calls on the holy trinity as one looking for Christian theosophy or the wisdom of God. After his own time he was called by others the divinely wisest among the teachers of God.

[Protestants have used the word *theology*. Its value is clear once one sets aside the polemical statements of the scholastic theologians.]

All of the holy antiquity of the church agrees with the Holy Scriptures on this matter, namely that to true theology or teaching about God there belongs an actual enlightenment, teaching, and influence from God himself, and that this must be found among teachers as well as students. This can be demonstrated in its place concerning the enlightenment. Gregory, the theologian who was mentioned above as one taught of God, describes the theologian in the following way: The best theologian is not one who has found everything (for our book does not embrace everything), but the person who is most impressed by it and who has gathered in himself the greatest impression or part of it. Elsewhere he gives this counsel: Do you ever wish to be a theologian or be worthy of the divinity? Keep the commandments and enter into their intentions. By this, he designates a theologian present before God or directed to God's community in Godliness.

Another teacher speaks of this, saying that all doctrine about God is communicated only from the love of Jesus as the mediator through whom man must receive everything from God. He adds that no one can study theology other than the person fitted for God, drawing near to the Lord, and following after Christ. This is very close to what Luther knew against all contemporary scholastic patterns: I know of no counsel other than a humble prayer to God which will give us doctorates in theology. The Pope, emperors, and universities can make us doctors of the fine arts. But be certain no one will make you a doctor or a teacher of the Scriptures except the Holy Spirit in heaven alone as Christ said in John 6:45. And following Luther, another Lutheran preacher says salvific theology consists in interior illumination in which the morning star rises in our hearts (2 Pet. 1:19), and God gives a bright beam in the heart (2 Cor. 4:6).

The basis for what we have been saying was set down by the Lord Jesus himself in his statements regarding the great light of the new covenant: True Christians or the anointed ones are all taught by God according to John 6:45. . . . This is also upheld by the ancient teachers who called St. Anthony expressly "theodidakton" even though he was an unlearned and common man. They said in fact: He could not even read but he understood the Scriptures by hearing them and by careful reflection on them.

The early fathers earnestly stressed this learning of God without which no one can be a Christian, let alone a teacher. . . .

[This theology comes from God Himself.] Therefore, they looked not merely to a mediated doctrine of God but chiefly to an unmediated one, without which a mediated doctrine would not be enough. On the part of man they demanded nothing other than faith and belief. . . . All human arts and endeavors they held as not useful and demanded only God's own activity. . . .

Concerning the necessary practice of true learning of God, one is to note that it flows freely from the divine light as from a true fountain, ceaselessly going forth. As a result the early fathers knew of no other theology than of the fruitful and active and saving theology so long as false, mere literal, theological, polemical, and scholastic concerns were as yet unknown.

Those taught by God called theology the special gift of the grace of God which above all other gifts inflamed the heart and awakened it to love God's goodness. Theology was the first morning fruit of the grace of God, and therefore it also brought the first fruit into the heart. It brought it about that one willingly and joyously set aside all the loves of this world because in place of vain desires, one now had much greater treasure in the Word of God. Thereafter, it so inflamed the mind with a fire that nature was changed, and one came into the community of the serving spirits. They confessed that a theologian was attracted and made alive by the words of God and that he endeavored to remain freely living according to them and to tame his affections accordingly. The Word of God is pure (Ps. 12), and he who is made firm by the experience of knowledge in practice has overcome all affections.

... If one endeavors to study the intention of the first Christians, it is clearly indicated in the last chapters of the first and second books of the *Church History* how simple, pure, and yet divine and powerful their theology was. Until then, the clergy and their book-learning and worldly ways which they learned from the heathens, along with their merely reasoned wisdom, had not been mixed in nor troubled the clear water. The final result of this under the great fall was a stinking cesspool full of contention, hatred, vain honor, human concern, and falsification. See the *Church History*, book 16. . . .

We need not continue to reflect on this unspeakable misery of contemporary theology, but we wish only for a short time to delight in the first purity and simplicity which a lover of the ancient Scriptures expressed in opposition to today's abomination . . . this simplicity of the first theology was defended for a long time and in spite of persecutions remained pure for a relatively long time. One can still find the testimony of it in Tertullian: There is one rule of faith which is alone unmoved and is not to be bettered, namely that one believes in almighty God and the Creator of the world and in his Son Jesus Christ (he here expresses the statements of the so-called Apostolic Confession). If this law of faith remains, all other things relating to purity and the walk of life will be improved in that the grace of God works and washes to the end. . . .

And this was the simple pure truth held by the early fathers which they sought alone with a pure holy mind. Therefore, they described truth as an informing knowledge of all divine things into which a pure heart gave itself with denial of all its own sensual judgments, and by which the glory of the divine image was again revealed. From these and similar descriptions, it can be seen how far that praiseworthy truth or pure teaching has been left behind in the polemical activity of the scholastics and their battles over words, or if it is still retained, it is retained in the form of mere knowledge or is sought in a pious appearance without Jesus Christ and outside of him. True religion is not a sectarian ban, made certain from statements and traditions brought forth out of the human will as so-called articles, but it is, in short, the true direct path to the lost fatherland, or to speak more clearly, the knowledge of oneself as one was before and after the fall and then of God in Christ Jesus through the Holy Spirit as our highest source and goal, by which we are to come again out of the manifoldness and contention into the One.

Moving toward this goal, the whole true learning of God moves preeminently and only into the interior, namely toward the reestablishment of the divine interior image, as a famous ancient teacher once said: The work of theological instruction is only to make man once again similar and like God insofar as it is possible to do so through grace, so that he will stand and know nothing more than God on the basis of his achieved glory. To this the whole of the Holy Scriptures gives testimony, when it teaches how the base and the matter of the whole apostolic doctrine is only the revelation of the kingdom of God inwardly in us (Luke 17:28 . . .) and moreover by Christ in us himself as the chief of the members (Col. 1:27 . . .). Therefore, one must wait and receive wisdom, knowledge, and learning about God from the Spirit of Christ alone to this end. . . .

234

Gottfried Arnold

EMBLEMATIC INSERT
TO ARNOLD'S
*VITAE PATRUM**
1700

TRANSLATION OF EMBLEM

Upper and lower margin: He who does not enjoy Jesus Christ as the Way, the Truth and the Light will be darkened, cunning, and in error even if he appears good.

Hill top, left to right, top to bottom: glory, righteousness, power, love, wisdom, consolation, strength, glory [*sic*], peace, love [*sic*], joy, life, much enjoyment.

Left-hand list, top to bottom (to gate): Outpouring of the Spirit, Isa. 11: (1) of the Lord, (2) of wisdom, (3) of understanding, (4) of counsel, (5) of strength, (6) of knowledge, (7) of the fear of the Lord; reception of the spirit of (1) love, (2) power, (3) chastity, 2 Tim. 1:7.

Right-hand list, top to bottom (to gate): Fruits of the Spirit, Gal. 5:22: Perfection, vision of God, rest in God, union, inner prayer, patience, long-suffering, goodness, meekness, truth, hiddenness, humility, modesty, separation, resignation, abstinence, chastity, purity of heart.

Center line, from gate to top: I will place my law in their hearts (Heb. 8:10); For the righteous there is no law (1 Tim. 1:9).

Gate: The words of the new birth; John 3:5; Matt. 7:13.
___
*Reprinted from Gottfried Arnold, hrsg., *Vitae Patrum* (Halle, 1732²).

Left side, top to bottom (from gate to first branch): (12) peace, (11) light, (10) victory and new life, (9) death of old man, (8) temptations, (7) refreshments, (6) purification, (5) daily repentance, (4) change of mind, (3) faith, (2) kneeling before God, (1) knowledge of oneself.

Right side, from top to bottom (from gate to first branch): (12) joy, (11) power, (10) breakthrough to divine birth, (9) birth pains, (8) battle with flesh, world, and devil, (7) spiritual gifts, (6) renewal, (5) spiritual practices, (4) battle against sin, (3) prayer, (2) conversion to the Father, (1) submission of heart.

Center trunk (bottom to gate): This is the way, in this we have the safest way; Isa. 30:21; I am the way, John 14:6, The holy way, Isa. 35:8.

Left branch: The way of Cain and Balaam, Jude 5, 2 Pet. 2:15; neither to the right [sic].

List below left branch (bottom to top): reason, blindness, lack of faith, certainty, despising chastity, pride, lust of eyes, lust of flesh, great hypocrisy, falsehood, disobedience, idolatry, false worship, false gospel, factiousness, polemics, falsely praised disciplines, sin, wrath, envy, covetousness, murder, theft, magic, lies [. . .].

Right branch: According to the statutes of the world and not according to Christ, Col. 2:8; Gal. 5:4; nor to the left [sic].

List below right branch (bottom to top): hypocrisy, pharisaic appearance, external carriage, casting aside interiority, false zeal, self-deception, one's own works and walk, spiritual pride, *opera operata* [sacraments practiced as effective aside from the spiritual state of the receiver], self-chosen worship, knowledge of forms [alone], self-praise, good intentions [alone], human laws, self-will, murmurings, disbelief, cowardice, fear, disobedience, haughty reasoning, empty talk, false consolation, doubt.

Lower left corner: Living waters Jer. 2:13.

Lower right corner: The vine of Sodom in the land of Gomorrah. Book of Moses.

Gottfried Arnold

SELECTED POEMS*

TRUE SOLITUDE

Let not your sense scatter this and that;
Your spirit must be completely gathered in God.
Soul, if you are to rejoice in a deeper peace
Enter continually into the One.
There you will find an altar and temple to
contemplate
There the priest stands continually adorned
before God.
Leave yourself and your self-centeredness
And you will in the world be freed from the
world.

ONE CHRISTIAN, ONE MIRACLE;
MANY CHRISTIANS, MANY MIRACLES

I dwell as yet in this world,
Yet I am already lifted up to Heaven.
I carry a yoke which falls to me.
I am no angel and yet can praise God.
I am called a needy child
And yet am worthy to receive this
In which one find nothing but holiness.
I already have him and yet I must desire him.
His cross grows light and yet is heavy.

*Translated from Gottfried Arnold, *Poetische Lob-und Liebes Sprüche* (Leipzig, 1700),
no. 7 ("True Solitude"); Gottfried Arnold, *Göttliche Liebes-Funcken* (Frankfurt am Main,
1968), no. 13 ("One Christian"); ibid., no. 87 ("Walk with Jesus"); ibid., no. 144 ("Hiddenness"); ibid., no. 44 ("Soul Refreshes Itself"); Gottfried Arnold, *Neue Göttliche Liebes-
Funcken* (Frankfurt am Main, 1701), no. 1 ("Double Light").

After I am so closely united with him
My heart is full and yet empty:
Full of love, empty of that for which I weep.
I am a man of miracles before others' eyes
And do not know if I count for anything among men.
The power of the Cross has made me a fool.
I marvel that men do not laugh in my face.

WALK WITH JESUS

It is true; outside it is pleasant
Where everything can bedeck itself with flowers.
I, however, go into my house
To walk in all stillness with my lamb.
There the sun shines and the nightingale sings;
There it is green, blossoms come forth, fresh
                                   springs rush out.
There I see nothing but Jesus.
His angelic choir fills all places.
He is the sun, love, song.
As a result hope is renewed and pure waters leap.
Is that not enough for my beautiful walk?
He is also to bring me to paradise.

*   *   *

Hiddenness,
Your sea is so wide
And marvelously deep; I cannot probe its source.
One knows not how to find mass or goal or end
So long as one is in mutability,
Hiddenness.

The Glory,
Which you have prepared,
Prepared here for the children of your love,
Is special. Who preserves this secret
Bears even in the most wretched time,
The Glory.

238

Therefore, the Lord
Conceals what he awakens;
His children always go into hiddenness
Who need fear no judgment
Until finally God reveals the Glory
Which was covered.

He wanders thus
Into holiness
With soft step. He cannot understand this
Who will satisfy himself eagerly with simplicity.
As he otherwise is accustomed to do almost nothing
He wanders.

What blessedness
Is prepared for those
Through whom God seeks honor in their shame!
Obedience breaks through the strongest bonds.
Therefore, a grade of the highest blessedness is
Hiddenness.

THE SOUL REFRESHES ITSELF IN JESUS

Thus the loving companions play together
And in play increase the heavenly flames.
The one increases the desire of the other
And both know nothing except love.
They struggle in love; they give themselves
                              to one another;
The manifold must finally fade into one.
He sings, she plays; he kisses, she rejoices;
He teaches, she listens; he laughs, she jokes.
He says: How eternally are you chosen for me!
She calls: You are born for my joy!
Both double the echo into one
And cry: My friend is perfectly mine.
                              Echo: I mine!
Thus true; thus the divine light increases.

DOUBLE LIGHT

O beam of glory, you our sun,
You the source and fountain of light,
Send us your fire from the joy of your kingdom
Until our spirit is perfected in One.
At the same time ignite us more in your power;
Keep us in your love life.
What your thought creates for our love and peace
Is only given for common use.
Your gospel is for all of us
And must reach out to others
So that they may be truly one in you
Until your knowledge covers the earth.
Ah, draw us completely into your hidden light
Where we will stand before your throne
As if light is broken off for a time;
Let a new beam go out from you.
No wavering moonlight, no erring star
No shadow, no night dare darken us
Here and there eternally we wish eagerly
Only to stand, burn, flourish for your glory.
Thus the doubly bright light will not be darkened.

Gerhard Tersteegen

FROM
SPIRITUAL LETTERS*

Beloved Brother,

It was a most pleasant experience for me to be assured of your thoughts in your letter. . . . I was also pleased to discover that on my part I still stand in the communion of the spirit with you and with all of you praise God. I hope eternally to so remain. . . .

But I wish to turn to a completely different matter than the one raised in your letter. It is most true, dear brother, that, as you say, we find within ourselves what others call an external Babel, which comes from the whore and the beast. It seems to us absurd when we read that Christ's disciples allowed their weak, indeed false, thoughts to go so far from the kingdom of Christ. Many disciples today, however, go even further. How many weeping travelers to Emmaus can one not now find who have spoken much, written much, who have listened, and have hoped that the Savior would establish his kingdom for Israel in the last days, who have shouted out "Hosanna" for this purpose and who now go about sad and downcast because they have found suffering instead of joy. Only if their and our hearts remain justified before the Lord will he meet us in an unknown way on the path of sorrow and place the characteristics of his kingdom and the way for its establishment in us with another tone. Did not also Christ have to suffer in such a manner so as to enter his glory? Too often we seek the kingdom of Christ completely outside of us even though our souls know this is not so. In a like manner, we look for the kingdom of the Devil with Babel, the whore and false prophets as outside of us. As we, unfortunately, know the kingdom of the Devil is outside of us in others just as the kingdom of Christ in its time stands outside of us

*Translated from Gerhard Tersteegen, *Geistliche und erbauliche Briefe über das inwendige Leben und wahre Wesen des Christenthums* (Neue Aufl.; Stuttgart, 1845), I; no. 2, 6, 101, 119; II; no. 5, 144, 150.

241

and needs to be awaited. In a like manner, the cunning man looks outside of himself, sets his mind outside of himself, and thus holds himself away from God. As a result he himself remains blind to the basic knowledge of God in himself as one can well imagine. For both these worlds in totality are also found in us. In our ground is the mystery of evil and the mystery of Godliness; the death of Satan and the death of the Divinity is to be discovered through the spirit.

What appears to the senses of both these parts in the external world is only a growth or twig from the tree, an image, impression, or copy of the original. Everything which is outside of us must be a mirror in which we can find what is inside. This is the reason that enlightened souls so eagerly press for stillness and inwardness. This is also the reason that they interpret and understand everything in nature and in the Scripture so inwardly or, as is said, so mystically. This understanding reason, which only has an eye for images, cannot grasp. It sees the image in the mirror as being exactly as it appears. It sees it as having this or that shortcoming, and so forth. If an enlightened eye says to reason that this image reflects another body, that is, it is related to oneself and one needs only to begin to acknowledge and do away with the spots within oneself so as to make that image pure in itself again, reason would look at this statement as that of a fool, as a foreign and dark teaching.

May the Lord guide us truly into ourselves and open for us the eyes of the mind so as to know ourselves properly. From this action true knowledge of God and all godliness will flow forth from the self. We are corrupted in our very roots. Our will, desires, thoughts, understanding are not only corrupted if they turn to evil intentions, but they are also corrupted in themselves even when they turn toward good intentions. This is spiritual deceit in heavenly things (Eph. 6:12). Therefore, we must remain before the Lord in ourselves as without will, without desire, and so forth, so that the Lord through the pure movements of his grace might live and work in us. Oh, how impure are all our actions and movements! May the whole of our earth remain still before the Lord!

Dearly Beloved Friends and Sisters in the Grace of God,
For some time now I have had an inclination to send you greetings in a letter and although the opportunity which I now have has come very late, I do not wish to let it go by again.

242

I hope that the face of your inner soul's desires is still directed strictly toward Jerusalem so as finally after long crying and thirst to reach that place. We see the face of God here first in faith in the temple of our hearts and finally we will see him in perfection face to face in the upper Jerusalem.

The union with God in the spirit is the goal which we must always keep in our eyes. Whatever leads us to it must be loved and counted as worthy by us; everything else, however, whatever meets us in external things, we must set aside, look upon with great indifference, so that we not be hindered in this one thing needful by allowing some foreign element to enter too deeply into us. Nothing of anything which occurs outside of us is worth being troubled over interiorly. All our concerns in all things must be that we please God and stand by him inwardly.

With this I admonish you and all those who seek God to look up to our true shepherd, Jesus. I also greet N. N. and remain your inclined friend.

Dearly Beloved Friend and Brother in the Grace of God,

Jesus Christ, the true book of life, wishes to imprint himself in the ground of our soul so that through his spirit we might become the written, living copy, and letters of him, which cannot be read by all men. To this end let us study eagerly in this book. There is no danger in reading much in this book. By doing so, one cannot damage the understanding and where this happens it is only seen to so happen in the eyes of the world whose greatest wisdom is foolishness with God. I hope, then, and I wish from the ground of the soul, that the Father of our Lord Jesus will daily more and more transfigure his tongue in us and make us great, so that everything else might become small and nothing, and our heart might be able to say with truth: Jesus, Jesus, nothing but Jesus, be my wish and my goal.

Dearly Beloved Friend in the Grace of God,

You do well to practice prayer in your own manner. Continue on without ceasing and you cannot fail; God will make his own precious promise true for you. Pray and it will be given to you. No art is more simple and easier in the whole world than to pray incorrectly; indeed, it is no art. If we think that we cannot pray, it is a sign that we have not yet properly understood what it is to pray. Prayer is to look to the omnipresent God and to allow oneself to be seen by him. What is now easier and more simple than to turn our eyes upward and to see the light which surrounds us on all sides? God is far more present to us than the light. In him we live, we move, and we are. He penetrates us, he fills us, he is nearer to us than we are to ourselves. To believe this in simplicity and to think of this simply as well as one can, that is prayer. How can it be difficult to allow oneself to be looked after by so kind a physician who knows better what is troubling us than we ourselves know? We have no need to bring this or that, to present ourselves in this way or in that way, or to look too much, or to experience much if we wish to pray, but we need only simply and briefly to say how we are and how we wish to be; indeed, it is not even necessary that we say this, but we need only allow the ever-present good God to see. We are not to let him see only the surface but at every point we are to remain by him and before him so that he can see us correctly and heal us. We must not say anything to him or allow him to see anything other than what is in us. What will be is what he wills. If you find yourself disturbed, dark, with no spiritual experiences, simply tell God, and let him see your suffering; then you have prayed properly. Is there a natural laziness or diffidence at hand? Take heart but a little and turn again with humility to God. If one can remain awake standing better than kneeling, let one fight sleep in such a way; if one can do so better by looking in a book, this is not forbidden him. In short, one must help oneself at a particular time as well as one can, so long as one does not disturb one's chief goal by doing so, namely, prayer, but, rather, always turns oneself again to this task. Deny your own will and desires and you will pray properly and easily. For the Lord will work prayer in your soul through his grace. Remaining in weakness, your trustworthy friend.

Mülheim December 4, 1731

Dearly Beloved Brother in Jesus,
I am greatly humbled knowing that so many dear hearts there and elsewhere have placed so much attention in my paltry life and in its existence in the flesh. Nevertheless their heartfelt love refreshes me and for this the divine love will again refreshen all their hearts.

Looking over my life's calendars I find much red and much black—I wish to say more and greater suffering, sin, foolishness, and weaknesses than others who love me might think possible of me. I call that black which is mispleasing to me in this hour, but no longer frightens me because the red (I mean the overflowing grace and the power of the red blood of Jesus) seems to fall upon and over such dark ground so much more beautifully before my eyes. Oh, may the Lord preserve and continue the inestimable work of his grace in me and in all these dear hearts who are known to me and who are bound to him according to his good hand, so that I and all of us might worthily walk not only with the Lord who purchased us and called us but also with his children of grace among whom we have been justified and have come to dwell so that none of us might remain behind but that my final birthday and that of all of us might be celebrated by the angels and the pious with joy and jubilation!

The children of God have a threefold birthday. Through the first natural birthday they come from the dark prison of their mother's body to the light of this lower world. The child then weeps, but the relatives rejoice. By the second birthday of grace, namely the new birth, they are moved step by step from the constricting dark state of nature into the light of grace. In this situation and very often the child weeps, but the angels in heaven rejoice if only one sinner is repentant.

What we call death the first Christians called and celebrated as a birthday of the martyred and the saints. This third birthday, physical death, frees the children of God from this sad world, from the narrow prison of this body of humiliation and from all suffering and danger to the soul so that they are joyously born and set in the widths of the dear sweet eternity. Likewise, in this last birth things often constrain and look unpleasant for the child of grace, with the result that that child often groans and weeps until he breaks through, but it is all for his best.

As soon as it is over, one can say with Jesus, "It is finished." The angels, like midwives, so to speak, stand prepared at this birth and take the child, blessedly born into blessed eternity, into their arms so as to carry that Nazareth in the lap of Abraham or of God. Then, as children, they rejoice that a child is born to the world of life, love, and joy. A birthday is celebrated. Then one sings as one sings there, and I, I know, have sung along with it: Love, you have made me to your image. And at each verse the dear angels sing their Gloria. Honor be to God in the highest, Hallelujah. And after this I and each of you are to go further with God, not afraid of the short pains of birth (I wish to say the many difficulties of this soon-to-be-ended pilgrim path) but we are to prepare ourselves well and to make ready, knowing that our work is not in vain in the Lord. Amen! Lord Jesus remain with us for the evening will come.

My heart sends greetings and blessings to you all and to each of you individually. May Jesus speak his own Amen as well.

Dearly Beloved Sister,

I have received your first pleasant letter and your last brief note. I have not had the opportunity to write to you earlier. Your answer is enough concerning what I asked you. You can thus let it go, forget it, and remain pleasantly at peace with God. Your desire for greater solitude and stillness is agreeable to God. In his own time God will give to you what is useful for you and pleasing to him; trust in a childlike manner to his fatherly concern for you. For the present however, this desire for solitude should be authenticated among men and human activity so that you do not leave yourself too far away from them, but might gain and preserve the internal sweet solitude and communion with your soul's friend, even at times of unrest. May your heart be your dearest place of retirement where Jesus waits on you and will hold communion with you. Be truly at one with him. He is enough for you. Even in public life strengthen yourself often with upright or peaceful loving looks toward him, even if you have no sensible experience [of him] at all. Such a lack of sensible experience arises for a completely different reason than the one you think. Do not concern yourself much with it. It is enough that you wish to be the Lord's completely. In time such sensible experiences will entice you out far too greatly into a visible joyousness. God, who wishes to keep you in this by himself, sees this. Bear whatever comes in a still and undisturbed manner. Do not become tired or lose hope. God is as near when it is night as when it is day. Believe that he is as close and as friendly and as loving when you do not feel anything of these things as when you do have sensible sensations of them. Love and praise him for he is truly worth loving and praising. The inner inclination of your heart, willing to be completely for God, is the best prayer which the Holy Spirit works. This is the continual fire on the heart's altar. Keep this fire carefully covered over and let it burn in a still manner and reach up to its source. The further it is kept away from other lusts, the freer and more inwardly it burns. The daily thorns of the life of the Cross which lie before your feet are good for the fire if one takes them up willingly.

May God bless your soul and prepare you according to the desire of his heart; this your betrothed brother wishes for you and prays for you from his heart.

Mülheim November 11, 1738

My Dear Brother in the Lord,
I received the delightful letter from yourself and your dear wife along with the enclosures. Our communion and union in the spirit remains and, through the mercy of God, will remain eternally as blessing and refreshment, although in my present circumstances there are few possibilities to gain the external signs of this.

All visible and temporal matters and our abilities to handle them incline to their demise and to loss. What can be seen is transitory; what is unseen is eternal, essential, great, and alone able to give peace, indeed, far more peace than we can even imagine. This is the truth in all situations and also in the matter of social community. Our own community, in spite of its light, is in every way given over to change and circumstance. Insofar as this community has come forth from eternity and is grounded in Jesus, however, it is essential and will remain eternally. The nearer it is to eternity, the nearer it is to God and his children.

Turn inward into your spirit for God is there,
And the influence of his children is near.
If you live in a scattered manner in your thoughts,
Then God and his children will be far from you.

Thus, dear brethren, let us love one another eternally and embrace one another in the spirit of the love of the Lord, and together, as one, offer ourselves to the Lord at his very feet through his grace. Finally, dear brethren, I am a poor man, although I have received much grace and I seem always to be more useless. If according to your circumstances you treat me in the best possible way, I do not know how to speak to you unless God gives me the gift to do so expressly as he did to Balaam's ass. The Lord is close to you interiorly; give yourself to him as a child and he will not leave you without counsel or help in any matter. Therefore I flee unto his mercy. Let us only flee to the

Lamb with bowed head and look more to him than to ourselves. At the beginning grace pours itself forth to our senses in many ways because we are gross; it does so to free us from the gross bonds of the world and sin. It seems as if we have grace in our hand and we work with it bravely and truly according to our knowledge so as to free our souls and become better. Well is it for those who work faithfully in prayer and mortification while it is day and who do not, through laziness or concern with secondary matters, destroy the time and the grace which is given to us to work with and who do not sleep through the bright day. For the night will come when no one can work. Then grace will draw itself away from the sensual powers and will sink deeper into the ground out of which it sprang. Praised be the Lord from eternity to eternity, Amen.

Mülheim 10 April 1739

Gerhard Tersteegen

FROM
SPIRITUAL FLOWER GARDEN*

TO THE READER
God is your beginning. If you have him in essence
You have already read this book through to its end.
If you seek him, read this on your way.
If you are not one who seeks him, it will be of no
use to you.
(I, 1)

PILGRIM'S THOUGHT
My body and the world are a strange dwelling place for me.
I think: Let it go; you soon will be leaving.
He who lives here as a citizen busies himself with great matters;
He calls me wretched and stupid, but is himself a fool.
(I, 281)

TREASURE
Where the treasure is, there is the heart.
If heart, thought, and desire eagerly fly out,
Then one does not yet have/know God; then one lives
wretchedly.
He who possess God in the depth is well satisfied
With this possession; therefore he turns continually
into himself.
(I, 2)

---

*Translated from Gerhard Tersteegen, *Geistliches Blumen-Gärtlein inniger Seelen* (Lancaster, Pa., 1823), *Lo, God is Here!* is a free translation by John Wesley from Terstee-gen's *Geistliches Blumen-Gärtlein* (John Wesley, *Hymns and Sacred Poems* [London, 1739]).

RESIGNATION

One who desires much will be greatly disturbed.
One who wishes for nothing remains ever in stillness.
In consolation and joy, in fear and suffering
Remain resigned in God's peace.

(I, 285)

THE HERO

A silent, consoled heart
In want, need, and pain,
In death and life
given eternally to God.
Where, where is such a hero
To be found in the world?

Without death, one does not come to life,
And not without suffering to death.
If you wish to withstand suffering,
You only cause greater need for yourself.

GOD IS PRESENT

God is present; let us pray
And in honor and fear enter before him.
God is in the midst; let all be silent in us
And bow inwardly before him.
He who knows him and calls him by name
Casts down his eyes;
Come, give yourself once more!

God is present, he whom the cherubim
Serve in obeisance day and night.
All the angelic choirs sing "Holy, Holy"
When they honor this being.
Lord, take our voice
Where we poor persons also
Bring our offering!

We reject willingly all vanity,
All earthly lust and joy;
Our will, soul, body, and life lie
Given as your possession.
You alone are to be
Our God and Lord,
To you the honor is due!

Majestic Being, may I properly praise you
And offer you service in the spirit.
May I, as the angels, always stand before you
And see you as present!
Let me completely
Endeavor to please you,
In all things, dear God!

Air, which feels all, in which we always move,
Ground and life of all things,
Sea without bottom or end, Miracle of all Miracles,
I sink into you.
I in you, you in me
Let me completely disappear,
find and see only you.

You penetrate everything. Allow your beautiful light,
Lord, to touch my face!
As the tender flowers willingly unfold
And in stillness hold the sun,
Allow me as still and happy
To embrace your beams and allow you to work.

Make me simple, inward, resigned,
Soft and in still peace.
Make me pure of heart, that I might see you clearly
In spirit and truth!
Allow my heart
To sweep upward as an eagle
And live only in you.

Lord, come dwell in me; allow my spirit on earth
To be a hallowed place of you;
Come, you close being, glorify yourself in me
That I might continually honor and love you!
Where I go, sit, and stand,
Allow me to see you
And bow before you.

(III, 11)

Württemberg Pietism

Johann Albrecht Bengel
1687–1752
&
Friedrich Christoph Oetinger
1702–1782

Johann Albrecht Bengel

FROM THE
GNOMON OF THE
NEW TESTAMENT*
1742

I. The Word of the living God, which had governed the primitive patriarchs, was committed to writing in the age of Moses, who was followed by the other prophets. Subsequently, those things which the Son of God preached, and the Paraclete spoke, through the apostles, were written down by the apostles and evangelists. These writings, taken together, are termed "Holy Scripture"; and, bearing this title, they are themselves their own best eulogy. For it is because they contain God's words and are the Lord's Book that they are called Holy Scripture. . . . The Scriptures of the Old and New Testaments form a most reliable and precious system of divine testimonies. For not only are the various writings, when considered separately, worthy of God, but they together exhibit one complete and harmonious body, unimpaired by excess or defects. They are the fountain of wisdom which is preferred by those who have tasted it to all the compositions of other men, however holy, experienced, devout, or wise.

II. It follows that those who have been entrusted with so great a gift should use it properly. Scripture teaches its own use, which consists in action. To act it, we must understand it, and this understanding is open to all the upright of heart. . . .

III. Many annotations were not written in the Church of the Old Testament, although the light was more scanty then; nor did learned men think that the Church of the New Testament required to be immediately laden with such helps. Every book, when first pub-

*Reprinted and rev. from Johann Albert Bengel, *Gnomon of the New Testament*, trans. Charlton T. Lewis and Marvin R. Vincent (Philadelphia, 1864), pp. xii–xxxii, 536–545, 932–933.

lished by a prophet or an apostle, bore in itself its own interpretation, as it referred to the existing state of things. The text, which was continually in the mouths of all, and diligently read by all, kept itself pure and intelligible. The saints were not busy with selecting the berries, as if the other parts were to be pruned away; nor with accumulating cumbrous commentaries. They had the *Scriptures*. Those who were learned in the Old and New Testaments were at hand to teach the unlearned.

IV. The purposes which can be attained by commentaries are chiefly the following: to preserve, restore, or defend the purity of the text; to exhibit the exact force of the language employed by any sacred writer; to explain the circumstances to which any passage refers; to remove errors or abuses which have arisen in later times. The first hearers needed none of these. Now, however, it is the office of commentaries to effect and supply them in some measure, so that the hearer of today, with their aid, may be like the hearer in those times who had no such assistance. Our late age has one advantage: It can interpret the prophecies more clearly by the event. Whatever things, of every kind, readers draw from the Scripture, they can and ought all to share with each other; chiefly by word of mouth, but also by written compositions; in such a manner, however, as neither to lessen nor supersede the perpetual use of Scripture itself.

V. Scripture is the life of the church: The church is the guardian of Scripture. When the church is strong, Scripture shines abroad; when the church is sick, Scripture is imprisoned. Thus Scripture and the church exhibit together the appearance of health, or else of sickness; so that the treatment of Scripture corresponds with the state of the church. That treatment has had various ages, from the earliest times down to the present day. The first may be called native or natural; the second, moral; the third, dry; the fourth, revived; the fifth, polemic, dogmatic, topical; the sixth, critical, polyglot, antiquarian, homiletic. That exposition and understanding of Scripture which is at hand in Scripture itself has not yet prevailed in the church. This is clear from our abundant discrepancies of opinion, and our dullness of sight in interpreting prophecy. We are called upon to advance further to such a proficiency in the Scriptures as is worthy of men and of kings, and answers nearly enough to the perfection of Scripture. But men must be prepared for this by passing through trials (whatever else some of the learned may think, who, relying on their own powers alone, suppose that nothing is effected toward the understanding of Scripture by trial and by prayer, but all by mere study; it is trouble that gives understanding). The history and description of those ages would furnish fitting matter for a judicious and useful treatise; but other things are more needed here.

VI. Whosever desires to render any help in interpreting Scripture should examine himself, to know by what right he does it. As far as I am concerned, I did not apply my mind to writing commentaries from any previous confidence in myself; but under divine guidance I was led into it unexpectedly, little by little. The nature of my public duties, which required me, for more than twenty-seven years, to expound the Greek New Testament to students first induced me to make some notes. As their number increased, I began to commit them to paper, and at the suggestion of a certain venerable prelate . . .

VII. I have long since given the name of Gnomon, a modest, as I think, and appropriate title, to these explanatory notes, which perform only the office of an index. . . . The intention is briefly to point out the full force of words and sentences in the New Testament, which, though really and inherently belonging to them, is not always observed by all at first sight, so that the reader, introduced directly into the text, may pasture as richly as possible. The Gnomon points the way well enough. If you are wise, the text itself teaches you everything.

VIII. Human selections of sayings and examples, taken from Scripture, have their use; the study, however, of the sacred volume should not end here; for it should be thoroughly understood as a whole, especially by teachers. In order fully to accomplish this, we ought to distinguish the clearly genuine words of the sacred text from those which various readings render doubtful, so as neither to pass by the words of apostles without profit, nor to expound the words of copyists for those of apostles. I have endeavored to furnish such a text, with all care and fidelity, in my larger edition of the Greek New Testament, published at Tübingen, and in the smaller one published at Stuttgart. . . .

Most learned men shun the spirit, and, consequently, do not treat even the letter rightly. Hence it arises that up to the present time, the most confused and contradictory opinions prevail as to the mode of deciding between conflicting readings, and of combining such decision with the received text. . . . We are convinced, after long and careful consideration, that every various reading may be distinguished and classified, by due attention to the following admonitions:

1. By far the greatest part of the sacred text (thank God) labors under no important variety of reading.

2. This part contains the whole scheme of salvation, fully established.

3. Every various reading may and ought to be referred to these portions as a standard, and judged by them.

4. The text and various readings of the New Testament are found in manuscripts, and in books printed from manuscripts, whether Greek, Latin . . . or other languages; in the direct quotations of Irenaeus, and so forth, according as divine Providence dispenses its bounty to each generation. We include all these under the title of codices, sometimes used comprehensively.

5. These codices, however, have been diffused through churches of all ages and countries, and approach so near to the original autographs, that, taken together, in all the multitude of their varieties, they exhibit the genuine text.

6. No conjecture is ever to be regarded. It is safer to bracket any portion of the text, which may seem inexplicable.

7. The whole body of codices form the standard by which each separately is to be judged. . . .

15. There are, therefore, five principal means of judging the text. The antiquity of witnesses, the diversity of their extraction, and their multitude; the origin of the corrupt reading, and the native appearance of the genuine. . . .

17. When, however, it happens that some of these favor one reading, and some another, the critic may be drawn now in this, now in that direction; or, even should he decide, others may be slow to agree with him. When one man has a keener eye than another, either in body or mind, discussion is vain. One man can force no view on another, nor take the views of another from him, unless, indeed, the original autograph Scriptures some day come to light. . . .

XII. For properly commenting on the New Testament, especial attention to the style of its authors is requisite. Certainly the wisdom of God employs a style worthy of God, even when through his instruments he accommodates himself to our grossness. And that which is worthy of God, it is not our part arrogantly to define, but humbly to believe (Cf. 1 Cor. 2:1, 14:21). The holy men of God, in both the Old and New Testaments, exhibit, not only an exact knowledge of the truth, but also a systematic arrangement of their subject, a precise expression of their meaning, and a genuine strength of feeling. Beyond these three characteristics nothing need be desired. The result of these was that the writers of the New Testament, however unlearned, wrote always in a style becoming their subject, and, raised far above the technical rules of Greek rhetoricians, produced an eloquence truly natural, and that without effort. We shall describe these characteristics one by one, showing at the same time what has been observed concerning them in the present work. . . .

XIV. It is the especial office of every interpretation to exhibit adequately the force and significance of the words which the text contains, so as to express everything which the author intended, and to introduce nothing which he did not intend. The merits of a good style are two, depth and ease. They are seldom combined in human authors; and as each man writes, so do others seem to him to write. He who himself weighs every word will find in the work of another a meaning unknown even to the author; he who writes with less precision himself interprets the words of others too vaguely. In the divine Scriptures, however, the greatest depth is combined with the greatest ease; we should take care, therefore, in interpreting them, not to force their meaning to our own standard; nor, because the sacred writers show no marks of laborious care, to treat their words as if employed without due consideration. The divine language very far surpasses all human elegances of courtly style.

God, not as man, but as God, utters words worthy of himself. Lofty are his thoughts: hence words of inexhaustible force. . . .

Any degree whatever of acquaintance with the Greek New Testament is useful and laudable; but they who are less expert therein frequently admire, seize on, and herald to others false emphasis, whilst they pass by that which is genuine. This renders it the more necessary that we should help one another. Even dull eyes can make use of light for the chief purposes of life; but he who has a peculiarly strong sight perceives many things more accurately than others. Thus in Scripture all may see as much as is essential, but the clearer the believer's sight, the greater is his enjoyment; and that which one once sees, others who of themselves saw it not are, by his direction, enabled to perceive. . . .

XV. Earth produces nothing to be compared with holy feelings, including in this term the character or disposition for the feelings, strictly so called, are impetuous and eager, but the disposition consists, as it were, of calmer feelings, diffused and at rest. Now the sacred writings, like all others, besides the thoughts and feelings they express, have a disposition or character of their own. Every interpreter treats of the thoughts; those who are wiser and endued with spiritual experience pay due regard to the feelings; but this character (let me say it without offense) has been almost entirely lost sight of, except that the modesty of Scripture has been sometimes mentioned. And yet it pervades in a wonderful manner all the discourses and epistles of the New Testament, forming a continual recommendation of him who acts, speaks, or writes, and constituting, in its fullest sense, decorum. . . . It is generally such that one can more easily reach it by a perception of the heart than by a circuit of words. And this will be a principal reason why our commentary may be considered frequently too subtle, frequently too frigid. I doubt not, however, that those who have by degrees become accustomed to it will agree with me in my admiration of the language of the sacred writers. The painter by the most delicate stroke of his brush, the musician by the swiftest touch of fleeting notes, exercises the highest skill of his art; and in everything that is highly finished, it is the most minute details, which escape rude ears and eyes, which yet bestow the most exquisite and profound delight. Such is the case with Holy Scripture. Let each one, then, take what he can, and avoid criticising the rest. . . .

XVII. He who comprehends the intention of this work will not expect to find differences of opinion carefully enumerated and laboriously refuted, with the names of their advocates and the titles of their works. It is expedient indeed that some should undertake that office, and follow the history of Scriptural interpretation from century to century; this, however, is in the power of few, though some do search out and collect many particulars for the general advantage. It is better, however, for the weak to be ignorant of foolish opinions, which would scarcely occur to anyone, than to have them recorded. We should fare badly, if, in order to ascertain the royal road of truth, it were necessary for us to examine and be familiar with all the bypaths. In fact, the true interpretation is more frequently buried than assisted by a multitude of conflicting opinions. I have, however, guarded the reader against some recent erroneous interpretations, without either naming the authors or quoting their words. The reader who is unacquainted with them will not perceive the allusion, nor is it necessary that he should do so, whereas he who is acquainted with them will understand what I mean. I touch also upon some rather probable interpretations as yet little discussed; and where my own opinion might appear paradoxical, I support it by the agreement of others, especially the ancients. . . .

XXI. No one has as yet called my orthodoxy in question. Whoever has examined my writings will acknowledge that I have followed the standard of Scripture, not only in doctrine but even in language, with a religious care which even to good men seems scarcely removed from superstition. For I consider that no aberration from the line of truth laid down in Scripture, however slight, is so unimportant that the recognition of the truth, corresponding with the knowledge of God, expressed according to his direction, and agreeable to his glory, is not to be preferred to it. Truth is one, and consistent with itself in its greatest and in its least parts. It is the reader's duty, therefore, to think well of me, until I am proved guilty of error by someone who does not err himself in accusing me. It too frequently happens that one man attributes to another a pernicious opinion which both equally abhor, and thus by a short and hasty assertion places a stumbling block in the way of a thousand others. . . .

XXV. . . . I have not thought it necessary to subjoin practical applications, improvements as they are termed, to each chapter; for he who submits himself to the working of divine love in the truth imbibes from the divine words, when he has once perceived their meaning, all things profitable for salvation, without labor and without stimulus. They, however, who read rightly, that is, who weigh all things, and will not be led from the text but introduced to it, will find some assistance in this work, we are sure, in arriving at the full meaning of Scripture. . . .

XXVII. The multifarious abuse, or I should rather say nefarious contempt, of Holy Scripture has in our day reached its climax, and that not only with the profane, but even with those who in their own opinion are wise, nay spiritual. The *gegraptai*, "it is written," wherewith the Son of God himself, in his single combat with Satan, defeated all his assaults, has come to be held so cheap that those who feed upon Scriptures whole and alone are considered grovelers or fools. Thus will the false prophet find the gates open. And well-intentioned writers emulously produce practical treatises, prayers, hymns, soliloquies, religious tales. Singly, they may be exceedingly useful; but the mass of them, when taken together, draws away many from the Book of the Lord, that is the Scripture, which in itself combines, in the utmost plenitude and purity, all usefulness. Let those who approve the

261

best things preserve the heavenly deposit, which God, by a revelation ever growing in clearness from the time of Moses down to that of the apostles, has bestowed upon us not in vain. Then, if anyone thinks that he can obtain from this work of mine any aid toward the saving treatment of the New Testament, let him employ it for the glory of God, and for his own and others' profit—and pray for a blessing upon me.

CHAPTER 1

In the beginning was the Word, and the Word was with God, and the Word was God—this is thunder brought to us by the Son of Thunder; this is a voice from Heaven, to which human conjecture objects in vain. . . .

1. Rendering. The general meaning of Logos in every such connection is the word, said symbolically of the law-giving, creative, revealing activity of God. This is naturally suggested here by the obvious reference to Gen. 1:1, 3.

Many have seen in this but a bold personification of the wisdom or reason of God, as in Prov. 8:22. But this sense of Logos does not occur in the New Testament, and is excluded by the reference to the history of creation. Besides, the repeated "with God," verses 1 and 2, compels us to distinguish the Logos from God; the word became flesh, verse 14, cannot be said of an attribute of God; and the Baptist's testimony, verse 15, in direct connection with this introduction (compare also such sayings of Christ as chap. 8:58; 17:5), show clearly that John attributes personal preexistence to the Logos. Similarly, every attempt to explain away this profound sense of Logos is inadequate, and most are ungrammatical.

Thus the fundamental thought of this introduction is that the original, all-creating, all-quickening, and all-enlightening Logos, or personal divine Word, became man in Jesus Christ.

2. Origin and History of the Idea. (a) John uses the term Logos without explanation, assuming that his readers know it to bear this sense. Accordingly, we find this conception of it not new with him, but a chief element in the development of the Old Testament theology. In the Mosaic account, God's revelation of himself in the creation was, in its nature, Spirit (Gen. 1:2) in contrast with matter, and in its form, a word (Gen. 1:4) in contrast with every involuntary materialistic or pantheistic conception of the creative act. The real significance

under this representation of the invisible God's revelation of himself by speech became the germ of the idea of the Logos. With this thought all Judaism was pervaded—that God does not manifest himself immediately, but mediately; not in his hidden invisible essence, but through an appearance, an attribute, emanation, or being, called the Angel of the Lord (Exod. 23:21, etc.) or the Word of the Lord. Indeed, to the latter are ascribed as his work all divine light and life, in nature and history; the law, the promises, the prophecies, the guidance of the nation. (Cf. Ps. 33:6, 9; 107:20; 147:18; 148:8; Isa. 2:1, 3; Jer. 1:4, 11, 13; etc. Even such poetic personifications as Ps. 147:15 and Isa. 55:11 contain the germ of the doctrinal personality of the Word.)

(b) Another important element of Hebrew thought was the wisdom of God. The consideration of it became prominent only after the natural attributes of God—omnipotence, and so forth—had long been acknowledged. The chief passages are Job 28:12, and so forth, Prov. 8 and 9. Even the latter is a poetic personification; but this is based on the thought that wisdom is not shut up at rest in God, but active and manifest in the world. It is viewed as the one guide to salvation, comprehending all revelations of God; and as an attribute, embracing and combining all his other attributes. This view deeply influenced the development of the Hebrew idea of God. At that stage of religious knowledge and life, wisdom, revealing to pious faith the harmony and unity of purpose in the world, appeared to be his most attractive and important attribute, the essence of his being. One higher step remained, but the Jew could not yet see that God is love.

(c) In the Apocryphal books of Sirach, chaps. 1 and 24, and Baruch, chaps. 3 and 4:1–4., this view of wisdom is developed yet more clearly and fully. The book of Wisdom (written at least 100 B.C.) praises wisdom as the highest good, the essence of right knowledge and virtue, and as given by God to the pious who pray for it (chaps. 7 and 8). See especially chap. 7:22, and so forth, where wisdom has divine dignity and honors, as a holy Spirit of Light, proceeding from God, and penetrating all things. But this book seems rather to have viewed it as another name for the whole divine nature than as a person distinct from God. And nowhere does it connect this wisdom with the idea of Messiah. It shows, however, the influence of both Greek and oriental philosophy on Jewish theology, and marks a transition from the Old Testament view to that of Philo, and so forth.

(d) In Egypt, from the time of Ptolemy I (300 B.C.), there were Jews in great numbers, their headquarters being Alexandria (Philo estimates them at a million in his time, A.D. 50) and there they gradually came under the influence of the Egyptian civilization of that age, a strange mixture of Greek and Oriental customs and doctrine. Aristobulus, about 150 B.C., seems to have endeavored to unite the ancient doctrines of wisdom and the Word of God with a form of Greek philosophy. This effort, the leading feature of the Jewish-Alexandrian school, culminated in Philo, a contemporary of Christ. Philo strove to make Judaism, combined with and interpreted by the Platonic philosophy, do the work of the idea of Messiah, affording, by the power of thought, a complete substitute for it. This attempt to harmonize heathen and Jewish elements, while it led in his philosophy to a sort of anticipation of certain parts of Christian doctrine, explains how he himself vacillates between opposite and irreconcilable views.

(e) Philo represents the Absolute God as hidden and unknown; but surrounded by his powers as a king by his servants, and through these as present and ruling in the world. (These powers, *dunameis*, are, in Platonic language, ideas; in Jewish, angels.) These are different and innumerable—the original principles of things, the immaterial world, the type of which the material is an image. The two chief of these in dignity are the *theos*, God, the creative power, and the *Kurios*, Lord, or governing power, of the Scriptures. But all these powers are essentially one, as God is one; and their unity, both as they exist in God and as they emanate from him, is called the Logos. Hence the Logos appears under two relations; as the reason of God, lying in him, the divine thought; and as the outspoken Word, proceeding from him and manifest in the world. The former is in reality one with God's hidden being; the latter comprehends all the workings and revelations of God in the world; affords from itself the ideas and energies by which the world was framed and is upheld; and filling all things with divine light and life, rules them in wisdom, love, and righteousness. It is the beginning of creation; not unoriginated like God, nor made, like the world; but the eldest Son of the eternal Father (the world being the younger), God's image, the Creator of the world, the mediator between God and it, the highest angel, the second God, the high priest and reconciler.

(f) Luke concludes that, such being the development of the doctrine of the Logos when John wrote, although there is no evidence that he borrowed his views from Philo, yet it is impossible to doubt the direct historical connection of his doctrine with the Alexandrian. . . . It must be admitted that the term Logos seems to be chosen as already associated in many minds with a class of ideas in some degree akin to the writer's, and as furnishing a common point of thought and interest with those speculative idealists who constantly used it, while presenting them with new truth.

(g) But any connection amounting to doctrinal dependence of John upon Philo is utterly contrary to the tenor of Philo's own teaching. For he even loses the crowning feature of Hebrew religion, the moral energy expressed in its view of Jehovah's holiness, and with it the moral necessity of a divine teacher and savior. He becomes entangled in the physical notions of the heathen, forgets the wide distinction between God and the world, and even denies the independent, absolute being of God, declaring that, were the universe to end, God would die of loneliness and inactivity. The very universality of the conception, its immediate working on all things, would have excluded to Philo the belief that the whole Logos, not a mere part or effluence of his power, became incarnate in Christ. "Heaven and earth cannot contain me," cries his Logos, "how much less a human being." And on the whole it is extremely doubtful whether Philo ever meant formally to represent the Logos as a person, distinct from God. All the titles he gives it may be explained by supposing it to mean the ideal world, on which the actual is modeled. At most, we can say that he goes beyond a mere poetic personification, and prepares the way for a distinction of persons in the Godhead.

(h) John's connection with the doctrines of the later Jews, though less noticed, is at least as important as that with Philo. In the Apocryphal books, as we have seen, the idea of the Logos was overshadowed by that of the divine wisdom. But it reappears, prominently and definitely, in the Targums, especially that of Onkelos. These were written, indeed, after John's Gospel (Onkelos, the earliest, wrote not later than the second century A.D.); yet their distinguishing doctrines certainly rest upon ancient tradition. They represent the Word of God, the Memrah or Dibur, as the personal self-revealed God, and one with the Shekinah which was to be manifested in Messiah. But it would be absurd to claim that John borrowed his idea of Messiah from the Jews, who in him looked for, not a spiritual revelation of God in clearer light, to save men from sin by suffering and love, but a national deliverer, to gratify their wordly and carnal desires of power. Not even for the divine Word become flesh, and dwelling among men, but for an appearance, a vision, a mere display; or at most an unreal, docetic humanity.

3. Summary of the doctrine. The Logos here is the real, personal God, the Word, who did not begin to be when Christ came, but was originally, before the creation, with God, and was God. He made all things, verse 3. (Philo held to the original, independent existence of matter, the stuff, *hulē,* of the world, before it was framed.) He is holy light, which shines in moral darkness, though rejected by it. (Philo has no such height of mournful insight as this.) This Logos became man in the person of Christ, the Son of God. (Philo conceives of no incarnation.) Thus John's lofty doctrine of the Messiah is not in any way derived from Jewish or Gnostic speculations, but rests partly on pure Old Testament doctrine, and chiefly on what he learned from Christ himself. His testimony to this forms the historical part of his gospel. In the beginning—John's style, especially in this passage, is preeminent for its simplicity, subtlety, and sublimity. That Beginning is meant when all things began to be and were created by the Word, verse 3, *ev archē,* he says; that is, In the Beginning, as the Sept., Gen. 1:1, and Prov. 8:23. That the beginning of no later period is here meant is proved by the whole course of events; for the beginning of the Gospel was made when John went forth, Mark 1:1; but the beginning here spoken of is more ancient than the incarnation of the Word. In turn, none is higher than this. In the beginning of heaven and earth, God created the heaven and the earth; in the same beginning of heaven and earth, and the world, verse 10, already the Word was, without any beginning or starting point. The Word itself is simply eternal, for the eternity of the Word and that of the Father are described in the same manner. He was, when first was made all that began to be. Artemon maintains that John means the beginning of the gospel, and thus explains the verse: In the beginning of the gospel was the Word; and the Word, through his first ascension to Heaven, was, in the same beginning, with God, and so forth. He attempts to support this explanation by the authority of some of the ancients, Photinus and the like. This gives us no anxiety; error gave birth to error as much of old as today. Artemon throughout contends that Justin Martyr first taught that Jesus was the Son of God before the world was made. But Justin praises that doctrine as new, not because recently invented, but because it had been unknown to Trypho and such persons. We will bring forward in this place a single testimony of Ignatius, who in his Epistle to the Magnesians, 8, says, "There is one God, he who manifested himself through Jesus Christ his Son, who is the Eternal Word of himself, and did not come forth from si-

lence." The objections with which Artemon meets this message (P. ii. chap. 36, etc.) are so farfetched that they ought not to carry away the reader, but to confirm him. Was—Not, was made. See the distinction between these words, verses 10, 14, 15; chap. 8:58. The Father also is called he that is, and so forth, Rev. 1:4. The Word was before the world was made, in which he afterwards was, verse 10. The Word— Gr. *logos*, Lat. *Sermo, Verbum*, or even *Logos:* that Logos of whom verse 14 speaks. Whence is it that John calls him the Word? From the beginning of his first epistle, says Artemon (Part ii. chaps. 14 and 19), it is plain that the expression may be more properly regarded as adopted from the gospel into the epistle. In both writings he names the Logos before he comes to the name Jesus Christ. But he so terms him, not in imitation of Philo, much less of Plato; but by the same Spirit which taught the prophets of the Old Testament to speak thus. See Gen. 1:3; Ps. 33:6, Sept., By the Word of the Lord the heavens were fixed: Ps. 107:20, Sept. He sent his word—hence the very frequent title, the Word of God, in the Chaldee paraphrase; also Wisd. 16:12, 18:15. One and the same mystery in the Old and in the New Testament is expressed in similar terms. God is a Spirit, or eternal mind; the Son of God is the Logos, the inmost and yet the most express Word of the eternal mind. He who spiritually knows the spiritual nature of God knows too the spiritual nature of his Word, and understands why he is called the Word even before he is called the Light and the Life; compare 1 John 1:1, and so forth. Hence just as the apostles, in speaking of Christ, often distinguish between flesh and spirit, so he, whom John terms Logos, the same is termed Spirit by Clemens Romanus, an apostolic man. One Lord Christ, who hath saved us, although he was spirit before, yet was made flesh, and so forth. The Logos is he whom the Father has begotten, or uttered as an only-begotten Son, by whom the Father speaking makes all things; who speaks the things of the Father to us. Verse 18 gives the reason he is called Logos, and the actual description of what the Logos is. It is the only-begotten Son of God, who was in the bosom of the Father, and hath taken the part of his declarer. This clause, in the beginning, and so forth, was followed by an explanation with an emphatic addition (*epitasis*) in the two clauses that follow in this verse. With God—therefore distinct from God the Father. *Pros*, usually, unto, for *para*, with, as *eis* for *ev*, in verse 18, denote a perpetual tendency, as it were, of the Son to the Father in unity of essence. He was with God in a singular sense, for there was then nothing out of God. Again, John speaks more absolutely here than in

1 Jn. 1:2, where he says, the eternal life was with the Father, in contrast with the manifestation made to believers that they might become sons. Thus we dispose of the difference, which Artemon (part ii. chap. 18) tries to establish between the expressions of the epistle and the gospel. In his Dissertation, too, and throughout, he interprets the words "to be with God" as an ascension of Christ to Heaven before his Baptism. But this interpretation, when once the beginning is rightly explained, falls at once. If Christ, before his Passion, had trodden the way to life by such an ascension, he would not have had it to say afterwards, thou hast made known to me the ways of life (Acts 2:28) and his whole journey, from birth to that ascension, would have been of no benefit to us; but the plan of our salvation would begin only with the descent which followed. Thus the first two chapters of Matthew and Luke would lose their force. The words of Ignatius (Epistle to Magnes, 6) are clear: Jesus Christ, before the ages, was with the Father, and in the end appeared; and of Hermas, the Son of God is more ancient than the whole creation, so that he was present at his Father's counsels for founding the creation. God—not only was he with God, but also was God, Gr. *theos*. The absence of the Greek article, especially in the predicate, does not weaken it as meaning the true God. Sept., 1 Kings 18:24. And when the predicate precedes the subject, there is an epitasis, chap. 4:24. Further, the same signification is confirmed in this passage, from the fact that then there was no creation, in relation to which the Word could be called God; hence the word God is here used absolutely (defended in my apparatus), the more precious to us. In this stronghold of the faith, in this most sure center, we stand unshaken, and fortify ourselves against all enticements which try to draw us off to everything but the subject. Was—not made God, but true God. The Word was God, and that in the beginning. The Word—said the third time, with the greatest force. The three clauses form a climax: the article, Gr. *ho logos*, marks the subject. The Godhead of the Savior had been openly declared in the Old Testament: Jer. 23:6; Hos. 1:7; Ps. 23:1; and its testimonies are taken for granted in the New Testament, for instance, Heb. 1. Accordingly Matthew, Mark, and Luke make it their aim to prove rather that the real man Jesus is the Christ. And when in consequence some at last had begun to doubt the Godhead of Christ, John asserted it, and wrote in this book a kind of supplement to the gospels, as in the Apocalypse he wrote a supplement to the prophets.

2. He alone. The word "he" comprises the whole of the verse

next preceding, as he, or the same, verse 7, comprises verse 6. With God—this is here repeated and is now put in contrast with his subsequent mission to men. This verse repeats, and sums up in a single statement, the three clauses stated severally in the preceding verse. This Logos, who was God, was in the beginning, and was with God. A striking antithesis; compare verse 14, and 1 John 2:1.

THE WORD

| Was in the beginning God, | Was made flesh, |
| With God: | And dwelt among us. |

Moreover the very congeries of this second verse manifestly supports this antithesis, the name Logos not occurring again until verse 14.

3. All things—Gr. *panta*. A large word, denoting the world, that is, the universe of created things, verse 10. All things which are out of God, were made; and all things which were made, were made by the Logos. Now at last "John the Divine" passes from the being of the Word to the being made of all things. In verses 1 and 2, the condition of things is described before the world was made; verse 3, in the making of the world; verse 4, in the time of man's innocence; verse 5, in the time of man's corruption. By him—opposite to without him. Were made—Gr. *egeneto*. This in some measure is earlier than the *ktisis*, founding, of all things, and evidently implies, as an inference, the making of all things out of nothing. Thus the phrase "all things" conveys the impression of something earlier than the completion of the whole *kosmos*, world, and especially than that of mankind, to which John comes down in verses 9 and 10. And without—this sentence expresses something more than the next preceding. The subject is, not even one thing, the predicate is, without him was made, which was made. And the "which" is evidently equivalent to "what," 1 Cor. 15:10, by the grace of God I am what I am. Not even one thing—Gr. *oude ev*, however superlatively excellent, which was made—after its kind; Gen. 1:11, 21, 24. The Preterite implies something more absolute than the Aorist *egeneto*, was made, though in Latin both are expressed alike. All things, without any exception, were made by him. This John explicitly affirms, against the false philosophy which excepted matter from creation.

4. In—first, John says, in him was life (cf. chap. v. 26). Then he calls him the life. So in 1 John 1:1 and 2, first he calls him the Word of

life, then the life; and verses 5 and 7, God is said to be light, and to be in the light. John especially imitates the expressions of the Lord Jesus. Life—the consideration next to that of being is that of life. Then there is no death, then no nature without grace. And the life—the subject: the life, bestowing life on all things, which were alive. Was the light—light and life together: chap. 8:12, 1 Tim. 6:16; Phil. 2:15, 16. As on the contrary darkness and death—yet quickening precedes illumination. Of men—all in the state of uprightness, from which the consideration of the Logos must not be severed. Men: nowhere does this mean Adam and his wife; so it denotes mankind. The evangelist here comes from the whole to the part—from those things which were made, or which were alive, to rational beings. In respect to each, the Word, Logos, Speech, has an appropriate meaning.

5. And—from this verse the doctrine of evil and its origin receives much light. In darkness—this darkness is not said to have been made. For it is a privation, incurred by men. In the darkness the glory of the light is the more conspicuous. Shineth—present tense, with the same force as in lighteth, verse 9. It always *phainei*, is shining. The light was always at hand, even in the Old Testament, to remedy darkness and sin. The same verb *phainei*, shineth, is said of the New Testament, 1 John 2:8. And—not—like and—not, verses 10 and 11. The darkness—that is, men wrapt in darkness, comprehended it not—men, it seems, disliked the light too much, were too deeply sunk in darkness. When they did not comprehend the *logos asarkov*, the Word without flesh, he was made flesh, verse 14.

CONCLUSION

Now, by the goodness of God, I have finished, in declining years, not only the criticism, but the exegesis also, of the Apocalypse and the whole of the New Testament, which I undertook in youth. Kind readers will find a text conformed to the most genuine copies, its meaning explained in dogmatical, prophetical, historical, and chronological matters; the form of evangelical doctrine religiously adhered to; all things connected by one uniform tenor of rules and arguments. There are five divisions of the work: the critical Apparatus annexed to the text itself, the Harmony of the Evangelists, the German exegesis of the Apocalypse, the Order of the Times, and, lastly, this Gnomon, but the web is one. My "Defences" too have the same design: I have only rewritten and digested again what I had before written.

This indeed is wearisome, and it seems uninteresting, but those acquainted with the subject will pardon me; for, on account of the weight of the subject, and the weakness of some, it must be so. It has long been evident how the world receives the Word of God; if I have treated it as the Word of God, as I trust, I ask to be received in no other way. Even students of the truth are often too slow to receive things to which they have not been accustomed. When they have long ago heard, this is so, they at length ask, what is it? And when the demonstration is ended, they complain that the postulates are set before them. Some only with their death cease to obstruct the truth in a portion which they do not understand. Still the labor is not in vain; while some come unexpectedly short, others unexpectedly yield, or will yield. Light grows daily; through difficulty to triumph truth toils onward; posterity will judge differently of many things. O God, whatever stands or falls, stands or falls by thy judgment; maintain what thou hast condescended to perform through me. Have mercy on my readers and myself. Thine is, Thine be glory forever!

Johann Albrecht Bengel

TOWARD AN APOCALYPTIC CHRONOLOGY*
1740

1. EXPRESSED ACCORDING TO THE TEXT

Earthly Year

3940   birth of Jesus Christ

3943   first year of Dionysian chronology [Dionysius Exiguus, d. 545, developed the present system of dating from the birth of Christ]

Anno Dion. 30   Jesus Christ suffers, dies, arises, gives a *preview* of his revelation (John 21:22–23; Acts 1:7) and ascends into Heaven

A.   96   *Revelation* is written by John: chap. 1. The coming of the Lord is announced to the seven congregations in Asia and to their angels: chaps. 2 and 3

B.   97, 98   The *seven seals* are opened and their significance indicated by the five seals of Chronus [measure of time]: chaps. 4–6. The seven trumpets are given to the seven angels: chaps. 7 and 8

C.   The Lord comes: John's remaining is no longer

D.   Sec. [centuries] 2–5   The trumpets of the four angels consecutively: chap. 8

E.   Anno 510–589   The first woe: chap. 9

F.   589–634   Standstill between the first and second woe

G.   634–847   The second woe: chap. 9

H.   Anno 800   Beginning of the non-Chronus [nontime measure] and the many kings: chaps. 10 and 11.

---

*Translated from Johann Albrecht Bengel, *Erklärte Offenbarung Johannes oder vielmehr Jesu Christi* (Franckfurt am Main, 1740).

272

I. Anno 847–947 Cessation between the second and third woe: chap. 11:14

K. Anno 940–1617 The 1260 days of the woman in the wilderness after which she gives birth to the human son: chap. 12:6

L. Anno 947–1836 The third woe: chap. 12:12

M. Anno 1058–1836 The three and one-half years: chap. 12:14

N. Between the three and one-half years: the beast in the three epochs of his full security: chap. 13:5

O. Anno 1208, 1209 War with the saints: end of the Chronus sub. lit. [under letter] B [above]: chap. 13:7

P. Anno 1614 The angel with the eternal gospel: chap. 14:6.

Q. Anno 1836 End of non-Chronus and the many kings; fulfillment of the Word of God and his mystery; end of the lesser time and the first, second half period; defeat of the beast; thousand year imprisonment of Satan: chap. 19, 20

R. After this: loosening of Satan for a short period. Beginning of the millennium, during which the saints reign: chap. 20:3

S. End of the short period: chap. 20:7

T. End of the world: chap. 20:11

U. All new: chap. 21:22

Such a table may be viewed as something useful or superfluous; whichever the case, it will be proper for those who use it properly and thoughtfully. I describe it as an *attempt,* and most diligently assert that I do not intend to have established the years in any way with the same certainty in all and every point. Rather, I have worked as do geographers who often fill out on their maps known lands, borders, and coasts by unknown but necessary coherence.

2. EXPRESSED ACCORDING TO HISTORY

If one takes the chief historical periods from John's time in sequence according to the characteristics indicated to them by history, the text falls into the following order.

Sec. II.	Dispersal of the Jews by Hadrian	chap.	8:7
III.	Invasions of the Goths and other Foreign People	chap.	8:8
IV.	Saeculum Arianium		

V.	Abolishment of Empire under Augustulius	chap.	8:12
VI.	Persecution of Jews on Persia	chap.	9:1
VII.	The Saracen Killings	chap.	9:13
VIII.	Iconoclasm	chap.	9:20
IX.	Empire under Charlemagne	chap.	10:11
X.	Saeculum Infelix	chap.	12:12
XI.	Saeculum Hildebrandium	chap.	13:1
XII.	Power of Pope	chap.	13:4
XIII.	Crusade against Waldensians	chap.	13:7
XIV.	Papal Power over All Nations	chap.	13:7
XV.	Adoration	chap.	13:8
XVI.	Reformation	chap.	13:9
XVII.	Protestant Teachers	chap.	14:6,8

The other points which fall between these, each person may set in according to his own liking from the explanation. The person who compares the two charts will understand the complete agreement of the prophecy and its fulfillment.

Friedrich Christoph Oetinger

A CONFESSION OF FAITH*

I was dead, but now I live; yet not I but Christ in me. Thus, I have died to the law and its ceremonies, living alone for him who freed me from all except the commandment of love.

He declared me of age and has entrusted my spiritual inheritance to the protection of my care; therefore, I need no guardian.

Spirit and truth are the essential elements of my saving religion; the narrow and specific fulfillment of all aspects of a proper and unselfish love is my unending worship.

My church is the temple of my body, purified externally as well as internally and prepared as a dwelling place for the trinity. Jesus alone is preacher in it; he chose and designated my conscience as his pulpit. Heart, senses, and all desires are the listeners who attend and maintain in inward morality and industry what proceeds from his gracious mouth.

When he mounts the chancel and proclaims his loving gospel, it is Sunday; a feast day if he stirs in my soul living and weighty thoughts of his good deeds or of those of a true friend and martyr. If, however, because of my errors and sins he speaks to me and punishes me, it is for me a day of repentance, prayer, and silence.

Oftentimes my teacher is completely silent; at such times I consider what I have previously heard, reach to meditate in my Bible as the best sermon for change, or if neither of these is available, I read in the great book of nature. Moreover, I remain completely submissive to him who wishes to make me a new creature.

If at times he grants me the pleasure of having a glimpse of his friends and travelers on his journey, members of my head and branches of my true vine, my heart rejoices with them in him and binds as a community of suffering those who are able to meet us on

---

*Translated from Karl Christian Eduard Ehmann, *Oetingers Leben und Briefe* (Stuttgart, 1859), pp. 181–183.

the way toward the goal before us; in this order I hold with them, according to the mind of the lamb, a love feast.

My baptism is that true burial after the complete mortification of all that which can be reckoned in me as the image of the first Adam.

If Christ, the second Adam, appears in essence in me, and if there is sensed in my activities and surrenderings the mind of his child, then I celebrate Christmas. It is Easter if my spirit proceeds triumphant through all suffering, death, and hell. I celebrate Ascension if I receive meanwhile the freedom to sweep myself up to God, my source. I celebrate Pentecost if grace is poured out from the heights into my heart through the Holy Spirit.

If pleasing beams of light are seen from afar it is day, and morning if the sun shines actively on my horizon; it is noon if it reveals itself in its most beautiful clarity in the firmament, but evening if grace, for a time, hides itself and sets. Yes, it is truly night, and midnight, if loneliness and temptation storm over me and darken my mind so that I am not even capable of catching a glimpse of my sun of grace. But if finally all that I am is increasingly renewed by the great restorer, then the New Year beams forth. After many harsh, cold winters follows a pleasant spring which grants me experience of beautiful sensations of the glorious might and power of my heavenly gardener. In summer the full fruit of the scattered seed first manifests itself. In autumn, among manifold changes, everything matures and is gathered in with joy by him who scattered seed and planted it. In winter my tree of life is often robbed of all its ornament and form; it seems as if completely withered. But this is only so that in new fruitfulness, it might be ready and strong where constancy is inconstancy. And this will continue until finally the tree after many misdirections will finally be planted by the unseen hand of the Lord in the heavenly paradise.

What will then be revealed will be those things which carnal eye has not seen nor mortal ear heard and taken up; indeed those who are least capable of seeing are best [prepared] to experience it more than to speak of it.

Lord, help me to this by grace—and what [delight] would that be if I saw you and stood there before your throne! Ah, teach me more of this that I might continually seek you with a prudent heart! Amen!

Friedrich Christoph Oetinger

A CONFESSION OF THOUGHT*

I seek to deal with principles in a nonsectarian way if I can and to explain the Holy Scripture but not without the works of God. In regard to chemistry, it belongs to the true knowledge of that which is necessary, simple, and useful for understanding. Not gold and silver, but the true way, wisdom in Holy Scripture brought me to this. In holy things there must be a harmony of all—in nature also; otherwise there will soon be a *nervus probandi* (nerve of testing). In so skeptical a time, the truth of God in nature and Scripture is my basis. I am in battle if I am abandoned before God, if I wish something other than God's eternal purpose, if I attend to any leader other than the Holy Spirit, if I do not walk truly in the order and proper path of work and suffering, in the fear of God according to Revelation 14 as it applies for this time to the message of the angel of the eternal gospel, if I am not crucified to the world and myself, if I do not stretch out my hand in any way to the tree of life or Christ's Cross. Then I am at war with myself until all phantasms here disappear through grace or truth. This is the true *reductio in materiam primam* [reduction into prime matter]; this gives basic preserving truth.

---
*Translated from Karl Christian Eduard Ehmann, *Oetingers Leben und Briefe* (Stuttgart, 1859), pp. 563–564.

Friedrich Christoph Oetinger

ON ENLIGHTENMENT*

In the gospel for today [Matt. 11:2–6] our Lord and Redeemer wished to bring the disciples of John as well as his own disciples to a new level of enlightenment. His own disciples had earlier seen him raise the daughter of Jairus and later the youth at Nain from the dead. After this the twelve apostles were sent out to do miracles and to preach. Indeed, in baptizing and teaching, the apostles went beyond John the Baptist. They returned without any doubt and told (as John learned when he sent his two disciples to Jesus) how the blind saw, the lame walked, evil spirits were driven out, and many sick persons were healed with oil. All this had to occur so that Jesus' answer might bring greater enlightenment to John.

See how greatly superior the enlightenment of the disciples of John and Christ was to ours. But the enlightenment of the apostles following Pentecost was greater than this. For this reason after the time of John the Baptist, the least among the persons converted by the apostles was named greater than John himself (Matt. 11:11).

Anyone reading the gospel will not find in it specific words concerning enlightenment, but the topic itself is treated; both John the Baptist and Jesus Christ deal with true enlightenment. I bring to your attention: Awake you who sleep and arise from the dead; and Christ will enlighten you (Eph. 5:14). God orders all things and all circumstances so that each person will be prepared by everything which happens for greater enlightenment. The new birth and enlightenment are the same: The new birth comes through water and the Spirit, that is, by the heavenly power which flowed out physically from Jesus' side and was never known by our reason; but the enlightenment indicates to us that we are to appropriate as small innocent children these spiritual elements and to preserve them as a witness until

---

*Translated from Otto Weber et al., *Die Stimme der Stillen* (Neukirchen Kreis Moers, 1959), pp. 145–149.

we see truly how they have brought forth the new birth. By this we are to bring to good use that which Jesus accomplished for us by his own love offered to God so that we might possess a more certain knowledge of it than a watchmaker does of his watch or a farmer of his plow. We take the words of Jesus and the apostles as words of life and they give more joy to the heart than the light of the sun, the moon, and the stars. It is a living knowledge, since the life of God himself is with it and by the joy arising from it we are made agile and swift, able to conquer the world, at least so to use the things in the world that they do not lead us away from the life of God. It is true that spiritual things, if they are made corporal by Christ, are opposed to the natural man, but by and by he sees how vain everything is and that it does not fill the desire of the soul. As a result he finally learns to freely decide to place the things of Jesus Christ before the things of the world and to hold teaching higher than gold. He then seeks first in the words of Jesus a more preeminent understanding than he has found in household or business affairs. The words are marks of heavenly matters.

This is the goal of enlightenment: that we see all in the glory of God which he poured out in Christ, without which there is no true understanding, no true agreement, no spiritual community in any matter. For as Paul says: God, who commanded the light to shine forth from the darkness, also made our dark souls bright with the glory of God in the presence of Jesus Christ (2 Cor. 4:6). But the minds of those who do not believe this are hardened and incapable of grasping it. This is because the god of this world by the spirit and sympathy of the world takes away their desire so that they cannot see the bright light of the gospel in the presence of Jesus Christ which in itself would be easy. In the world there is enough book knowledge which has no desire for life, but it does not reach enlightenment; indeed, book knowledge kills enlightenment. As a mocker it finds a twisted wisdom to destroy enlightenment and audaciously takes up company with the foolish maiden and yet desires that the Lord will open the door to eternal life. From this you see how necessary it is that you be trained by true knowledge. Therefore I propose to you how you are to come to true enlightenment through the apostles' holy words if you are truly inclined to the dispensations and preparations of God and if you truly understand the manifold nature of traditional holy teaching.

Send out your light and your truth, O Lord, that they might

bring us to your holy hill (Ps. 43:3). The light of your presence has brought all believers to enlightenment; therefore we ask for your grace that it will bring us to this goal.

If this matter of enlightenment is as important to you as it ought to be, note how you are to come to it by the dispensations and preparations of divine providence. This is made completely clear in the gospel in a twofold way. First, John sent two disciples to Jesus at the time Christ's works were most discussed and when the disciples had returned from their trips into the neighboring cities, among which was Nain. This is a work which in his foresight God had so ordained and directed that it should happen at exactly the same time. God therefore brought the disciples of John to a greater enlightenment. Second, there is the statement of Jesus after the disciples of John went away. In this statement Jesus pointed to a greater enlightenment. And because the people in their zeal went to hear John, they providentially were impressed by the dispensation of God in the precursor, John. You went out, he said, not to hear a street barker nor a pompously clothed court preacher but a prophet who was greater than Abraham, Moses, David, and all the prophets. Did you thus turn to the providence of God that you might be better prepared to come to me?

Thus God worked in the beginning so that for those who sought God all aids should be useful for greater enlightenment. Thus you can believe with certainty that all things which happened to you in school, in catechetical practices, and in confirmation were foreseen by God for your calling and enlightenment. But things happen as they always happen. Wisdom complains that she is not heard. The dispensations of God are not lacking although they do not have as great an impact as they did in Jesus' time.

All who come to enlightenment can say of it that certain exterior words from others or illnesses or chastisements or specific examples of pious people awakened them to consider the Word of God. For the most part they let it take its course; but they were frightened and pushed it aside for another time. There are also those who heard much, made many resolutions, and yet did not turn to earnestness, like those concerning whom Paul spoke (Heb. 6:7–8): The earth which receives the rain and yet bears thistles is to be cursed.

I admonish you, however: Consider what God wishes for you in all these things that he allowed to come to you: certainly nothing other than that for once you allow the enlightenment from the gospel to be sweet to you. For as long as you think "This is a hard saying, impossible for me," you will not have an open ear to come to the gospel. You will have hesitated to prepare yourself to see the loveliness of Jesus. You will have been frightened that you must stand aside from your unrighteousness, if you let it come so close to you.

We still have to discuss how we come to enlightenment by the manifold nature of traditional teaching. The disciples of John had already heard the doctrine from John (John 1:29) that Christ Jesus was the lamb of God. But although he himself was not certain, John in his love for them wished to make his disciples more certain. They must go to Christ himself as sent and ask him. Asking is a glorious thing, since by it one distinguishes between one's thoughts. If the answer properly illuminates the different thoughts, one becomes more certain. It is not without reason and it is fitting with the manifold nature of teaching that Jesus did not answer immediately. "Indeed I am he who is to come," but he left it to their free choice to decide after they heard and saw the returning apostles and after they saw Jesus and heard his answer. By this they gained a firm basis for enlightenment from which thereafter they received more grace and truth.

True enlightenment still works in the same way. Not in one but in a manifold way, God prepares the path to know truth. It is true that more doubts arise at present than did then, but God also gives more direction to truth in hidden ways. It must be that the costly pearls of Scripture raise doubts only in the unenlightened so that the justified might more greatly rejoice in the manifold nature of certain truth. One trusts oneself in the already established way and one does not seek enough in the inexpressible treasures of Jesus in which all wisdom lies hidden. Therefore there are many who take great steps on the way of natural knowledge and yet are far from true enlightenment. They do not understand the pleasures of God (Matt. 11:26) but bind themselves to the order of nature.

Do not think that true enlightenment is a minor matter; it comes by grace, not through the elements of the world. God indicates to each person in his inner being by the holy Word how delicate his movements are and how inward are his workings. True enlightenment leaves nothing aside which belongs to the whole matter. Man takes up everything himself. Man prays, seeks, knocks, does not tire, is not impatient in waiting for the time in which God locks up all.

Man does not seek God to have more enlightenment before the time according to the rule: He who has, to him it will be given (Matt. 13:12).

Give yourself to the task so that you use everything which God gives to all, to each and every one. Grace acts exceedingly above all we can pray and think (Eph. 3:20). May this bring each person on the loving way of the gospel to glory in the presence of Jesus Christ.

Friedrich Christoph Oetinger

FROM THE
BIBLICAL AND EMBLEMATIC DICTIONARY*
1776

Conversion, *Epistrophe*

... What is conversion? Answer: If one turns from false intentions and customs to the Word and law of God, takes as its chief purpose the directions of Psalm 1, and sees how he has been blinded to how he was in darkness and the power of Satan even though he was eloquent, then one is on the way of blessedness. All sermons are intended that a man who from his youth on has clung to many false intentions and covers over his heart might once look to Jesus as the highest law to love above all and that thus he might be free of the hardness of his understanding and the whole web of sinfulness with its hundreds of excuses, and stand in complete redirection toward the righteousness to which he has been called internally and externally. He is to do so, indeed, in such a way that he remain directed with all which he has, with all the powers and impulses of God, toward that which is preserved as beautiful and divine in righteousness. He is to do so until the Word comes fully into him from the kingdom and is a judge of hidden inclinations and revealed thoughts. For this reason, the proverbs of Solomon and Psalm 1:19 note that one is not only to be converted generally to the Lord, but also by his whole heart, soul, mind, and powers toward everything which the law testifies of Christ in particular. Therefore, Paul compares the Word of God to a surgeon's knife which sets aside all coverings and exteriors (Heb. 4:12). ...

---

*Translated from [Friedrich Christoph Oetinger], *Biblisches and Emblematisches Wörterbuch* (1776).

283

PIETISTS—SELECTED WRITINGS

Repentance, *Metania*

Repentance is, particularly, a change of mind, a turning around of thoughts. By it, under the influence of truth in the will, one reads the melody and learns how the decisions out of which judgments arise are deeply rooted. No one changes his mind; he only sees the shamefulness or his great need. By this God calls all men in their consciences to better life. And this is enough of an impulse for a change of mind; hereafter, by renovation the full reestablishment of the thoughts follows, and this is the purpose of this dictionary.

Experience, *Sensus, Aestisis.* Knowledge, *Epignosis*
(this is twofold, Phil. 1:19)

Experience is what one is inwardly when the life spirits are established in it according to their part. . . . According to 2 Corinthians 3:18, we are reformed in the same image. Knowledge on the other hand is an external expression of the matter according to its expressed characteristics; one sees the matter before oneself which is not manifest in the experience. By a long interior journey, the soul can draw to itself experiential instruments, as I acknowledge in Swedenborg, but such a journey is dangerous because spiritual evils can mix themselves into heavenly things (Eph. 6). One must take care, one must not cast aside experience, for without it there is no true knowledge. To know is to have a heightened experience by means of speech; without this one helps oneself with definitions which one does not learn by oneself but borrows. As a result there are so many empty words, *kenophoniae,* by which one thinks one knows something without properly knowing anything. Let one look at Shaftesbury. . . . He says that it is fortunate if one does not know philosophic information which one has borrowed. A true philosopher learns from oneself, as is proper (Luke 12). In the Proverbs of Solomon experience and knowledge are taken as one; at least they are so according to the translation of the Greek Septuagint because Adam the first man had both of them in one. In this life, we must now understand piece by piece and in according to syllogisms; to these one must remain true in the smallest ways. Solomon describes the arts of wisdom, knowledge, understanding, intelligence, essential order, self-scrutiny, the presence of mind, wit, but all these have a differing relationship to experience and understanding. . . . Concepts present themselves on the tablet of the imagination (Prov. 3:3), and the memory holds them. Judgment draws much from the binding of words, noting how what follows comes from what went before. According to the Word: "He who has, to him it will be given. . . ."

Faith, *Pistis*

Faith is a precious thing which makes the heart firm; it comes through the structure of grace and through discretion of foods. The heart is by nature inconstant, changing between desire and fear, consolation and despair (Jer. 17:9). If one has many revelations, visions, and dreams, one's heart is still not as firmly rooted as by faith. Faith is a *hypostasis*, a firmness from conviction (Heb. 11). Faith comes from hearing, that is, through the external planting of an assured mind (James 1:21). God certainly will not do away with the syllogistic ordering of the mind, but will give it life (Gal. 3:21). For the mind the structure of grace is given in the Gospel (Rom. 4:21). Logic is not a structure, but only a law. . . . In certain ways it brings about in a machinelike fashion a proper forming of the thoughts. But in the gospel, each true thought must not only be formed but must be born. The first thought must be for a new birth: Jesus is the Lord (1 Cor. 12:3) and whoever is born in Jesus and enters into his hypostasis [must know that] God looks over his many failings and sins of weakness until he comes to certainty by teaching (Eph. 4:13). The beginning of faith, because of which God holds man as righteous, is a strong impression by which desire and pleasure for the Son of God rises. By it one holds as certain and true (so that the whole life follows from it) the statement that one cannot help, that nothing can help the deep corruption, except the formation of grace. Therefore, one gives oneself immediately to grace with the desire to be led into all truth. The beginning of this can be very small and paltry (Acts 14:8). . . . Today one has exchanged faith for knowledge, for a logical demonstration, but in this one often errs if one holds the statements as true only like the statements of geometry, believing that one does not need as well the Holy Scripture but only human science. In this one deceives oneself, for such an idea has no root in the ground of life. Faith is an inner hidden *hypostasis;* be it ever so small, it will move forth into all truth by the indwelling impulse of the Spirit. Then one does not live, speak, think, or act for oneself, but only for the Lord, and one has all other concepts in Christ in God, if not at all times in one's thoughts, nevertheless in the Spirit.

Holiness, *hagiosyne*

Holiness is a hidden glory and the glory of hidden holiness (Ps. 99). The power of unceasing life is revealed by Jesus, the High Priest (Heb. 7:16). Glory and life go together (Rom. 6:4). They are given to those who are his people, for those people are holy. I will now take an extract from the thoughts of an author who had his basic concepts in this regard from Judaism. The question was if everything which is righteous is also holy. Answer: No. Holiness draws itself to God, righteousness toward men. A holy person is one who knows how to offer to God and to receive from God what God brings to him. We ourselves cannot bring anything to God. We have nothing other than what we have received from him. The body has been given to us from the elements; the complexion from heaven and earth; the nature of the soul is from the base of the soul, the invisible world, but the spirit is from God himself who impressed his image in us in the spirit. If we give that image back to God again we will have holiness, from which will flow Godliness and from which true worship will follow. . . . According to the New Testament, we know that God communicates his holiness and his life in Christ, and if we not only present our spirits but also our bodies in reasonable worship, we are holy (Rom. 12:1), for we have not received the spirit of the world but the Spirit from God in that we know what has been given by him (1 Cor. 2:12). Thus, giving thanks to God through Jesus Christ at all times belongs to holiness (Eph. 5:20), and therefore, all play formed in the world should be far from us (Eph. 5:4). In place of this there ought to be thanks for the marks of a holy pattern of life.

Sorrow, *metania ametameletos*

Sorrow is to feel fear for an evil deed. There is a distinction between *metania* and *metamelia*. Sorrow is concern over oneself. *Metania* is the best in that it is to see one's thoughts and change them. Both of these are often tied together. One can be happy at all times about the change of mind, if one thinks on it and on the fact that it has occurred (2 Cor. 7:10). There are two kinds of sorrow. The first occurs before

286

renewal and goes to the point that one knows that one is far from the glorious things concerning which one has heard and that one is worthy of death (1 Cor. 14:25). The second occurs after renewal in special cases where one acknowledges this or that sin with all its circumstances, and is brought to the holy experience of sorrow as in 2 Corinthians 7:11....

Woman, *gyne*

In the beginning woman was the glory of man (1 Cor. 11:7) when Adam was as yet undivided. Thereafter, however, woman was formed out of the softer powers. Now God, for Christ's sake born of a woman, has blessed all womankind, and as man and woman we bear the image of the earth in us until, in the resurrection, we become like the angels who are neither man nor woman. In the meantime, all must be made righteous in Christ as if the future were made present. As a result Paul says that in Christ, there is neither male nor female, neither slave nor free man (Gal. 3:28) but you are all justified as one in Christ. Nevertheless, a distinction must be made. In Christ, man is nothing without a wife, and a wife is nothing without a man. Therefore, Christ is the wife for the man and the husband for the woman, but this matter he will make clear in his own time. For the present, it is enough to say that God looks upon it as if it had already occurred even though it has not. In Christ God sees everything in a point. One thousand years are for him one point....

New birth, *anagennesis*

It is necessary to state that water and the spirit and the birth belong to the new birth, but one must not immerse oneself too far in this before one comes to the necessary age. The new birth is a restructuring of knowledge through the Word and truth according to Galatians 4:19. This change one can make real for oneself in God, if one attends to how the tuggings of God follow consecutively, and how from these, more yet will be given. In Psalm 19 there are always eight verses which tell what one desires, and eight more which tell what one will receive anew. One should hold to James 1:15....

Nicolas Ludwig, Count von Zinzendorf
1700–1760

Nicolas Ludwig, Count von Zinzendorf

THOUGHTS FOR THE LEARNED AND YET GOOD-WILLED STUDENTS OF TRUTH*
1732

1. Religion can be grasped without the conclusions of reason; otherwise no one could have religion except the person with intelligence. As a result the best theologians would be those who have the greatest reason. This cannot be believed and is opposed by experience.

2. Religion must be a matter which is able to be grasped through experience alone without any concepts. If this were not so a deaf or a blind or a mentally deficient man or a child could not have the religion necessary for salvation. The first could not hear the truth, the second would lack sense to awaken his mind and stir his thoughts, the third would lack the ability to grasp concepts to put them together and to test them.

3. There is less at stake in the truth of concepts than in the truth of experience; errors in doctrine are not as bad as errors in methods and an ignorant person is not as evil as a blockhead.

4. Understanding arising out of concepts changes with the time, education, and other circumstances. Understanding arrived at from experience is not subject to these changes; such understanding becomes better with time and circumstances.

5. If the divinity did not give itself to be understood by a man, it could not desire that a man understand it.

6. Revelation is indispensably necessary in human experience;

*Translated from Nikolaus Ludwig von Zinzendorf, *Der Deutsche Socrates* (Leipzig, 1732), pp. 289–296.

that revelation be reduced to conceivable concepts, however, is not so much necessary as useful.

7. All men can come to the necessary truths if only they wish to.

8. No one can accept the truth of a matter if it is presented to him as not true. There are two ways to convince a man: by appearances and by spiritual power.

9. As long as a religion treats only invisible things and all spiritual power is opposed to it, it will not be held as true by any one, for it will be presented as false.

10. Reason weakens experience.

11. Religion cannot be grasped by reason as long as it opposes experience.

12. The experience of a thing cannot be cast aside by any conclusion of reason.

13. There are three kinds of human minds. They are the passionate, the temperate, and the weak.

14. Passionate minds are of three kinds. The first desire only to have a great many things, the second also desire to enjoy a great many things, and the third desire that all things be for themselves alone.

15. Temperate minds are of three kinds. The first would like to have many things, the second would also like to enjoy many things, and the third would like all things to be for themselves alone; they would like this very much, and they use the opportunity to gain their ends when they arise, but they let the opportunities arise as they will.

16. Weak or lazy souls also would prefer to have many things. They would rather enjoy them and they would not refuse any opportunity to enjoy them if they did not have to devote any energy to getting something, to making friends, or to establishing themselves in a reputable position.

17. The first kind of people are either afraid to have no religion and seek to free themselves from the duties of their religion by means of scrupulosity, or they make for themselves completely new obligations so as to do away with proper religion, or they, as opportunity arises, either defend a more pleasant religious way or throw out all religion completely.

18. The second kind of people endeavor to consider all religions as one, or they engage in religion with great courtliness but without truth, or they banish cares concerning the practice of religion by emphasizing doctrinal statements.

19. The last kind of people are not concerned if there is a religion, and if there is one, they hope for the best or are willing to let the worst that can happen to them, happen to them.

20. The nature of each kind of mind brings with itself either a concept or an experience of religion. As long as the mind is in the body, it is possible that the sufferings which relate to this state will not allow the consideration which arises from the soul to clearly come forth.

21. The more the body has power, the more does one build up fantasies; the more the mind has the upper hand, the more does one consider situations carefully.

22. Not all movements of the body are evil and not all inclinations of the mind are good.

23. A spirit in the flesh must have another nature and characteristic than a living spirit.

24. All movements of a free nature insofar as they are considered aside from their effect whether they be of the body or of the mind are good.

25. If human nature loses its freedom, all the movements in the body and all the inclinations of the mind come under suspicion.

26. Where nature loses its freedom, it is ruled by another being.

27. A wise and good being would move bound nature toward its best end, but an unwise and evil being would rule over it for its injury.

28. Both have to work in man either through reflection or through experience.

29. Just as a child must be helped in the most necessary usage of the body, so must a man be helped in the first and most necessary operation of the mind.

30. If this does not occur, a child will remain either a blockhead or a fool; if this does not occur, the mind will remain either completely mad or at least stupid.

31. What is known from long experience as the most noble and most necessary part of a man must be helped in the first place.

32. What is known as a means for placing man according to body and soul in a good position must be tested and must be somewhat developed from the simplest to the most difficult; if the simplest matter was of use one would not need the means.

33. True fortune for the natural man, insofar as it concerns the body, consists in that one can be at peace in all activities if one wish-

es, and insofar as it touches the mind, it consists in that one can wish for what is good for one without compulsion.

34. It would be good if one could discover by zealous searching the creator of human nature; such a person would without doubt come to the best conclusions as to how human nature could be whole.

35. Every rational man will seek what is best for him.

36. Everyone who seeks what is best for himself will give ears to proposals for gaining one's best.

37. Everyone who accepts proposals for gaining one's best must allow tests to be made which cannot bring harm so as to see whether the proposals will bring about one's best or not.

38. If a proposal relates to reflection, one must reflect further on it; if a proposal relates to experience, one must seek further regarding it.

39. Every statement which is at the same time natural and clear to a free and unobscured consideration, is accepted by an undisturbed understanding, and is felt by a free and unbound power of imagination is true.

40. For a proper study of the truth it is necessary that one neither accept it nor throw it aside; if one wishes to experience the truth as authentic one must neither desire it nor shut it out; one must not be prejudiced or self-willed.

41. The necessary questions are the following: (1) If I am my own or from someone other. (2) If I can preserve myself or not. (3) If I am of myself or of another. (4) If the Lord is favorable or unfavorable to me, the Lord who can preserve me, and to whom I belong. (5) If he desires something from me by which I can please or displease him. (6) If he has ever revealed his desire and in what manner he revealed it and still reveals it. (7) How I can know if such a revealed desire is the will of my Lord or is the false commandment. (8) If I dare to be disobedient to the commandment of my Lord without hurt to my body or mind. (9) If my fellow preachers are in a position to protect me if I allow myself to be hindered by them in this search for consideration. (10) If closer relationships with my Lord can be pleasanter and more useful for me than the relationship I have with my fellow members. (11) If the means is at hand for me to learn my Lord better. (12) If and how I can discover the reason why so good and universal a Lord has so few servants and almost as few friends among my fellow men. (13) If the sad circumstances of myself and my fellow men are a necessary work of our Creator or a miscarriage. (14) If it is possible to become

once again a proper work of our Creator. (15) If this possibility brings with it so much laboriousness that one dare not even consider it possible. (16) If this labor lays upon us or is with us alone or if it is either a work of the Creator himself or a cooperative work of the Creator. (17) If we have had any thoughts which bring us to such a question, or have taken something from others which explains such things to us, or have discovered some powers which drive us to this. (18) If we have followed our thoughts, studied doctrines, and used the power. (19) If the thoughts arose by themselves or from other causes; if they were impressive or flighty. (20) If the doctrines were clear, rational and sensible at the same time, or in which of these aspects they fell short. (21) If the experience was free or the result of constraint. (22) If we were willing to follow that religion which our thoughts had prevailed upon, if its doctrines were perfect in all ways, and if experience arose in us in a most attractive way. (23) If there was anything present which could make us better inwardly. (24) What we have to do to make this something known. (25) If we could achieve this by our own activities, if only we decided to.

42. It is necessary for us to study carefully all and each of these truths so that our reason, insofar as we have it, might be freed of affections and intemperance, our thoughts might be released, encouraged, ordered, and made easy, and our imaginative power might be enlivened and grasped.

43. And since we cannot bring about these activities ourselves, because of the lack of necessary power and abilities, but must gain them elsewhere, there is nothing other necessary but that we wait for them with desire, note them with care, and bear them with docility.

44. It is necessary that we do not put trust in our powers, that we humble the understanding, collect our thoughts, and allow feelings to be at rest.

Nicolas Ludwig, Count von Zinzendorf

THE LITANY OF THE LIFE, SUFFERING AND DEATH OF JESUS CHRIST*

Congregation: Praised be Jesus, Lamb of God! May he be adored forever! How mightily and how marvelously are we saved by him. Praised be his grace which lives and has breath, and lets his praise be sounded in heaven and on earth. He is worthy of this.

Leader: Praised be Jesus who though he was in the form of God did not count equality with God a thing to be grasped, but emptied himself, taking the form of a servant, being born in the likeness of men. And being found in human form he humbled himself and became obedient unto death, even death on a cross. Therefore God has highly exalted him and bestowed on him the name which is above every name, that at the name of Jesus every knee should bow, in heaven and on earth and under the earth, and every tongue confess that Jesus Christ is Lord, to the glory of God the Father [Phil. 2:6–11].

Congregation: Indeed he is eternally worthy of this, that in a thousand ways all beings in Heaven and on earth praise him.

Leader: Lord God Father in Heaven, you so loved the world that you gave your only son that all who believe in him should not perish but have everlasting life.

---

*Translated from Hans Urner, *Der Pietismus* (Glabeck, 1961), pp. 56–59.

	Lord God Son, Savior of the world, like a human child you took on flesh and blood. Lord God Holy Spirit, you came to him and remained in him; in him the complete fullness of the Godhead dwelt bodily.
Congregation:	Holy Trinity, be blessed because of the Lamb of God. Amen, Halleluja! Halleluja! Amen, Halleluja!
Leader:	Christ came here in the flesh from the Father. He is God above all, praised in eternity. He left us an image which we are to follow in his footsteps. He was like to his brothers in all ways, because he was merciful and a true High Priest before God. He was tempted in all ways like us, but without sin. Because he suffered and was tempted, he can help those who are tempted.
Congregation:	Lamb of God, holy Lord God, hear our prayer of need; have mercy upon us.
Leader:	From the sin of not believing in you, From all sins of the flesh and the spirit, From all self-righteousness, From all lukewarmness and drunkenness, From all indifference to your wounds and death.
Congregation:	Defend us, dear Lord God. There is nothing in us but poverty. By your blood, death, and suffering give us a warm, completely submissive heart.
Leader:	O Immanuel, Savior of the World
Congregation:	Make yourself known to us!
Leader:	By your holy incarnation and birth
Congregation:	Make us love our humanity!
Leader:	By your poverty and servanthood
Congregation:	Teach us to be lowly in this world!
Leader:	By your powerlessness and weakness
Congregation:	Strengthen our weakness!
Leader:	By your gracious childlikeness
Congregation:	Help us reach the joy of children!
Leader:	By your correct understanding of the Scripture
Congregation:	Make firm the word of truth in us!

297

Leader:	By your holy simplicity
Congregation:	Make our hearts and minds simple!
Leader:	By your obedience and servanthood
Congregation:	Help us to be obedient in heart
	Make me like in mind to you, as an
	obedient child, meek and still.
	Jesus, now, help me that I might
	be obedient as you.
Leader:	By your holy life on earth
Congregation:	Teach us to walk peacefully!
Leader:	By your endurance and industry
Congregation:	Help us patiently endure!
Leader:	By your faithfulness
Congregation:	Make us faithful on our part!
Leader:	By your pilgrim life on earth
Congregation:	Teach us to be at home everywhere!
Leader:	By your watching and praying
Congregation:	Teach us to be wakeful in prayer!
Leader:	By your humility, meekness, and patience
Congregation:	Make us proud to bear your yoke!
Leader:	By your mildness and mercy
Congregation:	Teach us to be merciful!
Leader:	By your zeal for your Father's house
Congregation:	Make us zealous for your kingdom!
	Now, our King, you have our heart and mind!
	We are able to do little but we bring ourselves to you, so that each of us in our whole person might read your holy image.
Leader:	Christ, Lamb of God, you who take away the sins of the world
Congregation:	Give us your peace!
Leader:	By your willingness to die
Congregation:	Give us the mystery of your love!
Leader:	By your holy baptism of blood
Congregation:	Set us forth upon God's earth!
Leader:	By your tears and cry of dread
Congregation:	Console us in dread and pain!
	You shed so many tears for us,
	So many drops of blood flowed out from you,

298

So many are the voices which pray for us and plead for us.

Leader: By your head crowned with thorns
Congregation: Teach us the nature of the kingdom of the Cross!
Leader: By your outstretched hands on the Cross
Congregation: Be open to us at all times!
Leader: By your nail-pierced hands
Congregation: Show us where our names stand written!
Leader: By your wounded feet
Congregation: Make our path certain!
Leader: By your pale beautiful lips
Congregation: Speak to us consolation and peace!
Leader: By the last look of your breaking eyes
Congregation: Lead us into the Father's hands!

Holy Lord God,
Holy strong God,
Holy merciful Savior,
You eternal God.
Never let us fall
From the consolation in your death!
Kyrie eleison.

Leader: By the form of your suffering and death
Congregation: Remain continually before our eyes!
Leader: May the impression of your passing
Congregation: Be before us always.
Leader: May your martyrdom and blood
Congregation: Nourish us to eternal life!
Leader: May the permanent testament of death
Congregation: Be a rule for your heirs!
Leader: May the Word of your Cross
Congregation: Remain our confession of faith!

We wish to remain by the Cross, and to follow your martyrdom until we see you face to face.

Leader: Worthy is the Lamb who was slain to receive power and wealth and wisdom and might and honor and glory and blessing [Rev. 5:12].
Congregation: From eternity to eternity. Amen.

Therefore you, heart without comparison, in your beautiful death you are never to leave our sight until

Congregation: we look upon you forever. In the hymn "Jesus is
(cont.)   without compare" our voices are never to tire until
                 they are formed together in the highest congrega-
                 tion.

Nicolas Ludwig, Count von Zinzendorf

SELECTED HYMNS*

HEBREW MACARONIC

If one is Mechulle [corrupted]
He will find Geulle [redemption]
at Ose Isch [sign of man] in blood;
And if the greatest Rosche [wicked man]
as a Posche [transgressor]
falls to his feet, it is good.

What a good B'sore [message]
His blood is the Cappore [atonement].
We redeemed are by it
It cries for our Mechile [forgiveness]
God hears and grants the Meile [petition];
The heart feels it and is consoled.

I believe b'emune schleme [with complete faith]
a person as a B'heme [beast]
Which knows nothing of Mizvos [good works]
Can without much difficulty
by the blood become a Zaddic [righteous man]
Praise, honor and laud be to the blood.

ETERNAL DEPTH OF LOVE DIVINE

Eternal depth of love divine,
  In Jesus, God with us, displayed;
How bright thy beaming glories shine!
  How wide thy healing streams are spread!

---

*Translated from Albrecht Schöne, hrsg., *Das Zeitalter des Barock* (München, 1968), pp. 227–228 (Hebrew Macaronic); translations by Wesley from *Herrnhut Gesangbuch* (1735) are from John Wesley, *Hymns and Sacred Poems* (London, 1739).

301

With whom dost thou delight to dwell?
  Sinners, a vile and thankless race:
O God, what tongue aright can tell
  How vast thy love, how great thy grace!

The dictates of thy sovereign will
  With joy our grateful hearts receive:
All thy delight in us fulfil;
  Lo! all we are to thee we give.

To thy sure love, thy tender care,
  Our flesh, soul, spirit, we resign:
Oh, fix thy sacred presence there,
  And seal the abode forever thine.

O King of glory, thy rich grace
  Our feeble thought surpasses far;
Yea, even our crimes, though numberless,
  Less numerous than thy mercies are.

Still, Lord, thy saving health display,
  And arm our souls with heavenly zeal;
So fearless shall we urge our way
  Through all the powers of earth and hell.

                                    (translated by John Wesley)

            *   *   *

O thou to whose all-searching sight
The darkness shineth as the light,
Search, prove my heart; it pants for thee;
Oh, burst these bonds, and set it free!

Wash out its stains, refine its dross,
Nail my affections to the Cross;
Hallow each thought; let all within
Be clean, as thou, my Lord, art clean!

If in this darksome wild I stray,
Be thou my light, be thou my way;
No foes, no violence I fear,
No fraud, while thou, my God, art near.

When rising floods my soul o'erflow,
When sinks my heart in waves of woe,
Jesus, thy timely aid impart,
And raise my head, and cheer my heart.

Savior, where'er thy steps I see,
Dauntless, untired, I follow thee!
Oh, let thy hand support me still,
And lead me to thy holy hill!

If rough and thorny be the way,
My strength proportion to my day;
Till toil, and grief, and pain shall cease,
Where all is calm, and joy, and peace.

(translated by John Wesley)

Nicolas Ludwig, Count von Zinzendorf

FROM

NINE PUBLIC LECTURES*
1746

CONCERNING SAVING FAITH

Preached in the Brethren's Chapel in London, September 6, 1746
Text: 1 Peter 1:7–8: "At the revelation of Jesus Christ. Without having seen him you love him; though you do not now see him you believe him."

The special connection, "You love and believe now in Him," compels me to make a very necessary observation, namely, that in many places in the Holy Scriptures faith is called love; and this is so not only in the New Testament, but occurs already in the Old . . . (Gen. 22:12). It is necessary that we mark this well, for otherwise the whole thirteenth chapter of the First Letter to the Corinthians would be an unintelligible chapter, since Paul explicitly says, "Even if one believes, yet he will not be saved, if he does not love" (1 Cor. 13:2).
Now the Savior states positively that he who believes shall be saved (Mark 16:16); and Paul says, nevertheless, that even though one believes, he will not be saved, if he does not love.
Hence it is quite clear that the Holy Scripture wants to point out to us that there is no saving faith which is not simultaneously love for him who laid down his life for us, for him who has created us, without whom we cannot live and exist for one moment.
In order to make myself clear on this subject, I must now treat faith, and, out of necessity, I must divide my lecture.
I will call faith *fiducia implicita* and *explicita*. Faith as it is in our own selves shall be called *fiducia implicita*, and faith which is manifested to others, which unfolds itself, shall be called *fiducia explicita*.

*Reprinted with permission from Nikolaus Ludwig Count von Zinzendorf, *Nine Public Lectures on Important Subjects in Religion,* translated and edited by George W. Forell (Iowa City: University of Iowa Press, 1973), p. 39–42, 74–87.

Now both of them, when they are together, are such that they make the man who has them unspeakably happy and even here manifest eternal life.

But in any event, if they cannot be together, then it is sufficient if only the first is there, the *fiducia implicita,* the undisclosed but affective believing within the heart. And this faith within the heart which one has within himself I also view from two perspectives: the first is "faith-in-distress" and the second "faith-in-love."

No man can create faith in himself. Something must happen to him which Luther calls "the divine work in us," which changes us, gives us new birth, and makes us completely different people in heart, spirit, mind, and all our powers. This is *fides,* faith properly speaking. If this is to begin in us, then it must be preceded by distress, without which men have no ears for faith and trust.

The distress which we feel is the distress of our soul when we become poor, when we see we have no Savior, when we become palpably aware of our misery. We see our corruption on all sides and are really anxious because of it. Then afterward it happens as with patients who have reached the point of crisis; they watch for help, for someone who can help them out of their distress, and accept the first offer of aid without making an exact examination or investigation of the person who helps them. That is the way it went once with the woman whom the Savior healed. For twelve years she had gone to see all kinds of physicians and had endured much from them. And finally she came upon him too and said, "If only I would touch that man's clothes, it would help me; even if I could not get to the man himself, if I could only get hold of a bit of his garment, then I would be helped" (Matt. 9:21).

This is faith-in-distress. And here I can never wonder enough at the blindness and ignorance of those people who are supposed to handle the divine Word and convert men, for example the Jews and heathen, those abortive so-called Christians (who are indeed as blind as Jews and heathen) who think that if they have them memorize the catechism or get a book of sermons into their heads or, at the most, present all sorts of well-reasoned demonstrations concerning the divine being and attributes, thus funneling the truths and knowledge into their heads, that this is the sovereign means to their conversion. But this is such a preposterous method that if one wanted to convert people that way, reciting demonstrations to them, then it is just as if one wanted to go against wind and current with full sails, or as if one, on the contrary, would run one's boat into an inlet so that one could not find one's way out again.

For that same knowledge of divine things which is taken to be faith, although it appears only, other things being equal, as an adjunct of faith, puffs up and nothing comes of it. And if one has all of that together, says Paul, and does not also have love, and even if one can preach about it to others, still it is nothing more than if a bell in the church rings. As little as the bell gets out of it, as little as it is benefited by the fact that it hangs there and rings, just so little does the fact that a teacher makes the most cogent demonstrations benefit him as far as his own salvation is concerned.

But what results from this faith-in-distress, from this blind faith which one has out of love for one's own salvation? What comes of a bold trust in the physician that he can and shall help, without knowing what his name is and who he is, without having known and seen him before, without having clearly sensed what sort and nature of man he is? Thankful love results from it, as long ago with Manoah and his wife, who so loved the man who came to them; they did not know him, though, for they said, "What is your name? We do not know you, but we love you. We should like to know who you are, that we may praise you when what you have said to us comes true" (Judg. 13:17). So it is exactly with the faith-in-distress: It has to do completely with an unknown man, yet with a man of whom one's heart says, "He likes to help, he likes to comfort, and he can and will help." My heart tells me that it is he of whom I have heard in my youth, of whom I have heard on this or that occasion. They called him the Savior, the Son of God, the Lord Jesus, or however else one has heard him named and however anyone in anxiety and distress thinks of him. In short: "He must help me; oh, if he would only come to my aid! If he would only take my soul into his care, so that it would not perish! Kyrie Eleison! Lord have mercy!"

Now faith-in-distress has the infallible promise that one shall be helped; the man having faith-in-distress shall obtain grace. No one shall come in vain, no one ask in vain. This was the faith-in-distress of the thief on the cross (Luke 23:42). . . . Had the thief been so inclined in prison, then one doubt or another would probably still have developed in the meantime; but because the thief had no time, it went very well. With people who are healthy and prosperous, who can be distracted or deliberate in the interim, who can eat, drink, sleep, and go to work in the meantime, they will probably have second thoughts which will disturb their faith. Such disruptions do not consist in doubts whether there is a Savior, or whether this man could help, or whether the invisible Jesus of whom one has heard could rescue souls from their destruction. Rather, the question will really be whether he wants to help such a sinner, who is such a thoroughly miserable and wretched creature. Sin begins to dawn on one only after faith, after trust, after the yearning and longing for help, for rescue, when one has time for reflection, when the distress is not too pressing. When distress and aid do not succeed each other so quickly that one cannot think of anything in between, the doubt comes, saying, "I am too great a sinner." But doubt is no sooner there, it is no sooner arisen, than it is really refuted by the actual forgiveness of sins: "Take heart, my son; your sins are forgiven" (Matt. 9:2).

At the same time we must note that all this is God's work in us, *fides implicita*, which has to do with the heart alone. It is within the heart, regarding which one has nothing to demonstrate to anyone else. Here one has to do with God alone and with his work in the heart; and here, at the very moment when one knows and feels himself to be so wretched, grace and forgiveness of sins is preached into his heart. This happens with infallible certainty and without anxiety that it could come to nothing. Man emerges at once out of the deepest sorrow and dismay over himself into blessed rest and contentment and, at the same time, into love and thankfulness and attachment to him who died for his soul, who gained eternal life for him with his blood (whether he had thought more about the matter or less, knew more or less, does not matter). From that very hour he loves him as his highest good, and the Savior can say to him, "You do indeed truly love me, and I have also forgiven you a great many sins; I have rescued you from genuine misery, it is true; now you stand there and feel ashamed for all eternity and can hardly get over your astonishment at how much I have forgiven you."

> Were the patience of them all,
> In every heavenly hall,
> In nations all around,
> And in God's people true,
> In one heart to be found—
> Good friends, I say to you,
> His patient gentleness,
> Surpasses even this. . . .

All this is still *fides implicita*, the faith which is God's work in the heart in the middle of our stillness, where we and he have to do with each other alone, where nothing comes between us and him—no man, no book, no knowledge, no learning, not even the most necessary truths—but only the distress, the sinner's shame, and the faithfulness of the Shepherd.

Now I come to the other faith, which I have called *fides explicita*, the faith which unfolds and manifests itself. And this faith is also of two kinds: faith while one is still learning about the Savior, and faith when one expounds and teaches the Savior to others.

Not seeing and yet loving makes one ask afterwards, "Who is that? What is that which I love this way?" And then one soon enough gets information for one's heart.

The people who had seen the risen Lord, who had loved him so tenderly, went away with fear and joy and told no one anything. They knew now that he was not a mere man; they knew that something more profound, indeed something inexpressible lay behind the man; but they lacked the words, the fitting expressions. They felt it sufficiently that their Creator was their Savior. Thomas, when he had to do only with the eleven and the Savior, could cry out without reflection, "My Lord and my God!" (John 20:28). But if they would have had to go and tell the people that the Savior was God, that he had redeemed the whole world, then they would not have had words for it. This they could not yet explain, for this was for them not unraveled for speaking. They could not bring it into a discourse nor make it plain. It did indeed shine through all their expressions, but not in any orderly fashion. . . .

This is the great subject matter; this is the chief object of faith. I know nothing but that you have died for me out of love; you have laid down your life for me. I know that if you had not died for me, I should have been lost; I should have sunk into the bottom of hell, had you not extinguished hell for me, had you not (as Dr. Luther says) drunk up death.

This is the first part of *fides explicita*. One knows in his inmost person with whom he deals. One knows him from head to foot, in heart and body. One knows him in his most profound nature as it is now and was then. And when one has thought and felt this long enough and has arranged it in all possible drawers of the mind and has become a scribe instructed for the kingdom of Heaven, then one takes out one truth after the other, presents it and demonstrates it with reasons grounded deep within oneself, which grasp the hearers' hearts. For if one would speak to those who know and love the Savior about his glory and majesty, then they say, "There is no doubt about that; that is clear enough to me, and I have no hesitation here. But the trembling of God shakes my soul. His suffering, his death, his anxiety, his atoning-battle which he endured for me, the fact that he had to be absolved through the Holy Spirit for my sake, that with him all my sin is forgiven, that with him I have leave to be eternally blessed—this is the reality for which no word, no expression is adequate." One's feeling of this cannot be made plain to someone who does not have it himself. It all gets stuck or comes out only half and half. These are the *arrheta rhemata*, the unspeakable things.

> When the heart confronts my eye
> In all his godly greatness,
> Then I think, "I die!"
> To gauge again that greatness,
> According to his humanity,
> No heart can be so small,
> So weak no other ever can be,
> As this heart at all.
> Then I think: Good-bye,
> You self-empowered repenting.
> Like wax before the fire, I
> Want to melt in Jesus' suffering.
> My heart shall see the wrath
> In this suffering, pain,
> And see the cleansing bath
> For all my transgressions' stain.

When a person has this faith, this faith-in-distress, this faith made doubtful by reason of great unworthiness, this faith which has fallen in love through the real help, through the blessed happiness and grace which the heart has obtained, is that not beautiful? When a person has within himself the meditations of faith and the lasting feeling, the searching in Jesus even up to his eternal Godhead, finding his Father and his spirit, and all this coming from his side, out of his heart, is that not beautiful? And when he at last has, experiences, and obtains as a gift the learned faith which preaches from the wounds of Jesus to his Creator's power and from his Creator's power into the side of Jesus, into his wounded heart, and which makes everybody convinced and wise and brings them to an evident and demonstrative certainty, is that not beautiful? Is that not a great blessedness? Does that not make a blessed man who, as Paul says, believes all this from his heart (Rom. 10:9) and can say and confess it with a plerophory [subjective complete assurance]? His faith so flows from his heart that he can thus pour himself out before mankind.

But what grace, what patience and condescension it is, that the Creator, who knows his poor creature better than it knows itself, requires of it no other faith for being saved than the faith-in-distress, the first faith. When my anxiety, my sin, my corruption makes me believe, then I think, "He who appears before my heart, who has such a bloody appearance, who is said to have died for me, certainly it will be he. Yes! Yes! It is he! That makes me blessedly happy; that helps me into the eternal kingdom." Whoever does not learn to believe this way, that is, whoever does not have so much misery, so much distress that he must believe, how can that person be helped? He is already judged for this very reason, because he does not feel misery enough to cause him gladly to believe.

Faith is no great art; rather, the first beginning of faith, the very first faith, is an effect of misery. No man except one who has the spirit of Lucifer, who has a satanical pride and blindness so that he does not want to see his physical and spiritual distress, who has been brought to insensibility because he will not feel his daily plague (and that is a Satan's spirit, a Satan's pride), none but such a person is in danger of missing the faith-in-distress. For even though a man is proud and egotistic in a merely human way and finally nevertheless does find in himself the fibres of his utter corruption and distress, his excuses cease, he begins to inveigh against himself, to condemn himself. And as soon as he does this, as soon as he discovers himself lost, then he is so full of anxiety that he does not have to create any for himself; he does not have to imagine any misery. And if this anxiety remains in him and increases and pushes its way into all his business, into his well-being, and he is forced to cry out for help, then he is in faith, in the faith-in-distress, in the midst of saving faith, and does not know himself how he got into it: "I believe it gladly because I delight in it."

So easy is it to be saved; so completely without excuse remain those who perish through unbelief.

*On the Essential Character and Circumstances
of the Life of a Christian*

Preached in the Brethren's Chapel in London, September 25, 1746

Text: John 21:16: "Do you love me?" [RSV]

My purpose is to make clear from these words what constitutes the essential Christian. . . .

We want to look first at the essential character of a Christian, and secondly we will consider the circumstances of his life.

The genuine character of a Christian consists absolutely in this: When he speaks with the Savior, when he speaks with his brethren, when he has anything to straighten out with God the Father, when he needs the ministry of angels, when he shall present himself on the day of the Lord to join in judgment over the living and the dead—then he absolutely does not appeal to his religious denomination, but rather to his nature, to his descent. For the most serious objection on that day will be, "I do not know you nor where you come from" (Luke 13:25).

This is the *Crinomenon* [judgment], which decides on that day and in all similar circumstances and upon which it depends that one is received and the other cast away. The Savior does or does not call a person to mind. "I will acknowledge him; I will say, 'I know you'" (Matt. 10:32).

Therefore, it is a rule belonging absolutely to the character of the true Christian that, properly speaking, he is neither Lutheran nor Calvinist, neither of this nor the other religious denomination, not even Christian. What can be said more plainly and positively? What reformer, be it Hus or Luther or Wycliffe, or whatever his name might be, would be so presumptuous as to maintain that men are saved because they are his followers? For Paul excludes Christ himself when he says, "Not of Paul, not of Cephas, not of Apollos, not of Christ" (1 Cor. 1:12).

It is really a great misfortune that people read the Scriptures but read them without the proper attention and that such main passages are not noticed. For seventeen hundred years men have written this for all the world to see, *Christianus sum* [I am a Christian] and for as many centuries have put this into the mouths of all the martyrs,

311

Christianus sum, which is contrary to the plain words of the apostle Paul, who has expressly forbidden that any man call himself "of Christ" or Christian. Let our enemies call us that, let the Turks and pagans, let the Jews call us this in derision: *Vir bonus, sed malus, quia Christianus est* [He is a good man, and bad because he is a Christian], it is a pity that he is a Christian. But we must not speak this way. To be sure, the ancient fathers have themselves given occasion to this confusion: Prudentius says, *"Secta generosa Christi nobilitat Viros,"* that is, the noble, the excellent religion of Christ makes people even more noble than they were before.

Who directed the people to do this? Who directed them to make a religion out of the family of Christ, in direct contradiction to the Holy Scriptures? It does not matter that men have confessions of faith; it does not matter that they are divided into religious denominations; they may very well differentiate themselves according to their *Tropo Paedias* [form of doctrines]. An upright Christian man can say, I side with Calvin; an upright Christian man may also say, according to my judgment I rather side with Luther. But this gives neither the one nor the other the least warrant, the least right to salvation; this only distinguishes him according to his insight and as an honest man among the faithful; it entitles him not to be arbitrarily judged in his manner of acting, in his form, his method of treating souls, and in the outward appearance of his worship. Each thing has its peculiar external form, its external shape, and everything does not look alike. No man has the same point of view as another, and by this means he distinguishes himself innocently and inoffensively. For as soon as anyone appeals to the fact that he does not hold with another's logic, in that moment the other's right to censure him ceases. And it is a vulgar, mean disposition of mind when people of one religious denomination take pleasure in opposing people of another, or when on that account they show enmity toward each other. For as soon as someone says that he is of a persuasion different from mine, then he has taken away my spiritual right over him to censure him.

Now thus far it is good that we have many religious denominations; up to this point I am in agreement, so much so that I despise anyone who, without the deepest and most thoroughly examined reason, changes over from one denomination to another; so much so that nothing sounds more ridiculous to my ears than a proselyte. Only with the greatest difficulty can I make myself deal with such a person, when I become aware that he has left his former denomination, especially among the Protestants, who all take the Scriptures as the guiding principle of faith. Therefore, frivolity should not govern denominational matters. The differences in religious denominations are important and venerable concerns, and the distinction of religious denominations is a divine wisdom. No peculiarity should cause a disturbance. But all of these ideas still betray their human origin, of which it may be said that three hundred, five hundred, a thousand years ago things were not yet conceived in this way. There is only one of whom it may be said, "Yesterday, today, and forever he is ever still the same" (Heb. 13:8).

And his church stands as she has stood,
Jehovah the Father is her God;
She still retains her very first dress:
Christ's own blood and righteousness.

Now then, I have said what a Christian is not, what a person must not presume to comprehend under the name Christian, in what respect a person must not boast of Christ, what a Christian upon occasion must consider entirely *skybala*, refuse, as Paul calls it (Phil. 3:8), whenever it tends to interfere with the foundation, with the main point, even were it good and real in itself or could in a certain sense be valid.

Now, what then is the proper character of a Christian? Take notice, my dear friends, for here we must in advance set aside the common word as it is used in all languages, except the German, which has something special in its usage.

In all languages one says a Christian, and in our German alone one says, *ein Christ*, and that is the right word. "All things are yours; and you are Christ's" (1 Cor. 3:22b–23a); you belong to Christ, you are his heirs, you are his family. And in another place it is also put quite "germanly": "You are bone of his bone and flesh of his flesh," and this refers to Genesis 2:23. "She shall be called Woman [*Männin*], because she was taken out of Man [*Mann*]" (Gen. 2:23b). All the prophets make allusion to this when they say, "Those who are called according to my name" (Isa. 43:7). In no way are we called by the name of Jesus or Christ in the sense of a religious denomination, as if Christ were our teacher, as if Christ were our prophet, our lawgiver, as if he were the founder, the author of our religion, as it is sometimes expressed by a pagan historian, as for example in Lucian. "The founder of this religion was crucified" [Lucian, "The Passing of Pere-grinus," in *The Works of Lucian*, 8 vols. (Cambridge: Harvard University Press, 1936), 5:13]. "The man who was crucified in Palestine because he introduced this new cult into the world." In this sense we are not Christians. Rather, we are Christians in the same way that, in our European countries, a wife takes the name of her husband and afterward is called not by her maiden name but by her husband's name. Thus every soul who has the right to call herself by this name, "because she was taken out of Man" (Gen. 2:23), belongs to Christ, is Christian.

Now whoever will not grasp this and has no other support for himself than that he has read the teaching of Jesus and industriously given lectures on it, that he can recount this teaching, and that he is established in its principles according to his religious denomination—such a person can be considered nothing more than one of those Christianly religious people. And even though he discharges all the duties according to his religious denomination, so that there can be no objection to him, yet he cannot on that basis lay claim to this: "O Lamb of God, you who take away the sin of the world (John 1:29), acknowledge me!" Rather, whoever wishes to claim this, he must be christened in his heart, as here in England it is said of one who is baptized, "He is christen'd"; he must be made a Christian; he must be of the bone and spirit of Christ; he must in truth take pride in this: "My Maker is my husband" (Isa. 54:5); he has not only created me, and he is not only the potter of my clay, but "he is the husband of my soul, who has betrothed himself to me forever and has betrothed himself to me in grace and mercy, yet, has betrothed himself to me in faith" (Hos. 2:19f.). I am certain who my husband is; I know him.

Thus far I have spoken about the character of a Christian, of a man who can call himself Christian without being a liar or a foolish, stupid person who does not know what he is saying.

Now I come to the other part of my discourse, to the chief circumstances which are found in the case of such a Christian.

The character of a Christian, the entrance into this state, and the entire progress in it as well are based on the text which I have read: "Do you love me?"

First of all, it is undeniable that if a person had no other certainty concerning the Savior than what the schoolteacher dictated to him about him in his youth, he would certainly be in bad shape. For then this objection might be raised against him: "Who knows? If you had been born a Jew, then you would have believed what the rabbi had taught you; if you had been born a Turk, then you would have believed what the Mullah had taught you; if you had been born in a pagan religion, you would have believed what the bonze or the lama or some other pagan priest had taught you." And not much of a reply can be made to that. . . .

But what is the special factor which so distinguishes us from all the religions, from all the persuasions and opinions, that every reasonable person must admit it? It is just that very thing which the Apostle Paul calls the folly of his preaching.

Here one would like for God's sake to beg all theologians, if they would only listen, not to take such pains constantly to represent our religion as agreeing with reason, as being common sense. If writings of this kind are assigned to pamphlets, by which people earn a living for themselves, then it may pass. But as soon as it is taken seriously, as soon as they want to demonstrate to atheists and common deists and people like that, that our religion is a wisdom rooted in their heads, a discernment which they can take in their own way, then they are obviously threshing empty straw, according to all instruction of the Scripture.

This position is false from the very start, for Paul states positively that there is something foolish in our preaching, and none of the wise ones of this world can comprehend it. There is no ear that can hear our language; there is no eye that can see our concerns; there is no sight sharp enough, no natural understanding sufficient to penetrate our matters, and one must be prepared for this. As it is said in the Acts of the Apostles, *tetagmenoi*, "as many of them were ordained for eternal life" (Acts 13:48); there the work had been done, their head, their mind, and their heart had been set straight, they could apprehend these things as wisdom, as wisdom in spite of everything. "Teach me wisdom in my secret heart," said David, "You purge me, you wash me, you make my bones rejoice, which before were broken and you give me a ready spirit" (Ps. 51:6b–10); you give me ideas quite different from those I had before, and you do this, your wisdom in my secret heart does this. This is the wisdom in 1 Corinthians 1, which none of the wise people of this world were able to reach or obtain; and if a bet be made, says Paul, if there are contrasting opinions on how the gospel shall be propagated, how the teaching of Jesus shall grasp the hearts, and an honorable man says, "Our wise, our understanding people will do this; the vulgar certainly will not comprehend it, but if it comes first to the learned, wise, and devout people, they will understand it"—then Paul tells them to their faces: Now we do have Christianity, and we do have an example, a congregation of God; now, good friend, where are the wise, where are the intelligent, where are the nobles? Well? Show them to me.

This is the plain, true, and genuine meaning of all that Paul says in the place cited. This is to prove nothing else but that the ordinary means do not suffice, that the ordinary frame of mind is not enough, that the understanding of man, as man, is as insufficient for grasping our matters as is the understanding of a poor animal for comprehending our geometric or algebraic propositions. It is undeniable; it must first be given to us. . . .

Instead of this the proud spirit of man, that presumptuous creature, which, however, is only a poor wretched human being, says in a quarrelsome way to its Creator, "It is foolishness, nonsense; it is enthusiasm; it is good for fanatics." This is quarreling and striving against the Creator; for the people who say this have our Bible as well as we do; they read it, they print it, and they circulate it among men as God's Word. What right do they have to call these same biblical truths foolishness, just because they do not understand them? They have most certainly no right, but it is their pleasure. Every man loves to maintain his own assertion; every man is so disposed that if there is something he does not have, the other person shall not have it either, and what the other person does have is nothing at all, is not even worth the effort. Therefore I cannot help it: our theology, our mysteries, our Christianity I must let pass as foolishness for them, with the protestation that it is nevertheless wisdom for those who understand it; in this sense of it I will now mention what it is all about.

My friends, I will not dispute about how one enters into the state of being a Christian. Words are spoken, there is preaching; fine hymns and texts on glorious things contribute and are means to it, yes, may even be vehicles of it. But they are not the whole, not even the central concern. Then what is the central concern? My friends, it is this: Whoever will answer yes to the Savior's question "Do you love me?" must have caught sight of the Savior when the Savior looked into his heart for the first time. This is the order: First the Savior looks at us, and we perceive him; at that moment we have the matter in hand, and the Christian is ready.

My friends, not even a quarter of an hour, not even a minute, not even as much time as it takes to stop to think must intervene between the point when the Savior looks at us and when we perceive him. Afterward we again stop seeing; then we believe, and then it is the constant and unceasing act of the Savior to be looking at us: "His eyes remain open day and night toward us" (2 Chron. 6:20). "I will counsel you with my eye upon you" (Ps. 32:8b).

I want to explain these two points a little more closely. When a person becomes a Christian [*ein Christ*], when the Savior receives him, when a person is admitted to the power to be a child of God, then it happens this way: for a moment the Savior becomes present to him in person. In an hour, in a moment (it may be in an indivisible point of time which cannot be compared with any measure of time that we have, including moments themselves), a person comes into the circumstances in which the apostles stood when they saw him.

I do not pretend that we see a body with our corporeal eyes; I do not desire that the mind try to imagine a body or try to conceive a representation of it, or that the mind look into itself or turn its thoughts in toward itself until it sees a form standing before it. But I do ask for the essential in this, and that is that a person who has seen abstractly and purely must in the next moment realize that he has actually seen; that a person must know as certainly that his spirit has seen, that his heart has seen and felt, as when in ordinary human life one can be certain that he has seen or touched something. In the moment when this happens he does not need to have a sense experience or see something visible (this cannot be excluded with any certainty, but neither is it essential); it is only necessary that afterward the essential effect remain, that one can say not only, "I have seen, I have heard"; but rather, "Thus have I seen it, and thus have I heard."

The Scripture says that our entire work of the gospel is to portray Jesus, to paint him before the eyes, to take the spirit's stylus and etch—yes, engrave—the image of Jesus in the fleshly tablets of the heart, so that it can never be removed again.

Now the only question is, "In what kind of a form does one see the Savior?" In the Old Testament it was said, "You shall not make yourself a graven image or likeness" (Exod. 20:4), for this reason: In all your life you have never seen a likeness nor any original, and therefore you cannot make a copy. For I will not have my religion, my worship, profaned with masks and illusions; cherubim you may make, for you have seen some of them. But you shall make no god, for in your entire life you have never seen one.

In the New Testament this commandment is at an end: We have

seen. Therefore the Lutherans are right in leaving this commandment out of the catechism, for it no longer has any relation on earth to us. This makes the particular distinction between us and the Reformed, for they combine the ninth and tenth commandments to make room for the commandment forbidding images, which we Lutherans, according to our understanding, leave out of the Decalogue. We do not hold that a person should make himself no picture or image in the New Testament; a person may make an image, no, he should. It is a part of the Christian religion to form for oneself a picture of that God who took a body upon himself. Augustine wishes to see *Jesum in Carne,* Jesus in the flesh; and because I cannot do this, he said, he stands before my eyes as if I saw him being crucified.

Some of the theologians have wanted to find the whole suffering form of the Savior in the Song of Songs, in the bride's description of her beloved, "This is my beloved" (Song 5:26), and think that there he is painted piece by piece, as his figure was on the Cross. I do not want to enter into this discussion at present. But this is certain, that Christians can rightly, by divine right, sing:

> In that form appear to me
> As, for my great distress,
> Upon the Cross so tenderly
> You did bleed to death.

This they may claim; they have a right to speak this way, and all men, all souls have a right to say what Thomas said, "Unless I see in his hands the print of the nails, and place my finger in the mark of the nails, and place my hand in his side, I will not believe" (John 20:25).

And this is the advice which I give to all hearts. If anyone asks me about his salvation, I say to him, "Do not believe, if you do not want to be deceived, do not believe until you see the prints of the nails and place your finger in the prints of the nails and place your hand in his side: then believe."

But who must see? It is the heart which must see at least once. Afterward it goes on believing until it shall see him again. I must freely concede that this advice does not at first sight seem to conform to the advice of the Savior, "Blessed are those who have not seen and yet believe" (John 20:29b). Now how shall I reconcile my advice with the words of the Savior? Nothing is easier: There is a seeing and a not seeing. The Scripture shows that this is possible: "They have eyes and

318

do not see, they have ears and do not hear" (Jer. 5:21). Therefore a person may also not seem to see and yet be seeing; a person may not seem to hear and yet be hearing; a person may not seem to feel and yet be feeling. And so it is, "as dying, and behold we live" (2 Cor. 6:9). According to the external senses and the human disposition we neither see, hear, nor feel the Savior. But why then does he so often say, "I will manifest myself" (John 14:21)? Why does he say, "He who has ears to hear, let him hear" (Mark 4:9)? And that he did not say this only to those people who were speaking with him is made clear in that he repeated in the Revelation of John to those people who did not see him, "He who has ears to hear, let him hear" (Rev. 3:22). Why does the Apostle say, "You should seek him until you feel him" (Acts 17:27)? All his arrangement in the whole world was made for this purpose, that people may obtain a feeling of him (Acts 17:27). And from where comes the testimony of the apostle, "When it pleased God to reveal his Son in me, I set out immediately" (Gal. 1:15–16)? And from where comes the constant witness of all the other apostles concerning the direct and immediate special relationship with him?

Once one is involved in the Spirit, one comes into that extraordinary state concerning which John expresses himself thus, "I was in the Spirit on the Lord's day" (Rev. 1:10a). And this may happen with more or less sense experience, with more or less distinctness, with more or less visibility, and with as many kinds of modifications as the different human temperaments and natural constitutions can allow in one combination or another. One person attains to it more incontestably and powerfully, the other more gently and mildly; but in one moment both attain to this, that in reality and truth one has the Creator of all things, the fatherly Power, the God of the entire world, standing in his suffering form, in his penitential form, in the form of one atoning for the whole human race—this individual object stands before the vision of one's heart, before the eyes of one's spirit, before one's inward man. And this same inward man, who until now has been under the power of the kingdom of darkness, as soon as he catches sight of his Deliverer, this Deliverer reaches out his hand to him and plucks him immediately out of all corruption; he pulls him out of the dungeon of his prison and places him in the light before his face: "Take heart, my child, your sins are forgiven (Matt. 9:2); I will make a covenant with you, that you shall be mine (Jer. 31:33); I will be your advocate in judgment, and you shall be allowed to appeal to me; but, will you have me?" Do you receive me? Do I suit you? Am I acceptable to you? Do I please your heart? See, here I am! This is the way I look. For your sake I was made to be sin (2 Cor. 5:21), and for your sake I was made a curse (Gal. 3:13); for the sake of your sins I was torn, beaten, and put to death. I have sweated the sweat of fear and anguish, the sweat of death, the sweat of the strife of penance; I have laid down my life for your sake. I have been laid into the dust of the grave for your sake. Does this suit you? Is this important to you? Are you satisfied with me? Do I in this way please you? Do I please you better in the idea of a mangled slave who is thrown to the wild beasts in the circus, or in the form of the emperor who sits high on the throne and takes pleasure in the destruction of the poor creature? How do I please you the best?

He who in this moment, in this instant, when the Savior appears to him and when he says to him, as to Peter, "Do you love me in this figure?"—he who can say, "You know all things; you know that I love you"; he who in this minute, in this instant, goes over to him with his heart, passes into him, and loses himself in his tormented form and suffering figure—he remains in him eternally, without interruption, through all eons; he can no longer be estranged from him. No possibility can be imagined, though the whole universe should join together, that anything could separate him from that friendship which is formed at the moment of his bloody appearing.

Now this is the entrance to this state, that one receives him at that moment, looks at him longingly, and falls in love with him; that one says, "It is true; now I can do nothing more, now I want nothing more. Yes, God Creator, Holy Spirit! My eyes have seen your soterion [Salvation] (Luke 2:30), they have seen your little Jesus; my heart wept for joy when his nail prints, his wounds, his bloody side stood before my heart. You know this."

Then our perdition is at an end; then flesh and blood have lost. Satan, who had already lost his case in court, really lays no more claim on such a soul; and it is just as if a man, who had sold himself to Satan, gets back his promissory note, as if the slip of paper came flying into the meeting, torn to pieces. The signature, the note, says the Apostle, is torn up and fastened to the Cross, pounded through with nails, and forever cancelled; and this is registered at the same time, that is, we are set free; we are legally acquitted. When the books are opened, so it will be found.

What is called repentance in the world, what is called conversion, this David describes thus: "As the eyes of the servants look to the hand of their master, as the eyes of a maid to the hand of her mistress" (Ps. 123:2), so the eyes of the sinner look for him until he appears before them. Then a person begins to look and to listen in the hope of finding the Savior as his Creator in his true, human suffering form, with his corpse wounded for us, before our eyes. When that has happened, then the person has seen him and now believes continually, no more desiring to see and never again in his whole life losing the look of the tortured Savior; he remains engraved in one's heart. One has a copy of this deeply impressed there; one lives in it, is changed into the same image, and every year, I might say every day, is placed into a greater light streaming from the wounds: It looks more and more reddish around such a person, as the prophets express it (Isa. 1:18); he appears more and more sinful; as we express it, he keeps to the point of his sufferings. Then one can no longer fluctuate. One knows of no other presence of the Creator than in the beauty of his sufferings.

But what kind of authority, what kind of eternal and incontestable effect on our heart, does his perpetual look have afterward? This belongs to our progress. Here there is no need to tell people, do not steal, do not get drunk, do not lead a disorderly life, do not be so fond of the creature, do not set your heart on this and that, do not be hostile. Now there is no need to preach one point of morality after the other at a person, not even of the most refined and subtle. Even though a person were to be most adept in the matter and become an example to the whole country, still there would be no need for reasoning. For every loving look from the Savior indicates our morality to us throughout our whole life: One dissatisfied, one sorrowful, one painful look from the Savior embitters and makes loathsome to us everything that is immoral, unethical, and disorderly, all fleshly-mindedness, as often as it is necessary.

I suppose that we remain men; it is a part of the state of sin not to think more highly of ourselves. But we shall succeed, if our Head but look now and then, at some interval, upon us.

We are not people who from the first moment of our spiritual life until into eternity itself remain unassaulted and unattacked. From a distance something comes at us; there is something in our own selves which we cannot name, to which we have as yet been unable to give the right name, until the proper position of the soul has been determined. This must be handled with great caution and watched over carefully; and even if it should stick in the deepest recesses of the mind, even if it is also lying imprisoned, so that it is actually not able to block our course in following Christ, yet it is still there, and no reading, no hearing, no moral doctrine guards against it. For the only remedy against all such alluring demands, gross or subtle, is the doubtful glance of the Savior, when the form of Jesus does not seem so pleasing, so joyful to our hearts, when he seems to us to be no longer so sweetly before our hearts as usual.

People who have murdered someone have said that the person and image of the murdered one always hovered before their eyes; they have neither been able to bear it nor escape from the sight of it. We also say of people who are very important to us, I see him as clearly as if he were here; I could paint him right now. This David applies to his Savior, "I have placed him so directly before my eyes that I will never lose him from my thoughts, from my point of view; I need only look up, and I have him immediately there" (Ps. 139). Suppose, then, that one might fall into all sorts of questionable situations, if possible to go astray in something, to allow oneself to be implicated in something by one's thoughts, to wander from the Savior with one's senses. The Savior need only look at one, even though one does not look toward him, and the glance of his eyes goes through one like a flame of fire: One is transparent, known throughout by him; he knows the moment when he is to look at us, and he also knows how he is to look at us, for he has read our thoughts before they have formed themselves. When Judas came and betrayed him, he preached him a sermon: "My friend, you give me a kiss and betray me." When Peter denied him, he spoke no words but rather looked upon him. In the case of Judas the sermon availed nothing; the look had this effect on Peter: "He went out and wept bitterly" (Matt. 26:75); he bathed himself in tears. What kind of tears? Tears of love. He wept for love, for he had not owned, confessed, or affirmed his Master, for he had not risked his life for him. And when the Savior said a few days later, "Do you love me?" the answer was, O dear Lord! I appeal to you; you have looked upon me: you have seen not only the faithful Nathanael under the fig tree, but you have also seen me, an unfaithful heart. You do know what your look has effected; you know indeed how your look operated upon my heart; my eyes were wet with tears; it went through body and soul. Yes, the Savior was obliged to say, it is true; you already have the right doctrine, and you are a good theologian; you know what you shall set forth to the church; you shall be a bishop. Point your diocese only toward my merits; point them only toward this method of coming to love me, toward this method which I have used, the method which you have experienced, which immediately brings a person out of all labyrinths into the right way. "Strengthen your brethren" (Luke 22:32) with the example of your conversion by the glance of my eyes.

It is this also, beloved in the Lord, which we have to wish each other at the end of this discourse, that we may be looked upon by the Savior so graciously, so powerfully, so essentially; and that at the same time we may be so blessed, so happy that we turn away our view and our eyes from everything which otherwise seemed to us proper or improper and turn them toward him with no desire to look at or into anything else; that our eye may not be able to throw a glance anywhere else but to this point.

And when you have once caught sight of the beauty of his suffering, so that in all your life you will not be able to get rid of that sight, then he conducts you with his eyes wherever he will have you; then with his eyes he teaches you what good and evil is. Your knowledge of good and evil lies in his eyes; not in the tree from which Adam poisoned himself, from which Adam ate his curse, but rather in the eyes of the tortured Lamb, there lies your blessed, happy knowledge of good and evil. As far as this same image looks upon you, into the midst of your mortal bodies, so far shall you be changed, pervaded, captivated by the person of Jesus, so that your other brethren perceive you no longer as a man in your denomination, as a brother of the same persuasion only, but rather as a consort, as a playmate for the marriage bed of the blessed Creator and eternal Husband of the human soul.

PRAYER

My dearest Savior! We beg of you this same blessed look, this same irresistible look, which you always know to fix upon the souls who like to look upon you, who like to receive you, who, when you come, are ready to pass over into your heart and wounds, to whom the touching of your corpse is important, for whom the first savor of your corpse can banish all curse and guide them even to the sight of your wounds. And to this look help, according to your wisdom, all souls, high and low, rich and poor, in all the circumstances they are in, at the moment of their willingness. In the meantime let us witness so long and, as far as possible, propagate our testimony among mankind so long, until you have gradually accomplished the number of those who want to and will see your saving Cross's image here in time, and until nothing more is remaining which pertains to election, so that your witnesses, before they rest, may be able to bring you the answer: Lord, what you have commanded is done, and there is still room.

Nicolas Ludwig, Count von Zinzendorf

BROTHERLY UNION
AND
AGREEMENT AT HERRNHUT*
1727

1. It shall be forever remembered by the inhabitants of Herrnhut, that it was built on the grace of the living God, that it is a work
of his own hand, yet not properly intended to be a new town, but
only an establishment erected for Brethren and for the Brethren's
sake.

2. Herrnhut, and its original old inhabitants must remain in a
constant bond of love with all children of God belonging to the different religious persuasions—they must judge none, enter into no dis-
putes with any, nor behave themselves unseemly toward any, but
rather seek to maintain among themselves the pure evangelical doctrine, simplicity, and grace.

3. The following are the characteristics of a true member of
Christ's body, and these we, the inhabitants of Herrnhut, who simply
adhere to the foundation built on the Word of God, deem to be the
most sure. Whosoever does not confess that he owes his awakening
and salvation exclusively to the mercy of God in Christ Jesus, and
that he cannot exist without it for one moment of his life, that the
greatest perfection in life (were it possible to attain to it, without the
intercession of the Mediator, urged by the plea of his blood and merit)
would be of no avail in the sight of God, while it is made acceptable
in the beloved; and whoever does not daily prove it by his whole conversation, that it is his full determination to be delivered from sin,
through the merits of Jesus, and to follow daily more after holiness, to
grow in the likeness of his Lord, to be cleansed from all spiritual idol-

*Reprinted and modernized from *The Memorial Days of the Renewed Church of the
Brethren* (London, 1895), pp. 111–121.

atry, vanity, and self-will, to walk as Jesus did, and to bear his reproach and shame: such a one is not a genuine brother. But whosoever has this disposition of heart, though he maintain sectarian, fanatical, or at least defective opinions, shall not on that account be despised among us, nor in case of his even separating himself from us will we immediately forsake him, but we will rather follow him in his wanderings, and spare him, and bear with him in the spirit of love, patience, and meekness. But whosoever is not fully established on the above-named fundamental principles, though he do not wholly forsake them, shall be considered as a halting and wavering brother, and be reclaimed in the spirit of meekness.

4. It is laudable in itself for the Congregation to devote certain days to the special remembrance of the faithful leading of our God, celebrating them with fasting and prayer, or thanks and praise. Such days, for instance, as that of the emigration of the first Brethren on the twelfth of May, on which day in different years many remarkable events have taken place. In like manner every individual may consecrate those days, which to him are the most memorable, to the Lord, spending them as above with his intimate brethren and friends. But in both cases care must be taken that this appropriation of certain days does not degenerate into mere lifeless custom.

5. Those who, with an unfettered conscience, acquiesce in the present external regulations of the church will not hesitate to declare the ground of their acquiescence, to wit, that they do not consider human regulations and customs as an unalterable part of divine worship, but make use of them, agreeably to the dictates of Christian liberty, in a spirit of meekness, love, and obedience, till the Lord himself brings about a change. Should in aftertimes any particular order of things be introduced among us, in respect to the outward form of devotional rites, simplicity and edification must be aimed at exclusively.

6. Whoever has not been used to auricular confession, or has conscientious objections in his mind against it, shall not be forced to submit to it at Berthelsdorf; yet no one shall be permitted to go to the Holy Communion without the previous knowledge of the minister at Berthelsdorf, in order that all confusion and levity may be prevented.

7. No one is to enter into confidential intercourse with people that are notoriously wicked, or altogether worldly minded, lest offense should thereby be given; yet it is proper that such people should be treated as much as possible in an equitable and unassuming man-

ner, and none should allow themselves in any vehemences against them.

8. Everyone should be careful to comprehend the true foundation of the saving doctrine on which we are all agreed, so that we may be able to give an answer to all our adversaries in meekness, yet with wisdom and power, and all may mutually defend and support one another.

9. When any traces of a good work begin to show themselves in one soul or another, no premature judgment concerning them should be formed; but it is expedient to wait with patience till the fruits begin to appear, while we must feel thankful to God for the good beginning which is to be traced, and promote their welfare as much as lies in our power.

10. In general, we consider it an abominable practice for anyone to judge and condemn his neighbor rashly, and without clear and full evidence, and without previously using all the acknowledged and scriptural degrees of brotherly correction. Whoever, therefore, is guilty of this unjustifiable proceeding subjects himself to well-merited censure.

11. Ministers, laborers, and all whose official incumbency it is to care for and watch over the souls of others must be at full liberty to hold frequent and full intercourse with one or the other, and no suspicion is to be cast on them on that account.

12. As the conversion of souls is the chief object of most of the present inhabitants of Herrnhut, everyone must be permitted to choose those with whom he would, for the time being, be more intimately connected, than he could be with others; and to alter his choice according to circumstances without fearing to give offense.

The intercourse between single persons of both sexes must have its restrictions, and the elders are empowered to prevent it whenever in any case scruples arise in their minds against such intercourse, though the apparent aim of it might be ever so laudable.

13. Envy, suspicion, and unfounded prejudice against the brethren must be most carefully guarded against. As everyone is at liberty to cultivate an intercourse with others, no one ought to take it amiss if another should appear more familiarly acquainted with the elders than he.

14. For the sake of the weak, no light conversation is to be allowed concerning God and spiritual things, but such subjects ought always to be treated with the greatest reverence.

15. Agreeably to the practice of the primitive church, the Brethren are called upon to exert themselves in every possible way for the benefit of those who are of the same household of faith; and to all others they are to do as they would wish that others should do unto them.

16. Whosoever has received the needful gift for it is to speak, the others to judge.

17. Those who seem to be best suited one to the other may, without hesitation, live in the habit of close familiarity, join in prayer, and act in all respects as intimate friendship requires; yet such preference given to any individual must by no means be to the prejudice of cordial brotherly love toward all others; and it becomes the duty of those who are particularly acquainted one with the other to lend each other a helping hand as it regards doctrine, admonition, reproof, direction, yea, their whole spiritual course.

18. No brother is to enroll himself as a member of any particular trading or handicraft association without first acquainting the others of his design. And no business carried on among us is to be looked upon as in itself mean and despicable.

19. No one shall, even in the smallest way, overreach his neighbor, much less defraud him.

20. No marriage is to be contracted without the knowledge and approbation of the elders, and no promise of marriage is to be given and received, except in their presence, and with their consent.

21. No son shall require his father or mother to move from his house as long as they have a mind to continue there in peace and quietness.

22. All superstitious notions and practices are inconsistent with the character of true brethren; and idle tales of apparitions, omens, and so forth, must be looked upon as foolish and hurtful.

23. As there are those who more particularly stand in need of daily admonitions—there shall be daily opportunities given for exhortation and edification at Herrnhut; yet no one can be considered obliged to attend on these occasions, unless the whole congregation should be expressly called to assemble together.

24. If anyone should be overtaken in a fault, he must not consider it disgraceful to be spoken to on the subject, or to receive admonition or reproof. He ought to take it in good part, and not allow himself to retort, much less think himself warranted on that account

to withdraw from the fellowship of the Brethren. All matters of this kind should be judged and decided exclusively by those whose official incumbency requires their interference.

25. Whosoever spreads any unfounded report against another is bound to declare to the elders the reason of his allegations, and afterward to racant the report, whether required to do so in consequence of the complaint of the person injured thereby or not.

26. Whenever in public companies anything is said to the disadvantage of anyone not then present, everyone is authorized to acquaint the person alluded to of it, yet without naming the offender.

27. It is the special duty of some brethren to visit, from motives of self-denying charity and love, those fellow members of the congregation who are afflicted with sickness and ailments, and to attend to their wants. And as long as we shall be favored to have a physician who is one of us, every inhabitant of Herrnhut should speak to him and ask his advice about any ailments or illness of his before he seeks counsel from others. No one who is not properly qualified for it should venture to undertake the cure of others.

28. The names and circumstances of the patients are to be immediately mentioned to the sick-waiters of both sexes; and the prescriptions of the physicians, as well as the directions of the sick-waiters themselves, ought to be carefully observed both by the patients themselves and by those who are about them.

29. Everyone must conscientiously keep to himself what has been confidently, and as a secret, entrusted to him.

30. No one is to harbor anything in his mind against another, but rather immediately, and in a friendly and becoming manner, mention what may have offended him, without respect of persons. Complaints which have been purposely suffered to accumulate must not even be listened to, but quarrels, envy, and willful dissensions ought to be abominated by all, and those who are guilty of these things be looked upon as unbelievers.

31. A mechanic or tradesman ought to be most punctual in fulfilling the promises he has made; and in case circumstances should prevent his doing so, it is his duty to mention, in due time, the cause of his not being able to act according to his promise.

32. All judicial interference is to be grounded in the plain commandments of God, on these statutes, and on natural equity and justice.

33. Every effort shall be made to reclaim the erring by friendly reproof and discipline, but should this fail the offender is expected and required to leave the place.

34. The elders shall hold a conference every Saturday, and if any be cited to appear before that conference he is to obey the summons, and in case of reiterated and obstinate refusal he must leave the place.

35. The watchers are to sing a verse from a suitable hymn, at the change of the successive hours in the night, with a view to encourage and edify the Congregation.

36. The doctrine and example of Jesus and his apostles shall be the general and special rule of all our ministry and instruction.

37. Whosoever perseveres in an open course of levity and sin, though often before warned and admonished, shall be excluded from our brotherly fellowship, nor can he be readmitted till he has given sufficient proof of his being an altered character.

38. All the young people at Herrnhut who shall confess their faith in Christ are to be confirmed, after which these statutes are to be given them for their consideration.

39. No magisterial person, minister, elder, or warden, nor anyone else who may in this or the other respect have authority over others, shall use the power possessed by him, otherwise than to be a helper of the joy of those over whom he is placed, and to comfort them in sufferings, trials, and wants.

40. All who are influenced by the love of God must keep up a friendly and cordial fellowship with all who are like-minded, making in this respect no exceptions.

41. Everyone shall be at liberty in love to admonish and rebuke his brother, whether there be ground for it or not. But this must be done with great modesty, and all vehemence on either side be carefully avoided. If an explanation or exculpation be offered, the person who gave the admonition ought either to be satisfied with it or refer the case to other Brethren.

42. Should we be called to suffer persecutions, everyone should consider them precious and most useful exercises; love those that persecute us, treat them respectfully, answer their questions with modesty and simplicity, and cheerfully submit to what may befall us, according to the confession we make before God and man.

BIBLIOGRAPHY

Althaus, Paul. *Die Prinzipien der deutschen reformierten Dogmatik im Zeitalter der aristotelischen Scholastik.* Leipzig: Deichert, 1914.

Ames, William. *The Marrow of Theology.* Edited and translated by John D. Eusden. Boston: Pilgrim Press, 1968.

Arndt, Johann. *True Christianity.* Translated with introduction by Peter C. Erb. New York: Paulist Press, 1979.

Die Bekenntnisschriften der evangelisch-Lutherischen Kirche. Berlin: Deutsches Evangelisches Kircherbundesant, 1930.

Bente, F. "Historical Introduction to the Book of Concord." In *Concordia Triglotta.* St. Louis, Mo., 1921.

Boehme, Jacob. *The Way to Christ.* Translated with introduction by Peter C. Erb. New York, 1978.

Calvin, Jean. *Institutes of the Christian Religion.* Translated by F. L. Battles. Philadelphia, 1977.

Dorner, Isaac A., *History of Protestant Theology.* Translated by George Robson and Sophia Taylor. 2 vols. Edinburgh, 1891.

Heppe, Heinrich. *Reformed Dogmatics.* Translated by G. T. Thomsen. London, 1950.

Hirsch, Emmanuel. *Geschichte der neueren evangelischen Theologie.* Gütersloh, 1951.

Käsemann, Ernst. "New Testament Questions of Today." In his *New Testament Questions of Today.* Translated by W. J. Montague. Philadelphia, 1969.

Käsemann, Ernst. "Thoughts on the Present Controversy about Scriptural Interpretation." In *New Testament Questions of Today.*

Knox, Ronald A. *Enthusiasm.* Oxford, 1961.

Koepp, Wilhelm. "Wurzeln and Ursprung der orthodoxen Lehre der unio mystica." *Zeitschrift für Theologie und Kirche* 29 (1921).

Lang, August. *Puritanismus und Pietismus.* Neukirchen Kreis Moers, 1941.

Langen, August. *Der Wortschatz des deutschen Pietismus.* Tübingen, Max Niemeyer Verlag, 1968.

Leube, Hans. *Kalvinismus und Luthertum im Zeitalter der Orthodoxie.* Leipzig, 1928.

Leube, Hans. *Orthodoxie und Pietismus.* Bielefeld: Luther Verlag, 1975.

Leube, Hans. "Pietismus." In *Die Religion in Geschichte und Gegenwart.* Tübingen: J. C. B. Mohr (Paul Siebeck), 1931.

BIBLIOGRAPHY

Leube, Hans. *Die Reformbestrebungen der deutschen lutherischen Kirche im Zeitalter der Orthodoxie.* Leipzig, 1924.

Martin, Geck. *Die Vokalmusik Dietrich Buxtehudes und der frühe Pietismus.* New York: Barenreiter, 1965.

Neve, J. L. *The Lutherans in the Movements for Church Union.* Philadelphia, 1912.

Nigg, Walter. *Das ewige Reich.* Erlenbach-Zurich, 1944.

Obermann, Heiko A. *The Harvest of Medieval Theology.* Cambridge, Mass., 1963.

Obermann, Heiko. "Simul gemitus et raptus. Luther und die Mystik." In *Kirche, Mystik, Heiligung und das Natürliche bei Luther,* edited by Ivan Asheim. Göttingen, 1967.

Preuss, Robert D. *The Theology of Post-Reformation Lutheranism, A Study of Theological Prolegomena.* 2 vols. St. Louis, Mo., 1970.

Ritschl, Otto. *Dogmengeschichte des Protestantismus.* 4 Bde. Leipzig, 1908–1927.

Scharlmann, Robert P. *Thomas Aquinas and John Gerhard.* New Haven and London, 1964.

Schmid, Heinrich. *The Doctrinal Theology of the Evangelical Lutheran Church.* Translated by Charles A. Hay and Henry E. Jacobs. Philadelphia, 1876.

Weber, Hans Emil. *Der Einfluss der protestantischen Schulphilosophie auf die orthodox-lutherische Dogmatik.* Leipzig, 1980.

Weber, Hans Emil. *Reformation, Orthodoxie und Rationalismus.* 2 Bde. Gütersloh, 1937–1951.

Williams, George. *The Radical Reformation.* Philadelphia, 1962.

General Studies on Pietism

Aland, Kurt. *Pietismus und Bibel.* Witten, 1970.

Barthold, Friedrich Wilhelm. *Die Erweckten im protestantischen Deutschland während des Ausgangs des 17. und der ersten Hälfte de 18. Jahrhunderts.* 1852/1853; reprint, Darmstadt, 1968.

Baum, Friedrich. *Das schwäbische Gemeinschaftleben.* 2. Aufl. Stuttgart, 1929.

Baumgart, Peter. "Leibnitz und der Pietismus: Universale Reformbestrebungen um 1700." *Archiv für Kulturgeschichte* 48 (1966).

Benz, Ernst. "Pietist and Puritan Sources of Early Protestant World Missions." *Church History* 20 (1951).

Benz, Ernst. *Die Protestantische Thebais.* Wiesbaden, 1963.

Beyreuther, Erich. *Geschichte des Pietismus.* Stuttgart, 1978.

Bornkamm, Heinrich. *Mystik, Spiritualismus und die Anfänge des Pietismus im Luthertum.* Giessen, 1926.

Brown, Dale. "The Bogey of Pietism." *The Covenant Quarterly* 25 (1967).

Brown, Dale. *Understanding Pietism.* Grand Rapids, Mich., 1978.

BIBLIOGRAPHY

Gerdes, Egon. "Pietism: Classical and Modern." *Concordia Theological Monthly* 39 (1968).

Godfroid, Michel. "Le Pietisme allemend a-t-il existe? Histoire d'un concept fait pour la polemique." *Etudes Germaniques* 101 (1971).

Goebel, Max. *Geschichte des christlichen Lebens in der rheinisch-westphälischen Kirche.* 3 Bde. Coblenz, 1849–1860.

Goeters, Wilhelm. *Die Vorbereitung des Pietismus in der Reformierten Kirche der Niederlande.* Leipzig und Utrecht, 1911.

Greschat, Martin. *Zur neueren Pietismusforschung.* Darmstadt, 1977.

Günther, Hans R. G. "Psychologie des deutschen Pietismus." *Deutsche Vierteljahrsschrift* 4 (1926).

Hadorn, W. *Geschichte des Pietismus in der schweizerischen Reformierten Kirche.* Konstanz und Emmishofen, 1901.

Heppe, Heinrich. *Geschichte des Pietismus und der Mystik in der Reformation Kirche.* Leiden, 1879.

Kaiser, Gerhard. *Pietismus und Patriotismus im literarischen Deutschland. Ein Beitrag zum Problem der Säkularisation.* Frankfurt, 1973.

Kohl, Manfred Waldemar. "Studies in Pietism. A Bibliographical Survey of Research since 1958–59." Ph.D. Diss., Harvard University, 1969.

Miller, Daniel W. "A Comparison of the Theologies of the Anabaptist, Pietistic and Schwenckfelder Movements." BST Diss., New York Biblical Seminary, 1948.

Mirbt, Carl. "Pietismus." In *Realencyklopädie für protestantische Theologie und Kirche*, vol. 15 (1896–1913).

Moltmann, Jurgen. "Geschichtstheologie und pietistisches Menschenbild bei Johann Coccejus und Theodor Undereyck." *Evangelische Theologie* 19 (1959).

Namowicz, Tadeusz. "Pietismus in der deutschen Kultur des 18. Jahrhunderts. Bemerkungen zur Pietismusforschung." *Weimarer Beiträge* 13 (1967).

Neveux, J. B. *Vie spirituelle et vie sociale entre Rhin et Baltique au XVII siècle de J. Arndt à P. J. Spener.* Paris, 1967.

Ritschl, Albrecht. *Geschichte des Pietismus.* 3 Bde. Bonn, 1880–1886.

Ritschl, Albrecht. *Three Essays.* Translated by Philip Hefner. Philadelphia, 1972.

Sachsse, Eugen. *Ursprung und Wesen des Pietismus.* Wiesbaden, 1884.

Sann, Auguste. *Bunyan in Deutschland. Studien zur literarischen Wechselbeziehung zwischen England und der deutschen Pietismus.* Giessen, 1951.

Schmalenberg, Gerhard. *Pietismus-Schule-Religions-unterricht.* Bern/Frankfurt, 1974.

Schmid, Heinrich. *Die Geschichte des Pietismus.* Berlin, 1863.

Schmidt, Martin. *Pietismus.* Stuttgart, 1972.

Schmidt, Martin. "Pietismus." In *Die Religion in Geschichte und Gegenwart*, vol. 5. Tübingen, 1961.

BIBLIOGRAPHY

Schmidt, Martin, and Jannasch, Wilhelm, eds. *Das Zeitalter des Pietismus.* Bremen, 1965.

Stoeffler, F. Ernst. *German Pietism during the Eighteenth Century.* Leiden, 1973.

Stoeffler, F. Ernst. *Mysticism in German Devotional Literature of Colonial Pennsylvania.* Allentown, Pa., 1950.

Stoeffler, F. Ernst. *The Rise of Evangelical Pietism.* Leiden, 1970.

Tanis, James R. *Dutch Calvinistic Pietism in the Middle Colonies: A Study of the Life and Theology of Theodorous Jacobus Freylinghuysen.* Gravenhage, 1967.

Tanner, Fritz. *Die Ehe im Pietismus.* Zürich, 1952.

Trautwein, Joachim. *Religiosität und Soziolsturktur.* Stuttgart, 1972.

Urner, Hans. *Der Pietismus.* Glabeck, 1961.

Weber, Otto, et al. *Die Stimme der Stillen.* Neukirchen Kreis Moers, 1959.

Weigelt, Horst. *Pietismus-Studien, I. Teil: Der Spener-hallische Pietismus.* Stuttgart, 1965.

Zsindely, Endre. *Krankheit und Heilung im älteren Pietismus.* Zurich, 1962.

Spener and Pietist Beginnings

Aland, Kurt, ed. *Philipp Jakob Spener, Pia Desideria.* Berlin, 1964.

Aland, Kurt. *Spener-Studien.* Berlin, 1943.

Blaufuss, Dietrich. *Reischsstadt und Pietismus—Philipp Jacob Spener und Gottleib Spizel aus Augsburg.* Neustadt an der Aisch, 1977.

Blaufuss, Dietrich. *Spener-Arbeiten. Quellenstudien und Untersuchungen zu Ph. J. Spener und zur frühen Wirkung des lutherischen Pietismus.* Bern-Frankfurt, 1975.

Bruns, Hans. *Philipp Jakob Spener: Ein Reformator nach der Reformation.* Giessen und Basel, 1955.

Deeter, Allen C. "An Historical and Theological Introduction to Philipp Jakob Spener's Pia Desideria: A Study in Early German Pietism." Ph.D. Diss., Princeton University, 1963.

Grünberg, Paul. *Philipp Jakob Spener.* Göttingen, 1906.

Rüttgardt, Jan Olaf. *Heiliges Leben in der Welt. Grundzüge christlicher Sittlichkeit nach Philipp Jakob Spener.* Bielefeld, 1978.

Schicketanz, Peter. *Carl Hildebrand von Cansteins Beziehungen zu Philipp Jacob Spener.* Witten, 1967.

Spener, Philipp Jakob. *Christliches Ehren-Gedachtnüss . . . Schadens.* Berlin, 1698.

Spener, Philipp Jakob. *Erfordertes Theologisches Bedencken.* Ploen, 1690.

Spener, Philipp Jakob. *Sieg der Wahrheit und der Unschult.* Cölln an der Spree, 1692.

Spener, Philipp Jakob. *Theologische Bedencken.* Halle, 1700–1702.

Wallmann, Johannes. *Philipp Jakob Spener und die Anfänge des Pietismus.* Tübingen, 1970.

BIBLIOGRAPHY

Wildenhahn, Karl. *Pictures from the Life of Spener.* Translated by G. A. Wenzel. Philadelphia, 1879.

Francke and Halle

Beyreuther, E. *August Hermann Francke, 1663–1727.* Hamburg, 1958.

Beyreuther, Erich. *August Hermann Francke und die Anfänge der ökumenischen Bewegung.* Hamburg, 1975.

Dannenbaum, R. *Joachim Lange als Wortführer des hallischer Pietismus gegen die Orthodoxie.* Ph.D. Diss., Göttingen, 1952.

Deppermann, Klaus. *Der hallesche Pietismus und der preussische Staat unter Friedrich III.* (I.) Göttingen, 1961.

Francke, August Hermann. *Faith in Christ, Inconsistent with a Sollicitous Concern about the Things of This World.* Translated by Joseph Downing. London, 1709.

Francke, August Hermann. *A Guide to the Reading and Study of the Holy Scriptures.* Translated from the Latin by William Jacques. Philadelphia, 1823.

Francke, August Hermann. *A Letter to a Friend concerning the Most Useful Way of Preaching. . . .* Translated by David Jennings. London, 1754.

Francke, August Hermann. *Predigten über die Sonn- und Fest-Tags Episteln. . . .* Halle, 1741.

Francke, August Hermann. *A Sermon on the Resurrection of Our Lord Preached on Easter Sunday.* London, 1732.

Francke, August Hermann. *Sonn- Fest- und Apostel-Tags Predigten.* Halle, 1746.

Francke, Kuno. "Cotton Mather and August Hermann Francke." *Studies and Notes in Philology and Literature.* Boston, 1896.

Geistreiches Gesangbuch . . . samt seiner Vorrede von Johann Anastasio Freylinghausen. Halle, 1705.

Guerike, Henry, *The Life of Augustus Hermann Francke.* Translated by Samuel Jackson. London, 1837.

Hayen, Hemme. "The Autobiography of a Seventeenth Century Pietist." Translated and edited by D. E. Bowan and G. M. Burnett. *The Downside Review* 87 (1969).

Heinrichs, Carl. *Preussentum und Pietismus.* Göttingen, 1971.

The Journals of Henry Melchior Muhlenberg. Translated by Theodore G. Tapper and John W. Doberstein. 3 vols. Philadelphia, 1942.

Kramer, Gustav. *August Hermann Francke: Ein Lebensbild.* Halle, 1880.

Peschke, Erhard. *August Hermann Francke.* Berlin, 1981.

Peschke, Erhard. *Bekehrung und Reform: Ansatz und Wurzeln der Theologie August Hermann Francke.* Bielefeld, 1977.

Starck, Johann Friedrich. *Tägliches Handbuch in guter und bösen Tagen.* Konstanz, n.d.

BIBLIOGRAPHY

Stark, John Frederick. *Daily Handbook for Days of Rejoicing and of Sorrow.* Philadelphia, 1855.

Radical Pietism

Arnold, Gottfried. *Die Erste Liebe.* Franckfurt & Leipzig, 1712.

Arnold, Gottfried. *Das Geheimnisz der Göttlichen Sophia oder Weisheit.* Leipzig, 1700.

Arnold, Gottfried. *Göttliche Liebes-Funcken.* Frankfurt, 1968.

Arnold, Gottfried. *Historie und Beschreibung der Mystischen Theologie/oder geheimen Gottes Gelehrtheit.* Franckfurt, 1703.

Arnold, Gottfried. *Neue Göttliche Liebes-Funcken.* Franckfurt, 1701.

Arnold, Gottfried. *Poetische Lob-und Liebes Sprüche.* Leipzig, 1700.

Arnold, Gottfried. *Unparteiische Kirchen- und Ketzer-Historie, Vom Anfang des Neuen Testaments Bisz auf das Jahr Christi.* 2 Bde. Franckfurt, 1699–1700.

Arnold, Gottfried. *Vitae Patrum.* Halle, 1732.

Blankenagel, Werner. *Tersteegen als religiöser Erzieher.* Emsdetten, 1934.

Chauncey, David Ensign. "Radical German Pietism (c. 1675–c. 1760)." Ph.D. Diss., Boston University School of Theology, 1955.

Dibelius, Franz. *Gottfried Arnold.* Berlin, 1873.

Durnbaugh, Donald F. *The Brethren in Colonial America.* Elgin Ill., 1967.

Durnbaugh, Donald F. *European Origins of the Brethren.* Elgin, Ill., 1958.

Durnbaugh, Donald F. "Johann Adam Gruber: Pennsylvania Prophet and Poet." *Pennsylvania Magazine of History and Biography* 83 (1959).

Durnbaugh, Donald F. "Work and Hope: The Spirituality of the Radical Pietist Communitarian." *Church History* 39 (1970).

Erb, Peter C. "Gerhard Tersteegen, Christopher Saur and Pennsylvania Sectarians." *Brethren Life and Thought* 20 (1975).

Erb, Peter C. "The Role of Late Medieval Spirituality in the Life and Work of Gottfried Arnold (1666–1714)." Ph.D. Diss., Toronto, University of Toronto, 1976.

Miller, Donald E. "The Influence of Gottfried Arnold upon the Church of the Brethren." *Brethren Life and Thought* 39–50 (1960).

Moltmann, Jurgen. "Grundzüge mystischer Theologie bei Gerhard Tersteegen." *Evangelische Theologie* 16 (1956), 205–224.

Renkewitz, Heinz. *Hochmann von Hochenau (1670–1721).* Breslau, 1935; reprint Witten, 1969.

Sachse, Julius F. *The German Pietists of Provincial Pennsylvania.* Philadelphia, 1895.

Sachse, Julius Friedrich. *The German Sectarians of Pennsylvania 1708–1800: A Critical and Legendary History of the Ephrata Cloister and the Dunkers.* 2 vols. Philadelphia, 1899–1900.

BIBLIOGRAPHY

Seeberg, Erich. *Gottfried Arnold. Die Wissenschaft und die Mystik seiner Zeit.* Meerane, 1923.

Tersteegen, Gerhard. *Geistliches Blumen-Gartlein inniger Seelen.* Lancaster, Pa., 1823.

Tersteegen, Gerhard. *Geistliche und erbauliche Briefe über das inwendige Leben und wahre Wesen des Christenthums.* Neue Auft. Stuttgart, 1845.

Tersteegen, Gerhard. *Das verborgene Leben mit Christo in Gott, aus den Schriften des erleuchteten Johann v. Bernies Louvigne.* Ins Deutsche übertragen und kurz zusammengezogen von Gerhard Ter-Stegen. . . . Stuttgart, o.J.

Thune, Nils. *The Boehmenists and the Philadelphians.* Uppsala, 1948.

van Andel, Pieter. *Gerhard Tersteegen.* Wageningen, 1961.

Weiser, Max. *Peter Poiret.* München, 1934.

Weiser, Max. *Der Sentimentalische Mensch.* Gotha und Stuttgart, 1924.

Württemberg Pietism

Bengel, Johann Albrecht. *Abriss der 50 genannter Bruder-Gemeine.* Stuttgart, 1751.

Bengel, Johann Albrecht. *Erklärte Offenbarung Johannes oder vielmehr Jesu Christi.* Frankfurt, 1740.

Bengel, Johann Albrecht. *Gnomon Novi Testamenti in qvo ex natvra verborum vi simplicitas, concinnitas, salubritas, sensvvm caelestium indicatur.* Tübingen, 1742.

Bengel, Johann Albert. *Gnomon of the New Testament.* Translated by Charlton T. Lewis and Marvin R. Vincent. Philadelphia, 1864.

Bengel, Johann Albrecht. *Sechzig erbauliche reden über die Offenbarung Johannes.* Stuttgart, 1748.

Ehmann, Karl Christian Eduard. *Oetingers Leben und Briefe.* Stuttgart, 1859.

Fullenwider, Henry Francis. *Friedrich Christoph Oetinger.* Göppingen, 1975.

Grossmann, Sigrid. *Friedrich Cristoph Oetingers Gottesvorstellung.* Göttingen, 1979.

Lehmann, Hartmut. *Pietismus und weltliche Ordnung in Wüttemberg. Vom. 17 bis zum 20. Jahrhundert.* Stuttgart, 1969.

Mälzer, Gottfried. *Johann Albrecht Bengel: Leben und Werk.* Stuttgart, 1970.

Oetinger, Friedrich Christoph. *Biblisches and Emblematisches Wöterbuch.* n pl., 1776.

Oetinger, Friedrich Christoph. *Inquisitio in Sensum Communem et Rationem.* Tübingen, 1753.

Oetinger, Friedrich Christoph. *Theologia ex Idea Deducta.* hrsg. von Konrad Ohly. 2 Bde. Berlin, 1979.

Yeide, Harry E. "A Vision of the Kingdom of God. The Social Ethic of Friedrich Christoph Oetinger." Ph.D. Diss., Harvard University, 1965.

BIBLIOGRAPHY

Zinzendorf and the Moravians

Hahn, Hans Christoph, and Reichel, Helmut, eds. *Zinzendorf und die Herrn-huter Brüder. Quellen zur Geschichte der Brüder-Unität von 1722 bis 1760.* Hamburg, 1977.
Lindt-Gollen, Gillian. *Moravians in Two Worlds.* New York, 1967.
Mälzer, Gottfried. *Bengel und Zinzendorf.* Witten, 1968.
Sessler, Jacob John. *Communal Pietism among Early America Moravians.* New York, 1933.
Taylor, J., and Hamilton, Kenneth G. *History of the Moravian Church.* Bethlehem, Pa. 1967.
Weinlick, John R. *Count Zinzendorf.* New York, 1956.
Zinzendorf, Nickolaus Ludwig von. *Hauptschriften und Ergänzungsbände.* Hildesheim, 1962–1972.

Neo-Pietism and Pietism's Influence

Aland, K., ed. *Pietismus und moderne Welt.* Witten, 1974.
Bacon, Isaac. "Pietistische und rationalistische Elemente in Klopstocks Sprache." *The Journal of English and Germanic Philology* 49 (1950).
Barth, Karl. *Protestant Theology in the Nineteenth Century.* Translated by Brian Cozens and John Bowden. London, 1972.
Busch, Eberhard. *Karl Barth und die Pietisten.* München, 1978.
Forsthoff, H. "Goethe und der westdeutsche Pietismus." *Monatshefte für rheinischer Kirchengeschichte* 15 (1921).
Franz, Erich. "Uber Goethes Verhältnis zur Mystik und Pietismus." *Mitteilungsblatt für den evangelischen Religionsunterricht* 21 (1928).
Friedmann, Robert. *Mennonite Piety through the Centuries.* Goshen, Ind., 1949.
Gaskill, P. Howard. "Hölderlin's contact with Pietism." *Modern Language Review* 69 (1974).
Grossman, Walter. *Johann Christian Edelmann: From Orthodoxy to Enlightenment.* Berlin, 1976.
Kindermann, Heinz. *Durchbruch der Seele, Literarhistorische Studie über die Anfänge der deuschen Bewegung vom Pietismus zur Romantik.* Danzig, 1928.
Lowen, Harry. *Goethe's Response to Protestantism.* Bern, 1972.
Meinhold, Peter. *Goethe zur Geschichte des Christentums.* Freiburg-München, 1958.
Nagler, Arthur. *Pietism and Methodism.* Nashville Tenn., 1918.
Pinson, Koppel S. *Pietism as a Factor in the Rise of German Nationalism.* New York, 1934; reprint New York, 1968.
Reed, Ray Alonzo. "Spenerian Pietism and the Cantatas of Johann Sebastian Bach." Ph.D. Diss., Boston University, 1968.

BIBLIOGRAPHY

Schneider, Robert. *Schellings und Hegels schwäbische Geistesahnen.* Würzburg, 1938.

Söhngen, Oskar, ed. *Die Bleibende Bedeutung des Pietismus . . . Zur 250-Jahrfeier.* Witten und Berlin, 1960.

Tillich, Paul. *Perspectives on 19th and 20th Century Protestant Theology.* New York, 1967.

Trobridge, George. *Swedenborg: Life and Teaching.* New York, 1962.

Uwoke, Tadakazu. *The Significance of Philipp Jakob Spener in the Development of Protestant Thought.* S.T.M. thesis, New York Union Theological Seminary, 1924.

The Journal of John Wesley. London, 1872.

INDEX TO PREFACE, FOREWORD AND INTRODUCTION

INDEX

INDEX

Neo-Pietists, 24–26
Newton, Isaac, 19
Non-partisan history of church and heresy, 11, 14
North America, 7, 25

Obedience, 5
Oetinger, Friedrich Christoph, 17, 18–19, 24
Oglethorpe, James, 22
Ordo salutis, 6, 12, 13, 19
Orphanages, 9
Oxford Greek Testament, 17

Pansophist theology, 17
Parents, family prayer and, x
Pastors, 6, 7; "call", ix; education, xiii, 6, 7, 9
Pelagianism, 25
Petersen, Johann, 16
Petrucci, Cardinal, 16
Pharisaism, 13, 14
Philadelphianism, 16
Pia desideria (Heartfelt Desires for a God-Pleasing Improvement of the True Protestant Church), 5
Pietism, ix–xi, xiii–xiv; enlightenment and, 24
Piety, 5, 6
Poetry, 16
Poiret, Pierre, 16
Porst, Johann, 14–15
Prayer, Kelpius on, 16
Prayer books, 10; Starck's, 10
Prayer groups, 5
Preaching, influence on, ix, xiii
Preservation of believers, 6
Priesthood of the laity, 5, 7
Prophecy, 15
Protestant Church, reform and renewal, 6
Protestant orthodoxy, 3
Purification, 13

Quietism, xiii, 10, 11, 12, 16

Radical pietists, 8, 10, 11, 15; marriage rejected by, 22

Radical Reformation, xiii, 4
Reason, 24
"Reborn" Christians, xiii, 5, 6, 9, 12, 13, 21; mysticism and, 14
Redemption, 6, 21, 24
Reform, 5; church, 7; individual, 5
Reformed Church, 11
Regeneration of believers, See "Reborn" Christians
Reitz, Johann Heinrich, 15
Religious experience, 3
Renewal, church, 6; personal, x, 3, 6, 13
Repentance, viii, 5, 9, 17, 21
Revelation, 24
Revivalism, 2
Rock, Johann Friedrich, 18
Roman Catholic Church, 6, 7, 11
Romanticism, 24
Rothe, Johann Andreas, 20, 21

Sabbatarianism, 15
Sacraments, mediating role of, 3
Salvation, necessities for, 2
Sanctification, 13
Scandinavia, 7, 25
Schade, Johann Kaspar, 11
Schäffer, Melchior, 20
Schleiermacher, Friedrich, 2
Scholasticism, Protestant, 3
Schools, x
Schwenckfelders, 4
Scripture, commentary, 18; interpretation, x, 14, 18; preaching and, xiii; translations, 10, 17, 18
Scripture studies, x, xii, xiv, 2, 5, 12, 17–18
Sectarianism, diminution of, x, 22, 26
Separatism, 6
Sin, 3, 13
Social gospel, 25
Spangenberg, August Gottlieb, 22–23
Spener, Philipp Jakob, 8–9, 12, 20, 22; Pia desideria, xiii, 5–6
Spener-Halle school, 17, 18
Spezial-Gott, 21
Spirit, See Holy Spirit
Spiritual body, 19

INDEX

INDEX TO TEXTS

INDEX

INDEX

INDEX

INDEX

thanksgiving, of, 91, 192–193; Zinzendorf on, 323–324

Preaching, 34, 35–36, 47–48; call to, 54; Francke on, 117–127; Scripture and, 31–32, 33, 34; topics for, 118–127; training in, 47

Pregnancy, 210–215

Pride, 65, 73, 153

Priesthood of laity, Luther's view, 34–36; source, 50–51; spiritual, 50–64

Prophecy, 54, 256

Proselytism, 312–313

Prudentius, 312

Ptolemy I, 263

Pure and Unblemished Worship (sermon), 159–162

Radical Pietism, Arnold, *See* Arnold, Gottfried; Tersteegen, *See* Tersteegen, Gerhard

Reason, 292–295; experience and, 292

Rebirth, Oetinger on, 278–279, 287; wisdom and, 224

Reformation and Scripture accessibility, 34

Religion, morality distinguished from, 118

Religious instruction, communion classes, 164; family and, 33; Scripture study groups, 32–33, 34

Renewal, 121–122; sin after, 116

Repentance, Arnold on, 222, 225; Francke on, 116, 119–120, 143, 152; Oetinger on, 284, 286; Spener on, 68, 70, 73, 79, 80, 82, 86, 90; Zinzendorf on, 320–321

Reproof, 61–62, 64, 111, 328, 329, 330

Resignation, basis and method of, 84; hindrances to, 86; meditation and, 86; sacraments and, 85; Scripture and, 85

Resignation (Spener), 83–87

Resurrection, bodily, 130; conversion as, 129–130; Francke on, 128–134

Revelation, 68, 69, 291–292; Book of, 272–274

Roman Catholic Church, 35, 69; fasting in, 81; mystical theology and, 68; Scripture reading and, 34, 35

Rule for the Protection of Conscience and for Good Order in Conversation or in Society, 108–113

Sabbath devotions, eve of, 181–184; morning, 185–186

Sacraments, 85, 95; Baptism, *See* Baptism; Holy Communion, *See* Holy Communion

Sacrifice, priestly, 52–53

Salvation, certainty of, 145–148

Sanctification, theology of, 68

Scholastic theology, 68, 70, 229, 230, 231, 232

Scripture, access to, 31–32, 34, 56; commentaries, 255–257, 258, 260; denominations and, 311–313; election and, 147; enlightenment and, 221; faith and, 31, 275; following Christ and, 143, 144; *Gnomen of the New Testament,* 255–271; improper use of, 58; joy and, 95; Luther on, 71–72, 73, 75; mysticism and, 228; Passion narratives, 80–81; prayer and, 71, 72–73, 91; preaching and, 119; reading and study, 32–35, 54–59, 63, 71–75, 165, 255–261, 277; resignation and, 85; resurrection, 130–131; revelation, as, 69, 70; Revelation (Bengel's chronology), 272–274; theology and, 229–233

Scrupulosity, 292

Secular affairs, duty toward, 59, 63

Self-control, 45

Self-deceit, 131, 134, 142

Self-denial, 65, 125, 152, 165–166; fasting, 81, 92, 326

Self-examination, 118

Self-love, 37, 146–147, 221

Self-will, 86, 87

Shaftesbury, 284

Shekinah, 265

349

INDEX

Sin, 96; awareness of, 307, 309; conquest of, 309; death to, 130, 131, 134; habits of, 114–115; meditation on, 78–79; wisdom lost by, 220

Sobriety, 159–160

Solitude, 246

Solomon, 284

Sophia, See Wisdom (Sophia)

Sorrow, 286–287

Spalatin, George, 44

Speech, rules governing, 108–111, 112–113

Spener, Philipp Jakob, *Christian Joy,* 94–96; evangelism, on, 37–40, 61; *God-Pleasing Prayer,* 88–93; *Hindrances to Theological Studies, On,* 65–70; love of neighbor, on, 36–40, 60; *Necessary and Useful Reading of the Holy Scriptures, The,* 71–75; *Pia desideria,* 31–49; *Resignation,* 83–87; Scripture study, on, 31–36, 54–56, 58–59, 63, 71–75; *Spiritual Priesthood, The,* 50–64; *Sufferings of Christ, Meditation on the,* 76–82; *Theologica Germanica,* 44; training of ministers, on the, 41–49

Spiritual Flower Garden (Tersteegen), 249–252

Spiritual Letters (Tersteegen), 241–248

Spiritual Priesthood, The (Spener), 50–64

Spiritual sabbath, 152

Spiritual Songbook, 167–180; Preface, 167–170

Starck, Johann Friedrich, 181–215; exhortations, 181–182, 184, 186–188, 190, 191–192, 193–195, 196–198, 200, 201–202, 203–204, 207, 210, 212–213; hymns, 183–184, 199–200, 205–206, 209, 211–212, 214–215; prayers, 182–183, 184–185, 188–189, 190–191, 192–193, 195–196, 200–201, 202–203, 204–205, 207–209, 210–211, 213–214

Statius, Martin, 126, 166

Study groups, 32–33, 34

Suffering, exhortations and prayers during, 200–204; grace and, 138; Jesus, Passion of, 76–82; Oetinger

on, 286–287; Spener on, 76–82, 87; Starck on, 200–204; Tersteegen on, 241, 244; value of, 87

Superstition, 328

Targums, 265

Tauler, John, O.P., 44, 68, 69

Teaching, 64; laity, by, 61, 63

Temperance, 111, 159

Temptation, 145

Tersteegen, Gerhard, *Spiritual Flower Garden,* 249–252; *Spiritual Letters,* 241–248

Tertullian, 232

Thanksgiving, 91

Theologians, 291; defined, 229

Theologica Germanica (Spener), 44

Theological studies, 66; character development and, 41–43, 45–46; hindrances to, 65–70; practical training during, 47–48; Spener on, 41–49, 66; temporal gains from, 65, 67

Theosophy, 230

Thomas Didymus, 308, 318

Threefold sabbath, 188

Transfiguration of Jesus, 151–153, 154–158

True Christianity (Arndt), 37, 39, 75, 154

Unbelievers, 37–40, 96, 315

Varenius, Heinrich, 70

Vengeance, 37

Vergil, 73

Vernacular, disputation in, 43

Vitae Patrum (emblematic insert to), 234–236

Wesley, John, 301–303

Wisdom (Sophia), 263; Arnold on, 219–226

Women, 62, 287

Word of God, *See* Scripture

Worldliness, 65, 96

350

INDEX

Other Volumes in this Series